(Continued)

Multiple Worlds of Child Writers

Friends Learning to Write

Anne Haas Dyson

Teachers College, Columbia University
New York and London

Published by Teachers College Press, 1234 Amsterdam Avenue
New York, NY 10027

The project discussed herein was performed pursuant to a grant from
the Office of Educational Research and Improvement/Department of
Education (OERI/ED) for the Center for the Study of Writing. However,
the opinions expressed herein do not necessarily reflect the position
or policy of the OERI/ED, and no official endorsement by the OERI/ED
should be inferred.

Grateful acknowledgment is made to the following for permission to
reprint the material indicated:

Table B.1, from Dyson, A. Haas. (1986). Transitions and
tensions: Interrelationships between the drawing, talking, and
dictating of young children. *Research in the Teaching of
English, 20,* 379–409. Copyright by the National Council
of Teachers of English.
Tables 1.2, 1.3, 8.5, D.1, and D.2, from Dyson, A. Haas.
(1988). Negotiating among multiple worlds: The space/time
dimensions of young children's composing. *Research in the
Teaching of English, 22,* 355–390. Copyright by the
National Council of Teachers of English.
Figure 1.3, from Dyson, A. Haas. (1989). Research currents: The
space/time travels of story writers. *Language Arts, 66,* 330–340.
Copyright by the National Council of Teachers of English.
Chapter 3 is adapted from Dyson, A. Haas. (1988). Unintentional
helping in the primary grades: Writing in the children's world.
In B. Rafoth & D. R. Rubin (Eds.), *The social construction of
written language* (pp. 218–248). Norwood, NJ: Ablex. Copyright
by Ablex Publishing Corporation.

Library of Congress Cataloging-in-Publication Data

Dyson, Anne Haas.
    Multiple worlds of child writers: friends learning to write/
Anne Haas Dyson.
    p. cm. — (Early childhood education series)
    Bibliography: p.
    Includes index.
    ISBN 0-8077-2972-8 (alk. paper). — ISBN 0-8077-2971-X (pbk.:
alk. paper)
    1. Children—Writing. I. Title. II. Series.
LB1139.W7D97 1989   89-34699
372.6'23—dc20   CIP

Printed on acid-free paper

Manufactured in the United States of America

96 95 94 93 92 91 90 89   8 7 6 5 4 3 2 1

For David, Mary, Ruthy, and Joanne,
and for our mother

Contents

List of Tables

List of Figures

Acknowledgments

Within this book, a developmental drama unfolds, a drama enacted by a primary school teacher and her five- to eight-year-old students. During the course of this drama, the children grow as writers of imagined worlds, and that growth is linked to their lives together as friends and scholars, as fellow reflectors on the world they share. In a similar way, the writing of this book was itself a drama, one supported by friends and colleagues. Here, I offer my thanks to many of them.

I thank first the school district personnel who allowed me entrance, the school faculty who graciously welcomed me, and, most important, the dedicated teacher and the spirited children who shared their school lives with me. While "my" teacher and her children must remain anonymous, I hope this book reveals something of the compelling aliveness—the hard work, lively play, and earnest reflection—so in evidence in their classroom.

In my own work and (sometimes playful) reflection, I was aided enormously by Carol Heller, a doctoral student in the Graduate School of Education at the University of California—Berkeley. Not only did Carol assist in data collection, she also edited every page of this book (at least twice), tracked down needed writing samples and bibliographic entries, and remained excited by the project and committed to the teacher and the children. While Carol has worked with me on this project for over three years, we have at varied times benefited from the assistance of others. As graduate students at UC—Berkeley, Mary Gardner provided much valued assistance in data collection, while Jim Slagel and Mark McCarvel helped with the organization and analysis of the children's texts. Alice Guerrero and David Ziegler, of the Center for the Study of Writing, and Adriana Artega, of the Division of Language and Literacy, Graduate School of Education, helped produce this book's many tables.

My study was supported by the Center for the Study of Writing, funded by the Office of Educational Research and Improvement/Department of Education. The center's Director, Sarah Warshauer Freedman, and Administrative Director, Sandra Schecter, were interested friends as well as able administrators. They listened many times to my stories about the children, always with much-appreciated attentiveness, as did many of my colleagues at UC—Berkeley. Bernard Gifford, Dean of the Graduate School of Education, has been a consistent source of support and encouragement.

In this book about "friends learning to write," it seems especially important, too, to acknowledge friends who have helped and continue to help me write. Celia Genishi, of Ohio State University, has long played that role for me; she is editorially and child-worldly wise. As a student at the University of Texas at Austin, I first found encouragement as a writer from Julie Jensen, a writer with clarity not only of prose but of commitment to teachers and children.

Finally, I thank my brother and sisters and my mother. I come from a family of fine storytellers, and so I dedicate this book to them.

Prologue

Six-year-old Maggie is having some difficulty figuring out what to write. So, she makes a chain by hooking colored markers together, balances the chain on her head, and calls it her "thinking cap." Maggie's friend Manuel admires that cap.

MANUEL: Thanks for making red the first color [in your cap].
MAGGIE: Why?
MANUEL: Because it's my favorite color.
MAGGIE: Red's your favorite color?
MANUEL: Yeah.
MAGGIE: Purple's mine. Purple's at the end.
MANUEL: Unless you look at it in another way.
ADULT: Then where would purple be?
MANUEL: At the beginning.

Inspired by Manuel, Maggie, and their peers, I hope in this book to offer a new way of viewing beginnings and ends—not the beginnings and ends of thinking caps, but the beginnings and end goals of school writing growth.

Manuel and Maggie are just two of the children I met in January of 1985 when I visited their classroom and met their teacher, Margaret.[1] I had anticipated that first visit with tempered optimism. I had been visiting many schools in the East San Francisco Bay Area. New to the area and interested in young children and their writing, I was looking for kindergarten and primary classrooms in which children had extensive opportunities to write their own thoughts. I had hoped for a classroom that reflected the social and cultural diversity of the area and, beyond that, one in which I, too, might blend in. Quiet classrooms with whisper-

---

[1] All names given to the teacher and children in this classroom are fictitious.

ing children and orderly tables made me feel conspicuous—too large, too old, too loud.

A friend, Victoria Purcell-Gates, had told me about Margaret's school, an urban magnet school attracting children from across its socially and ethnically diverse city. And, she assured me, I would feel comfortable in Margaret's room, where parents and tiny siblings often visited; I would be just another adult. Moreover, Margaret's children wrote regularly. Margaret taught language arts to all the children in the primary grades—kindergarteners through third graders—and they all kept journals that were filled with their own stories.

When I arrived that first morning, however, it was not the writing that I noticed. Margaret's classroom was full of children talking and drawing. There was writing, too, but, for me, as for the children, writing did not initially seem as colorful, as compelling, or as noisy, as those other symbolic media—speech and pictures.

Talking and drawing were tools the children initially used to organize their understanding of their world and to forge links with each other. Over the course of the next three years, as I continued to visit Margaret's classroom, I watched as the children's writing too became the scene of social connections and worldly reflections. Their once flat, black-and-white texts gradually became more colorful, more compelling, as writing found a niche within the children's repertoire of symbolic tools and within their ongoing social world and wider experienced worlds.

This book is the story of that change. It portrays the process through which Margaret and her children formed a community, one that was both supported by and supporting of the children's growth as writers. And it presents detailed views of the developmental histories of four young members of this community, as they grew—through writing—as classmates, artists, and particularly as creators of imaginary worlds.

The details of Margaret's classroom and her children's growth may well be particular to them; however, this close viewing of their school lives should allow insight into the developmental challenges children may face as writers and the symbolic and social resources upon which they lean for support. More important, their experiences should contribute to a broad interpretive framework for observing, understanding, and fostering writing growth, a framework that places learning to compose within the context of learning to symbolize experiences and to form social relationships with others.

The framework, like Manuel's view of Maggie's thinking cap, considers children's writing development from a different perspective than the currently dominant one. Most considerations of writing's growth stress that children must "disembed" or "decontextualize" their written texts from any dependency on other symbolic media and other people (Donaldson, 1978; Olson, 1977). Margaret's children suggest a different, although not incompatible, perspective. For children to develop as writers, especially writers of imaginary worlds, their written texts must become progressively *more* embedded in their social, affective, and intellectual lives. For authors of imaginary worlds attempt to move in many worlds simultaneously; thus, their imaginary worlds are their means of organizing their own experienced worlds while at the same time reaching out to and socially connecting with others, their readers.

In the end, what matters about writing in school is not simply the quality of the texts children produce but the quality of life they experience at school and beyond. In a community that values written language, writing can become an important means for individual reflection and social connection. And it is that feeling of belonging to a community—of connection to other people—that helps make teachers' and children's school lives together personally satisfying and socially meaningful.

1

Introduction: Becoming a Writer in School

In this chapter, I set the stage for Margaret's children by briefly considering the developmental roots of writing, the nature of story or literary discourse, and the potentially nurturing environment of the classroom community. I discuss the theoretical assumptions about children and their language learning that influenced my perceptions of the classroom and the children who populate this book. The following classroom scene highlights some of the issues to be explored here:

> Margaret has just announced to her kindergarten class that today is Alex's birthday. Christopher grabs a can of colored markers and a sheet of paper and heads for the classroom's back table, an area usually allowing for ample elbow room. "Alex! What's your favorite color?" he calls out. And then, the favored red marker in hand, Christopher begins to draw a big smile, two appropriately placed eyeballs, and a floating bunch of balloons. Alex wanders by occasionally as Christopher works, looking very pleased but not interfering with the work at hand. With a little help from an available adult, Christopher ends his production by spelling out "Happy Birthday to Alex." Soon, after a brief stay in Angela's box (the common initial A's causing some confusion), the birthday card is deposited in Alex's cubby.

This small moment of classroom life suggests the powerful forces that give rise to and engender literacy growth. Christopher was led to write by his desire to engage in a social activity that, in his culture, often involves print—the giving of a birthday greeting. While Christopher undoubtedly engaged in birthday card writing at home with family members, here he was motivated by his desire to please his friend Alex. Christopher's behavior suggests two major questions to be explored in this chapter:

- What social forces bring children to writing and energize their early writing efforts?
- What is distinctive about the classroom, as different from the home, as a social environment for literacy growth?

Christopher's actual message was not conveyed so much through the printed letters as through the use of the preferred red color and the pleasing images—a large smile and bright eyes, surrounded by cheery balloons. Christopher's written message was made more meaningful by the use of the more comfortable medium of drawing. These observations lead to additional questions to be explored here:

- In what ways do young writers lean on more fully developed symbolic tools?
- How do children discover the distinctive possibilities of writing as a symbolic tool?

In discussing these questions, I consider the symbolic tool of drawing, which Christopher highlighted, and two other tools much in evidence in early childhood—talk and dramatic play.

Finally, in the example, Christopher both made a physical object— a birthday card—and engaged in a communicative act—designing the card for his friend Alex. In so doing, he made use of symbols that have, in many children's worlds, certain meanings for both the symbol producer and the recipient of those symbols; that is, smiling faces and balloons, like the words *Happy Birthday*, convey good cheer and, more concretely, parties. In this chapter, I am concerned with children's writing as making and as communicating, but I focus on a use of writing that involves more complex symbols and more subtle means of communication, namely, the writing of imaginary worlds. This focus gives rise to still other questions:

- In what ways do children make imaginary worlds with marker and paper?
- How do written symbolic worlds, like the drawn balloons and

smiling faces, connect to children's personal experiences, their perceived real worlds?

• How do imaginary worlds, like birthday cards, serve as symbols that form social links between children?

In the sections to follow, I discuss these questions, drawing upon observations of young children made in previous studies in order to develop a theoretical framework for Margaret and her children. Underlying this framework is the notion that children's written language learning is both social and developmental. I assume first that written language is, as Vygotsky (1978) argued, a complex social tool that functions in varied ways in our society. Children learn about this tool—its purposes, its features, its processing demands—as they encounter it in meaningful activities. At the same time, however, children do not simply attempt to imitate adult models. I also assume that children's written language behavior changes in complex ways over time. Children actively construct or "figure out" written language, just as they do other sorts of symbol systems, making it sensible from their point of view (Clay, 1975; Ferreiro & Teberosky, 1982; Piaget & Inhelder, 1969). Further, these two assumptions help lay the groundwork for the third, namely, that different children will develop written language in different ways, which can be described and understood, even if their underlying causes cannot be explained. Individual children's ways of figuring out written language reflect the uniqueness that results from the complex interplay of their genetic and social histories.

Finally, after presenting this theoretical backdrop, I briefly describe the physical stage itself—the school setting and the classroom participants—and the procedures through which I watched the unfolding drama.

THE SOCIAL FORCES THAT ENERGIZE WRITING GROWTH

In the following anecdote, two children from a previous project (Genishi & Dyson, 1984) illustrate some of the social forces that engender and sustain literacy use. In particular, we can observe the very human desires to create and enact relationships with others and to organize and store information about a jointly shared world. (For the following and all other transcripts presented throughout this book, please refer to Figure 1.1, which provides a key to the typographic conventions I've used to indicate various aspects.)

Figure 1.1.   Conventions used in the presentation of transcripts.

( )   Parentheses enclosing text contain notes, usually about
      contextual and nonverbal information; e.g., (sighs,
      looks at her)

      Empty parentheses, on the other hand, indicate
      unintelligible words or phrases; e.g.,
      Jesse: You're supposed to have one ( ).

[ ]   Brackets contain explanatory information inserted into
      quotations by me, rather than by the speaker.

[A single large bracket is used to indicate overlapping
      speech; e.g.,
      Sonia: I wish I were in the land of [cotton candy.
      Jake: [cotton candy.

N-O   Capitalized letters separated by hyphens indicate that
      letters were spoken or words were spelled aloud by the
      speaker.

NO   A capitalized word or phrase indicates increased
      volume.

/n/   Parallel slashed lines indicate that the speaker made
      the sound of the enclosed letter or letters.

/n:/ A colon included in the previous symbol indicates that
      the given letter sound was elongated by the speaker.

...   Ellipsis points inserted in the middle of a blank line
      indicate omitted material; e.g.,
      Jake: Yeah. Buck Rogers, twenty-first-century person.
             ...
             You wouldn't see your brother ever again, ever
             again, Marcos.

      Conventional punctuation marks (periods, question
      marks, exclamation points) are used to indicate ends of
      utterances or sentences, usually indicated by slight
      pauses on the audiotape. Commas refer to pauses within
      sentence units, as when the speakers paused between
      words or word phrases during dictation. Dashes (--)
      indicate interrupted utterances.

Jack, 7-years-old, and his sister Emmy, 5-years-old, are playing in Jack's bedroom creating a fantasy in space, sometimes referring to a model spaceship they built earlier.

JACK: Fire! Pew pew pew! (sound effects)

EMMY: Uh, sir, that Spider [the enemy] did some damage to us. He tore out the whole back.

JACK: Damage report. Lieutenant!

EMMY: Yes, sir!

JACK: Damage report. What is it?

EMMY: All the levels have been blown off.

JACK: (sighs)

. . .

Would you quit lounging around?

EMMY: Sir, there's nothing to command. You're not moving. I might as well take a nap.

JACK: Why take a nap? Go to your headquarters.

EMMY: But, sir, this is my headquarters.

JACK: Go to your headquarters. (firmly)

EMMY: Yes, sir.

JACK: I want a damage report on paper. You have 11—

EMMY: But, sir, I already brought you the damage report on paper.

JACK: Oh, you did? You don't even know how to spell! (intonation changes here, as if no longer pretending)

EMMY: Yes, sir.

JACK: I want it right. I want a report on everything the Spider did, what it was, what damage it did, and all that.

EMMY: Okay, two hours later. Sir, I've got it made up. Here.

JACK: It's about time.

(Genishi & Dyson, 1984, p. 56)

As Emmy and Jack demonstrate, written language is a tool that helps the characters who populate a child's world accomplish social ends. Through writing, people convey information needed—or, as in Emmy's case, demanded—by others. With checks, people pay for their purchases; with grocery lists, they remember what those purchases should be. With calendar jottings, they remind themselves of special occasions; with birthday cards, they acknowledge those occasions. In such ways, writing establishes many social relationships: commander and commandee; families and grocery clerks; long-distance friends; customers and waiters; waiters and cooks; parents and babysitters. Parents and young children may be bonded through bedtime stories, and grandparents and children are often linked through letters and cards. In Nelson's (1985) terms, print is part of the scripts of children's everyday lives.

Indeed, even in communities where literacy assumes a relatively minor role, children are not isolated from written language (Heath, 1983). As a society, we are surrounded by traffic signs; dotted lines for signatures; and labeled cans, boxes, and even clothes. So children may take to pen and paper, too, participating in literacy activities with more-skilled others, exploring and playing with print's functions and features, and thus using it as a means of social connection, self-expression, and individual and joint exploration of a basic cultural tool (Bissex, 1980; Clay, 1975; Gundlach, McLane, Stott, & McNamee, 1985; Tizard & Hughes, 1984).

WRITING AS THE DEVELOPMENT OF A SYMBOLIC TOOL

While children may understand many social functions of written language in a general way, they do not necessarily understand specifically how it is that the black-and-white squiggles on the paper mediate between them and other people. There is a long "prehistory" to this understanding, as Vygotsky (1978) explained:

> It seems clear that mastery of such a complex sign system [as writing] cannot be accomplished in a purely mechanical and external manner; rather it is the culmination of a long process of development of complex behavioral functions in the child. Only by understanding the entire history of sign development in the child and the place of writing in it can we approach a correct solution of the psychology of writing. [p. 106]

Vygotsky located the seeds of children's writing in their first visual signs, gestural depictions. He argued that other visual symbols—play objects and drawings—derive their meaning first from gesture. For example, a box becomes a baby because it can be cradled. Drawn lines depict jumping because the fingers jumped as they drew them. Eventually play objects and drawings become independent visual signs, capable of symbolizing meaning on their own.

As children develop as visual symbolizers, talk is an accompaniment to and then an organizer of their symbolic action. For example, as she draws, a very young child might say, "Oh, look. I made a house," with genuine surprise; but an older child might say, "I am going to make a house." Here, speech may serve to guide and even to invest the visual symbol with meaning.

Similarly, as children explore the visual system of writing, they lean on other kinds of symbols (Dyson, 1982, 1983, 1986a), as both Christopher's birthday card and Emmy's report illustrate. In Christopher's card, the written graphics are interwoven with drawn symbols, while Emmy's report does not even have a physical form—its existence is conveyed through talk alone. For both, writing emerges couched within other symbolic media over which they have already gained control.

Indeed, children seem to rely on their understanding of how drawing symbolizes meaning as they refine their early lines of squiggles and letter-like marks to represent messages more precisely. Speech is again important, serving not only to organize and invest early written graphics with meaning, but also to form the raw material for the graphic symbols themselves. As Vygotsky (1978) explained, children discover that people draw not only things but also speech.

Vygotsky's student, Luria (1983), illustrated children's grasp of this principle and, moreover, linked children's discoveries about the written symbol system to their grasp of the specific function of print as an aid for recalling messages. Luria argued that children's discovery of this function follows from, rather than precedes, their first writing efforts and that that discovery in turn generates new discoveries about the system, as children figure out how "lines, dots, and other signs" function to help them "remember and transmit ideas and concepts" (p. 239).

The grasping of a new function or meaning for a potential sign is established in social situations as children interact with others; that is, children's signs evolve new functions as those signs are seen to serve new human ends—as they are invested with new social energy. Vygotsky (1978) offered this example: A child's initial attempts to grasp an object are interpreted by the adult caregiver as communicative; thus the caregiver responds to the child accordingly, and thereby the child's grasping movement begins to become the communicative act of pointing. Thus, the initial grasping movement acquires new functional meaning, becoming a communicative gesture. Meanings are thus established interpersonally before they become intrapersonal. In a similar way, children's first writing efforts may be given new meaning as they are responded to by others.

To document children's first writing efforts, Luria (1983) engaged in a series of writing tasks with young children and talked to them about their written products. He observed the following:

[Three-, four-, and five-year-old children] grasped the outward form of writing and saw how adults accomplished it; they were even able to imitate adults; but they themselves were completely unable to learn the specific psychological attributes any act must have if it is to be used as a tool in the service of some end. [p. 241]

The act of writing is, in this case, only externally associated with the task of noting a specific word; it is purely imitative. The child is interested only in "writing like grown-ups"; for him the act of writing is not a means of remembering, or representing some meaning, but an act that is sufficient in its own right, an act of play. But such an act is by no means always seen as an aid to helping the child later remember the sentence. [p. 242]

When children begin to grasp this function of print—that graphics not only represent meaning but can mediate the reading or recall of a specific spoken message—they begin to invent ways to differentiate one squiggle from another. Through manipulating the requests he made of the children—what he asked them to write—Luria (1983) aimed to help children grasp that function. He discovered that certain messages led children to use color, shape, size, and number of graphics to help mediate recall of a dictated message; that is, the child "gets the idea of using drawing (which he is already quite good at in play) as a means of remembering" (p. 257). Luria's procedures are illustrated in the following adult/child interaction (adapted from Luria, 1983, p. 259):

ADULT DICTATES: Here is a man, and he has two legs.
CHILD RESPONDS: Then I'll draw two lines.
ADULT DICTATES: In the sky there are many stars.
CHILD RESPONDS: Then I'll draw many lines.

Similarly Ferreiro (1980, 1986; Ferreiro & Teberosky, 1982) documented how children gradually begin to differentiate print forms, as they move from using the quantity of the object to be represented as a distinguishing characteristic, to using the number of syllables in the object's name, to characteristics of the sound of the name itself. Luria (1983) highlighted a functional context that helps explain the gradual differentiation Ferreiro not only observed but undoubtedly facilitated through her tasks and questions. This is the complex dialectic that takes place between the child's own graphic activity and the child's sense of the possibilities inherent in that graphic activity, a sense that evolves as the child interacts with others about print.

Luria (1983) focused on only one function of written language, to help children recall (or, I would add, to help someone else to figure out) what precisely has been written. Written language, though, serves many functions, and the discovery of them also leads children to write in new ways, as they adapt old symbolic means to achieve new ends. The particular functions of interest here are those served by children's creation of imaginary worlds.

THE MULTIPLE FUNCTIONS OF IMAGINARY WORLDS

Young children's imaginary worlds evolve primarily through dramatic play, talk, and drawing, although writing may be embedded in those worlds. Consider, for example, five-year-old Sara's creation, shown in Figure 1.2. When she was nearly done drawing, Sara did not read her product but, rather, explained it to me: "She likes swings so—*he* likes swings. He says, "WOW" 'cause he likes swings, 'n' he says, "OH"— How do you spell *boy*?"

Figure 1.2. Sara's happy boy with swings.

Over time, children will differentiate the boundaries between the written, drawn, and spoken symbols (Dyson, 1982, 1986a; Harste, Woodward, & Burke, 1984). Gradually, more of the meanings of their stories will appear within the written graphics themselves, rather than only in their drawing and their talking to themselves and to friends. As many scholars have pointed out, one of children's developmental challenges is to "disembed" or "decontextualize" their written texts from any dependency on other symbolic media and other people (Donaldson, 1978; Olson, 1977). And, as suggested earlier, I assume that understanding print's role in helping them to remember—and others to retrieve—their ideas will provide one reason for that differentiation.

At the same time, however, children's dramatic and narrative language serves multiple functions. It not only helps children to create an imaginative world that may be recalled or retrieved by others, but also links children to each other, just as Emmy and Jack came together in their spaceship. It also helps children to make sense of and evaluate their perceived real worlds, as the essence of their experiences are replayed via language, such as being frightened and nurtured, delighted and saddened, imperiled and rescued, given and denied (Corsaro, 1985; Paley, 1986; Wolf, Rygh, & Altshuler, 1984). In these ways, the imaginative worlds children construct are *embedded* in their social and experienced worlds.

Very young children develop an implicit understanding that creators of imaginary worlds move in multiple worlds. Wolf and Hicks (in press) describe the play narratives of preschoolers as young as age three, who speak with varied voices. These young story creators built imaginary worlds as they played with small replicas of human figures. The children used the dialogue voice, as they became characters acting within their imagined worlds; the narrative voice, as they became observers relaying the happenings within those worlds; and the stage manager's voice, as they became interlocuters with their audience in the ongoing social world, discussing and negotiating their evolving imaginary world.

Children's use of these varied voices became more differentiated over time, as different tenses and pronouns were used to mark certain voices. Past tense and third-person nominals and pronominals were used for the narrative voice ("Once upon a time, there was a daddy, a mommy, and a baby"); present tense and first-person pronominal forms were used for dialogue ("Oh, how beautiful I am"); and, while Wolf and Hicks do not specifically comment on this, stage-managing functions sometimes referred to the future ("This is going to be her baby"). Eventually, though, by five or six years of age, the observed children could double up these functions through the use of a unified voice. The narrative plot, for example, could be advanced through characters' dialogue, or dialogue could be reported indirectly through narration ("And then she told him to go").

Similarly, adult authors of fiction play with space and time structures, moving among multiple worlds, as both sociolinguists interested in literary discourse (Nystrand, 1982; Polanyi, 1982; Rader, 1982; Tannen, 1985, 1987) and literary theorists themselves (Barthes, 1974; Booth, 1961; Rosen, n.d.) have illustrated. Literary artists do not function as isolated, disembedded souls. An author may first be the real-world director of the unfolding imaginary plot; then, deep in that imaginary world, an actor speaking a character's words, feeling a character's emotions; then, inside a remembered world, a reflective storyteller reliving past experiences where the roots of the story may lie; and then, a socially astute communicator, adjusting words and phrases to ease interaction with real-world readers. Indeed, like their young counterparts, the challenge of adult story writers is to find a way to meld their varied voices within their texts. Authors, like storytellers, face "the problem of finding a place to stand" among these multiple worlds (Polanyi, 1982, p. 169).

It is in fact the controlled meshing of the author's experienced world with the imaginary world that ultimately allows authors and readers to connect within the ongoing social one: Authors evaluate their own life experiences through writing, and readers draw on their own "repertoires of conceptions about human plights" to experience the sights and sounds cued by print (Bruner, 1986, p. 34, drawing upon the work of Barthes, 1974, and Iser, 1974).

Tannen (1987) suggests that authors evoke these sights and sounds in their readers by drawing upon, "first, uses of language that sweep the audience along with their rhythm, sound, and shape; and second, those that require audience participation in sense-making, such as indirectness, tropes, imagery and detail, and constructed dialogue" (p. 69). The discourse tools Tannen cites are the stuff of children's dramatic play and of many children's interweaving of pictures and talk (i.e., shapes and sounds) to create dramatic drawn and oral worlds. By extending this into a developmental view, we can see another way in which children might build from old symbolic means as they work toward new writing ends. As previously discussed, children's realization of print's function in information storage and recall may lead to the differentiation of the specific alphabetic characteristics of writing (as distinct from drawing and speech). So, too, their realization of print's social and evaluative functions may lead them to find new ways to capture their experiences and engage in social interactions within the flat spaces and colorless squiggles of written text. And, as children's writing becomes progressively more embedded within their social and experienced worlds, they confront and work to resolve the tensions among all these worlds. Children learn to adopt multiple roles as they move among multiple worlds; that is, to build upon Vygotsky's (1978) ideas, they learn to write not just speech, but voices.

THE DEVELOPMENTAL CHALLENGE OF LEARNING TO WRITE IN SCHOOL

Children come to school with varying kinds and degrees of experience with written language, including with written stories (Heath, 1983; Schieffelin & Cochran-Smith, 1984; Teale, 1986). Given the opportunity to create imaginary worlds, most children's forte lies in their dramatic play (McNamee, McLane, Cooper, & Kerwin, 1985; Paley, 1981, 1986) and in their drawings (Gardner, 1980). Perhaps that is why, in the common school task of drawing pictures and writing "stories," it is the drawing that generally receives the greatest attention (Graves, 1983; Newkirk, 1987; Newkirk & Atwell, 1982). Children's written texts sometimes seem to be simply afterthoughts to their drawing and talking; that is, their texts may in fact not be embedded in their social and intellectual lives. Brian and Sara, two kindergarteners I once knew, expressed the sentiment well:

> BRIAN: Why do we always have to write words? (Translation: Why can't we just write the pictures?)
> TEACHER: Well, I like to see what you're going to write.
> SARA: Why can't you just ask us?

As I have just argued, over time, through the complex dialectic that evolves between children's own graphic activity and their interactions with others, children come to discover the range of functions served by written language, including its capacities for social interaction and individual reflection. Indeed, in whole societies, literacy finds a permanent and prominent niche when the information conveyed through written language becomes part of the social network—when people talk about written materials and when those materials can affect their views of themselves and their participation in the world (Elasser & Irvine, 1985; Elasser & John-Steiner, 1977; Freire, 1985; Heath, 1986).

How might such discoveries come about in school? Generally, in thinking about significant social relationships in the classroom, we highlight the one between teacher and child, just as the relationship between parent and child has been emphasized in research on literacy learning in the home. Yet, there is only one teacher, and there may well be 30 or more children. In such a group setting, children, like any people brought together under the authority of others, react to the official classroom structure by forming their own social structure (Corsaro, 1985; Goffman, 1961). In the child collective that arises in a daycare setting or classroom, children find the comfort of being members of a group that is "in this together" and, at the same time, the opportunity to define further their individual uniqueness as they compare themselves with their peers (Rubin, 1980).

Children's interest in each other has been cited by many skilled teachers and researchers who have worked with children from a variety of backgrounds (Ashton-Warner, 1963; Gilbert & Gay, 1985; Gillmore, 1983; Paley, 1986; Philips, 1972; Tharp et al., 1984). While the teacher does establish the larger structure within which school literacy occurs, the children's own social concerns may come to infuse school literacy activities with social meaning (Dyson, 1987b, 1988b). Children's daily writing activity may become a way for them both to link themselves with others and to display their own specialness, as a complex dialectic is set up between their own drawing, talking, and writing activity and the response of others to that activity.

To illustrate, consider the following interaction between Jake and Sonia, two children in Margaret's classroom:

> Six-year-old Sonia is hard at work on a picture of a heart in her journal. Jake, a classmate, notices that she is unusually silent.
>
> JAKE: How come you're not talking to me like you usually do? Are you scared or something?
> SONIA: Yes.
> JAKE: Of what? Please. Tell me.
> SONIA: I'm thinking about one of my dreams. I'll get rid of it.
> JAKE: Oh, it's a nightmare.
> SONIA: No, it's a really nice one.
> JAKE: Huh?
> SONIA: It's a nice one with a mean person in it. (returns to her drawing, explaining to Jake that it has something to do with her dream)
> JAKE: Oh. Is it a person who's mean and doesn't like hearts?
> SONIA: (ignores his comments, talks quietly to herself) There's the witch. (draws a female figure with a heart-shaped chest)
> JAKE: Oh. Somebody got turned into a frog. Heh, heh, heh.
> SONIA: No. Here's the nice person now. (draws a male figure, also with a heart-shaped chest; later adds a rainbow)

Despite Sonia's talk with Jake about her dream, she proceeded to write a text that seemed to have very little to do with her dream, but much more to do with the picture itself. Indeed, while she began with a third-person stance toward a more distant world, she left that stance to state her very much first-person-present enjoyment of her picture:

Once upon a time the Queen and King of hearts They saw a Beautiful rainbow. I Love This Picture.

In the above anecdote Sonia was engaged in the classroom activity of "writing a story." And that activity involves other symbolic media, most notably talking and drawing, and, while it is designed to allow for individual symbolic expression, it is also clearly an occasion for participating in the ongoing social world, in which, as Jake noted, Sonia usually participated. At the same time, through drawing and talking, Sonia was reflecting on her own experienced world—on her dream. Sonia's interaction happened primarily through talk and centered on the drawing.

Sonia's written text, like that of most of her peers, is simply a representation of her ideas and feelings; and, more particularly, it is governed by her picture. In time, in part by virtue of the children's spontaneous responses to each other's work, their texts themselves will assume some of the functional power of their pictures and their talk, conveying their images and linking them to each other socially. Their texts will become more dynamic worlds that mediate between their own lives, those of their friends, and their experiences in the wider world. It is this process by which writing, through the children's activity, finds a niche in their artistic, social, and intellectual worlds, that was revealed through the study described in this book.

The theoretical frame presented on the preceding pages sets writing growth firmly within the broad context of children's growth as symbolizers and socializers. This theoretical frame emerged from my experiences in the very human frame of these children's classroom, where writing quite literally existed amidst the social and artistic lives of children.

THE STUDY SITE AND DATA COLLECTION AND ANALYSIS

I studied Sonia, Jake, and their peers intensively over a two-year period. Although less intensively, I have continued my involvement in their school to date. In the following chapters, I will detail the nature of their classroom life together. Here, however, I briefly introduce their school, teacher, and classmates, as well as the procedures through which I came to know them.

The school is a magnet elementary school in a large urban area. It was begun in 1974 by a small group of parents who wanted an alternative to the public school system for their children. The intention was to begin a small K–3 school that would bring together an ethnically and economically diverse group of children and that would teach the basics (reading and math) through the expressive arts. According to the founders' own description, the "most important ongoing-element of this Magnet Project" was the continuous emphasis on teachers expanding and extending the children's talk, for, "without the extension of expressive language, there is no 'expression'" (Continuation Application for Urban Magnet Program in the Arts and Humanities, 1974).

The project initially survived with outside funding, but, when this funding was exhausted and the school district itself assumed financial responsibility, the school's existence was (and continues) to be periodically threatened. Parents and teachers have consistently protested the school's closing, however, and it has been relocated on several occasions to various parts of the city. At the time of my two-year study, it was located on a site with two other schools that also were based on the expressive arts—a middle school and a high school.

The children attending the school were indeed diverse, including Anglo, Asian, African-American, Hispanic, Middle Eastern, Native American, and mixed ethnicities. The school's approximately 80 children were separated into three "home classrooms": a kindergarten, a first/second grade, and a second/third grade. Margaret, an Anglo woman in her sixties, taught the kindergarten. For the first part of the year, the children stayed with their homeroom teacher, primarily so that the kindergarteners could adjust to the rhythms and rules of formal schooling. Beginning in January, the primary-grade children moved among the three teachers' classrooms during the school day. From that point on, Margaret taught all of the children language arts.

Margaret had been with the school since its founding. She thus had begun teaching kindergarten relatively late in her career, having previously been a secondary school teacher. She was not herself a visual artist, but she appreciated art, including children's art, and she loved to write. While she had once harbored the hope of writing "the great American novel," she had instead kept a diary, written letters and telegrams (the latter to politicians), and sometimes composed poetry as well. So, not surprisingly, Margaret was a strong supporter of the "journal" activity as the center of the school's language arts program.

The journals she used were books with construction-paper covers; inside was alternating blank and lined paper. In Margaret's classroom, journal time was a regular activity. The children drew and wrote in their journals, as Margaret circulated. She talked to them about their story ideas and mechanics of production and, in the kindergarten, acted as scribe for the children's dictations. When individual children finished all the pages in their journals, she allowed time for them to share two or three entries with the class.

While Margaret was only intermittently available to any individual child, she allowed them ongoing symbolic and social sources of support. Symbolically, the children could lean on drawing and on talking to help form and convey their ideas. Socially, they could lean on each other, since they were free to ask each other questions and to comment on each other's work.

As the children and Margaret worked, I observed. My times of intense involvement and more distant reflection on the fruits of that involvement are laid out in Table 1.1.[1]

At first I observed the class as a whole, getting a sense of the classroom's rhythm and tone and, just as important, of what exactly might be learned there about writing, language, and children. And, as noted earlier, what was initially most compelling to me was not the children's writing, but their drawing and talking. Thus, my initial questions about the interrelationships among the children's use of these varied symbol systems began to form.

As the project progressed, I began to focus on the eight children who, with Margaret, serve as the major characters of this book. All of these eight were judged by Margaret and me to fall within the broad range of "normal," both academically and emotionally. During the 1984–1985 school year, four of the children were kindergarteners and four were first

---

[1]During my first few weeks at the school, I established my role as a friendly, "reactive" adult (Corsaro, 1981, p. 118); rather than directing the children's activities, I followed their leads. However, the precise nature of my role in the classroom was determined by the nature of the relationships expected in that room between adult observers and children and by my own sense of appropriate adult behavior. To elaborate, I told the children that, when I was watching them, I was very busy; I had to write down everything that was happening so that I could remember it; remembering was important because I wanted to think about what school was like for "little kids." Therefore, when I wasn't "too busy," I would respond to their questions, but I did not offer the children advice during their drawing and writing. Further, I selected case study children who attended to their peers rather than to me. Yet, though the children acknowledged my role verbally (by such remarks as "She's not a teacher. She's just a person that watches children.") and nonverbally (by breaking class rules in my presence), I did respond in teacherlike ways in two kinds of circumstances.

graders. Their pseudonyms, ages, gender, and ethnicity are given in Table 1.2. I chose these children in part because I could comfortably observe them. None expressed any dismay at being observed, but, on the other hand, none attended to me rather than to peers. More important, the children all made use of the available sources of support in this classroom—the opportunities to use colorful strokes, dramatic voices, and lively dialogue to support their forming of text worlds. And yet, they did not do so in the same ways.

As will be discussed in Chapter 4, the children differed in their ways of interacting with symbolic tools such as drawing and speech, as well as in their ways of interacting with other people (Bussis, Chittenden, Amarel, & Klausner, 1985; Wolf & Gardner, 1979). I could not tap the complex personal and social sources of those differences, but I could describe them and study how they played themselves out in school. Since writing grows out of children's experiences with other people and other tools (gesture, speech, dramatic play, drawing), and since children's ways of using other media and of interacting with their friends vary, their ways of coming to write also vary (Dyson, 1986a, 1987a). This project, then, promised me the opportunity to understand both how children's written texts develop or find a niche within children's symbolic and social worlds and what might be the nature of the possible differences among children in this development.

To do this, I began to focus intensely on one child during each journal session. I sat behind and to the side of the focal child, making written notes on behaviors and, using a small tape recorder placed on the table, recording spontaneous talk. After the child had left Margaret's

---

First, I occasionally responded to the first graders' completed products as their teacher did, in order to maintain the children's trust. I thus followed Margaret's practice of proofreading children's completed products for story and sentence sense, spelling, and punctuation. I did this because my original tack of observing a child make an error, smiling and nodding when the child showed me her work, and then watching as the child confidently approached Margaret led to anger and distrust. (One child told me, "I figured out you're not very good at writing.") I, therefore, did respond to their completed work as Margaret did, when requested to do so and when such a response would not interfere with my observing any particular child (i.e., when I was not "too busy"). I did not, however, intervene in any ongoing drawing, writing, and talking.

For a similar reason, in the kindergarten, I took the children's dictations as well as observed them dictating to Margaret. She asked parents to come whenever they could to help the kindergarteners during journal time; the children, therefore, were used to adults other than Margaret responding to their requests, "I'm ready for a story." Moreover, my sitting there while a child raised his or her hand for many, many minutes could lead to anger, so I followed Margaret's procedure in taking dictation, when I was not "too busy." This involvement aided me in gaining the favor and respect of both Margaret and the children.

TABLE 1.1.   Data Collection Procedures

Academic Year	Month	Major Procedures
Year 1: 1985	Jan.	Dyson begins visiting school
		Familiarizing self with kindergarten and first/second-grade classroom routines and class members
		Selecting 8 case study children: 4 kindergarteners and 4 first graders
	Feb. through May	Dyson begins formal data collection
		Observing/audiotaping in kindergarten and first/second-grade classrooms 2 to 5 times weekly
		Photocopying kindergarten and first-grade children's journals
	June through July	Dyson begins intensive analysis of kindergarten data
Year 2: 1985-1986	Aug. through Nov.	Dyson begins intensive analysis of first-grade data
	Nov. through Dec.	Dyson, Heller, and Gardner begin visiting school
	Jan.	Teacher strike postpones beginning of observation
	Feb. through May	Dyson, Heller, and Gardner continue formal data collection
		Observing/audiotaping in first/second- and second/third-grade classrooms by each observer, 2 times weekly
		Photocopying first- and second-grade journals

TABLE 1.1.   (continued)

Academic Year	Month	Major Procedures
	June through July	Dyson begins writing case studies
Year 3: 1986– 1987	Aug. through Sept.	Dyson and Heller begin visiting new kindergarten class
		Documenting teacher's initiation of children into school life
	Oct. through Dec.	Dyson and Heller continue observations in kindergarten classroom
	Jan. through May	Heller continues visiting school, including kindergarten, first/second-grade, and second/third-grade classes; Dyson begins more concentrated period of data analysis and writing

classroom for the day, I photocopied the drawn and written products. Audiotapes were transcribed and integrated with the notes after each observation was completed. (The work sheets used to integrate data are contained in Appendix A.)

A child's composing of a journal entry often extended over a two- or even three-day period. Thus, weekly observations were generally conducted on consecutive days. Since school days were never entirely predictable (children were absent; their process took three or four days rather than one or two; Margaret unexpectedly began a whole-class activity, thus temporarily eliminating journal time), this schedule did not insure viewing the focal child's complete composing process within a school week. Nonetheless, beginning the second month of the study, at least one complete process was observed for each case study child each month of the project. During any observation session, data were also gathered on all children sitting near the focal child. In addition, many observations were made at other times of portions of a focal child's composing process; these partial observations served as comparison data for the full observations.

TABLE 1.2. Age, Gender, and Ethnicity of Focal Children

	Age*	Gender	Ethnicity
Kindergarteners			
Maggie**	5.0	Female	Anglo
Regina	6.0	Female	Black
Jesse	5.6	Male	Anglo
Ruben	5.1	Male	Hispanic
First graders			
Sonia	6.2	Female	Hispanic
Mitzi***	6.3	Female	Anglo
Jake	6.5	Male	Mixed (Black/Anglo)
Manuel	7.3	Male	Mixed (Hispanic/Anglo)

* Age as of January 1, 1985, given in years and months.

** During 1985, Christopher, a kindergartener, was a focal child; Maggie was a "back-up." She was observed, although less intensively, and all her journal entries were collected. During 1986, Christopher withdrew temporarily from the school, and so Maggie became a regular case study participant with Christopher as a back-up.

*** During the observations from February through May 1986, Mitzi was in the second/third-grade classroom; all other children were in the first/second-grade room.

At the end of the first two years of data collection, my two assistants, Carol Heller and Mary Gardner, and I had collected approximately 144 hours of audiotaped data and 246 journal entries produced by the case study children. Margaret provided an additional 100 "preobservation" entries produced by the four kindergarten case study children in the fall of year 1 before our data collection had begun. (Generally, the older children did not do extended writing in the fall, before they began language arts classes with Margaret.) Table 1.3 shows the number of entries, collected for each child and the average number of words they contained.

These data were studied in order to develop a set of coding categories—a specialized vocabulary—for talking about the children and their ways of composing. This vocabulary was to be used to construct each child's history as a composer in Margaret's classroom. In Appendix B, I provide a complete description of the coding categories and the procedures used to develop them. Here, I present a brief overview of the kinds of categories developed.

TABLE 1.3. Number of Journal Entries Collected from Each Child and Average Number of Words per Entry

	Kindergarten (fall)*		Kindergarten (spring)		1st Grade		2nd Grade	
	No. ent.	No. wds**	No. ent.	No. wds**	No. ent.	No. wds**	No. ent.	No. wds**
Maggie	25	22.9	13	22.6	9	40.4		
Regina	21	19.0	14	27.4	16	24.0		
Jesse	27	15.1	19	21.8	21	14.0		
Ruben	27	19.7	21	19.8	21	22.4		
Sonia					10	18.2	9	29.1
Mitzi					22	20.2	17	49.2
Jake					14	22.9	20	50.7
Manuel***					8	17.8	12	22.6
Totals:	100	19.2	67	22.9	121	22.5	58	37.9

* These products were collected by the classroom teacher before the project formally began.

** The figures for numbers are averages per entry.

*** Manuel's entire second-grade journal comprised one story; he, however, divided the story into "parts" that could be "finished" (as in, "I finished that part."). Therefore, "parts," rather than "entries," are counted for second grade.

The basic unit of analysis was the *composing event,* defined as all behaviors involved in the production of one journal entry. More than one observation session (activity periods in which the child was observed) could comprise one composing event, and although less likely, more than one composing event could occur during one observation session. The composing event was the framework for describing how individual children used drawing, any accompanying gesture and talk, and written text to represent meaning.

The *function* categories described how the children used talk during journal time. In brief, the children used language to represent real and imaginary situations or worlds (referred to as *representational* language); to monitor and direct their own behavior, including their drawing and writing behaviors (*directive* language); to seek information (*heuristic* language); to express their feelings and attitudes (*personal* language); and to manage social relationships (*interactional* language). (The labels for these functional categories were based on those by Halliday, 1973.)

The *meaning elements* categories described the meanings the children expressed not only in their talk, but also in their drawings and in their written products. Thus, these categories were the key to understanding the interrelationships among the meanings children expressed in varied media and how those interrelationships changed over time. The meaning elements included objects, actors, actions, placement in space and time (past, present, future), and sensorimotor qualities (direction, force, speed, volume).

Most important, perhaps, the coding system of *topics* described what the children were talking about and, more dramatically, which of their multiple worlds the children were focusing on (see Figure 1.3). The children might be talking about their own imaginary worlds; that is, their talk could be "task involved," as shown in Part A of the figure. This talk first revealed the children both leaning upon and confronting the tensions among the differing (but overlapping) symbolic worlds—space/time structures—created through drawing and any accompanying representational talk and gestures, on the one hand, and written text, on the other. For example, children initially drew a picture in their journals before they wrote an accompanying text. When they began to write their journal entries, their pictures existed in the present but any talk and dramatic gestures that had accompanied the drawing of that picture were cast in the past. Thus, Jesse dramatized a motorcycle race as he drew swirling lines (see Figure 1.4), and then he wrote, "This is the motorcycle guy" [a description of his picture]. "And then the motorcycle guy won" [a record of past told and dramatized action].

As my study progressed, the children's relationships with each other grew. Their imaginary worlds were increasingly embedded within their

Figure 1.3.   The children's talk: References to multiple worlds.

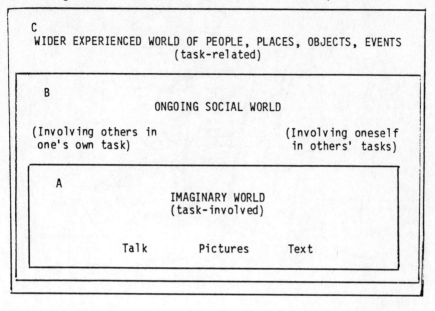

ongoing social world, and thus each child's case history became inter-twined with that of others. The children's talk could involve others in their own worlds or involve themselves in others' worlds (See part B of Figure 1.3).

This more deliberate coming together of the children's social and imaginary worlds also led to struggles with the borders between worlds. These struggles left little footprints in the children's texts—shifts of tense and of person or stance. To illustrate, consider Mitzi's text about her drawing of a cowboy:

> Once there was a cowboy. I hated the cowboy a lot. Do You LIke cowboy's? but I like YOu a lot. Sometimes I LIke The cowboy. TueSdaYs I liKe The cowboy. The End

In this piece, Mitzi leaves her perch as a third-person observer of an imaginary world to extend a first-person invitation to "you" to enter into her story with her.

Finally, the children's comments on each other's work could lead to talk that was task-related; that is, talk about the wider experienced world

Figure 1.4.   Jesse's motorcycle guy.

of people, places, events, and things. The children's imaginary worlds were thus increasingly embedded within yet another world (see part C of Figure 1.3). This embedding, too, could lead to struggles, as the children wrestled with how true experiences and personal opinions figured into their imaginative worlds. The following piece by Mitzi, who had very ambivalent feelings about her little brother, suggests tensions between imaginary and real worlds:

> Once there was a girl. I like the girl. I hate the Girls Brother a Lot. The End.

In the kindergarten and early first grade, most of the children's talk about each other's worlds or about the wider world of experiences happened during drawing. The children's written products were often controlled by their pictures; that is, their written texts had little independent existence. As will be illustrated, children's talk with each other about their imaginary worlds seemed important for both loosening the texts' ties to drawing and for embedding those texts in the peer social world and in the wider experienced world. That embedding posed, for all the children, the following challenging questions, which are refined versions of those that opened this chapter:

- In the classroom, the peer social world can infuse school literacy with social meaning. That world is built up through peer talk. Children may thus face this question: How does one interact socially through written monologues?
- For children, drawing is one of the earliest means of graphic representation over which they gain control. Their drawings and the process of creating them are often infused with and surrounded by talk. Thus, children may confront this question: How do meanings formulated in colorful drawings and/or lively talk "fit" onto the flat symbolic surface of written text?
- Finally, children's dramatic play and their imaginative drawings are their own replayings and graphic organizations of their experienced worlds. How, then, in the more deliberate process of writing, does one make up "pretend" stories about "real" experiences?

In brief, the children must discover how one negotiates among multiple worlds—the symbolic or imagined worlds brought to life through various media, the social world, and the wider experienced world.

In the next chapter, I take readers more deeply into Margaret's classroom, describing the classroom community formed by Margaret and her children, the community within which the children confronted and began to resolve these questions.

2

The Classroom Community: Nurturing Writing Growth

It is the second day of school, and Margaret is discussing journal writing with her kindergarteners: "I'm also going to show you another journal of a kindergarten person from year before last. . . . This was a little girl whose dad was the preacher of the church that I go to. She started kindergarten here and this was her sixth journal. We put [the number] one on the first journal you do. . . . This was the last journal she did before she moved to Oregon, and I asked her if I could keep it, and she said yes. But her grandmother keeps asking me for it."

Margaret's remarks, as she shared a favorite journal from the past with her new kindergarten class, reflected the message she seemed to be conveying to her children: When you enter my classroom you are entering into a community, a community with a history and bylaws, a community to which you will contribute. In this chapter, I consider the structure of this community—the daily routines, including the routines of journal writing, the central activity of Margaret's classroom. As the chief architect of this structure, Margaret was guided by values and goals for teaching, learning, and writing, some of which she explicitly stated and others of which seemed implicitly embodied within her daily decisions.

The major foci of this book are Margaret's children, their writing, and the role of that writing in their social lives. My intention in detailing the classroom structure and Margaret's goals and teaching procedures is not to evaluate them, although there is much to admire. Rather, my intention is to describe the classroom within which the children's social world was taking form.

THE CLASSROOM STRUCTURE

Space

The school building itself was a one-story, L-shaped building. Margaret's classroom was at the angle in the L, separated from her colleague Rebecca's first/second-grade homeroom by a bookcase, and from the classroom library on the other by a set of stairs and a half-wall (see Figure 2.1). Beyond the library was a small "home center," which was a dramatic-play area equipped with play stove and sink, boxed and canned goods, dishes, dolls, dress-up clothes, small tables, and huge blankets. Beyond that was Bill's second/third-grade classroom. Thus, Margaret's room was a cross-station for all the children as they moved between Bill's and Rebecca's rooms.

In the center of Margaret's classroom was a large oval, drawn with a marker on the rug. This oval was the center of classroom life. Each of Margaret's class sessions—whether she was meeting with the kindergarten class, the first/second-grade class, or the second/third-grade class—began and ended with the children sitting "on the oval." As suggested by Figure 2.1, most of the areas bordering the oval were used for specific activities, as follows:

- *Music*: The children sat on the floor and on the section of the oval nearest Margaret's desk when they sang songs, directed and accompanied by Margaret on the piano. Sometimes they performed on rhythm instruments as well.
- *Puppet theater*: A small group of children could perform spontaneous dramas with puppets. In the kindergarten, this activity could attract a large audience of children who clapped and applauded and, at times, dissolved into wild and rather unfocused giggling and dancing about. At such times, Margaret would call for a rather early intermission.
- *Books*: Individually or in pairs, children could look through the books; small groups of two or three sometimes listened as another child read a book out loud.
- *Puzzles and small manipulables*: Children generally did puzzles individually, except when it was clean-up time, when several children helped those sitting amongst scattered pieces with undone puzzle boards. The small manipulables attracted groups of three or four children, who enjoyed constructing buildings, vehicles, robots, and other objects.
- *Paint easels*: Strategically located by the sink, the easels accommodated four painters at a time. Throughout the building were special places on

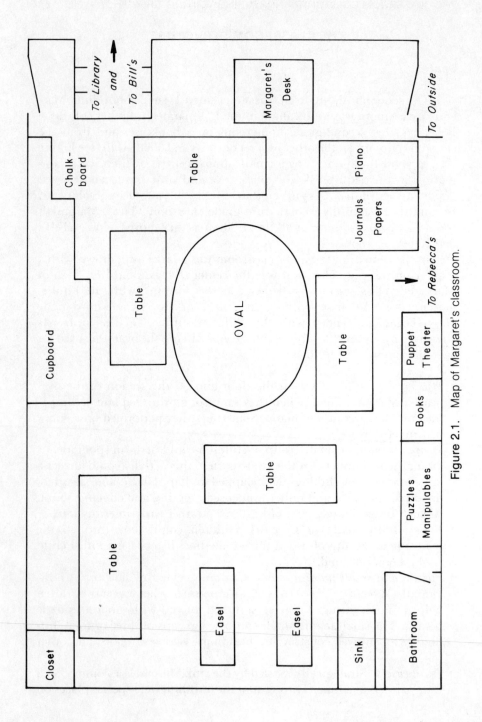

Figure 2.1. Map of Margaret's classroom.

the wall for all of the children's work. So, each day, after the paintings had hung to dry on a small clothesline, Margaret displayed the new work.

• *Tables*: Journals and art activities were done on the tables. The first/ second- and second/third-grade classes had approximately 30 children each, and there was just enough (or perhaps not quite enough) elbow room for them to fit at the tables. The kindergarten class was smaller in number, as well as in physical size. It typically had 20 children, who could comfortably spread out as they worked at the tables.

Time

The daily routines were tied more to space than to time. Class began on the rug and then moved to the tables or activity areas. Margaret sometimes got quite involved with the opening activities, while at other times she kept them short to allow more time for other activities. Margaret was not a clock-watcher, and time seemed to speed by. There were so many children and so much going on that time to change classes or to go out to recess always seemed to arrive abruptly, causing a rush of activity. Tables needed to be cleaned and materials put away, and the children usually needed to be calmed down. One of the children, Jesse—who looked forward to recess—found this lack of clock-watching distressing, as illustrated by his remarks in the following excerpt.

> JESSE: What? Look at the clock! We've got to go out. We're gonna be late today. That's why we gotta start on time.
> DYSON[1]: Well, nobody's perfect.
> JESSE: Everybody's perfect. Bill, Rebecca.
>
> . . .
>
> Rebecca is really perfect. She looks at the clock before anybody else.

Despite the fluidness of time, Margaret did have a fairly fixed daily schedule. During the time I observed at the school, children flowed in and out of her classroom in this order:

8:50– 9:55	Kindergarteners
9:55–10:10	Snack/recess

---

[1]Throughout the text, my participation in the classroom dialogue will be indicated by the use of my last name, as done here.

10:10–11:00	First/second graders
11:00–11:10	Recess
11:10–12:00	Second/third graders

The Curricular Context

While Margaret concentrated on all language arts, Bill took major responsibility for mathematics and science, and Rebecca for the reading aspect of the language arts. I closely observed the children as they flowed in and out of Margaret's room, and I gained some sense of the life surrounding her room through casual observation, through examining the school's curricular documents, and by attending to the noise that traveled from Bill's and Rebecca's rooms to Margaret's.

The math and science programs seemed to fit the written description given in the school's grant application:

> Specific attention will be given to actively involving individual pupils and groups in handling measuring containers with sand and water in order to develop a firm grasp of . . . quantities and shapes and weights. The school environment itself . . . will be measurable and dividable in terms useful for beginning learners. Natural phenomena in the school garden, fish tank and small animal cages will be discussed and analyzed so that pupils will develop a "scientific" method of recording and comparing information. Useful . . . skills will result from the application of basic math to life . . . [For example,] the children will measure and weigh themselves. [Continuation Application for Urban Magnet Program in the Arts and Humanities, 1974]

In addition to these elements, the children were introduced to and practiced basic arithmetic processes and facts.

The central aspect of the language arts program was the journal activity, which took place in Margaret's room. In addition, Margaret organized a home reading program, in which all the children took home books to read and discuss with family members or friends. In Margaret's, Rebecca's, and Bob's rooms, the children sang songs, and both Margaret and Rebecca recited finger plays and action rhymes with the children.

During her daily sessions with the children, Rebecca read to them regularly and also had them read a variety of literature. Rebecca enjoyed drama, and all classes engaged in some drama activities. During a daily silent reading period, the first through third graders read books selected from the school library. First graders who were just beginning to read also read simple sentences Rebecca composed, using their names. The first, second, and third graders read in a basal reader as well, and Rebecca organized the children into small groups for this purpose.

After lunch, the kindergarteners went to daycare centers or to their homes, and the first through third graders participated in a long activity period, centered around social studies and science themes. For example, for one unit, Margaret had the children interview their parents about their family history. The children then prepared family trees, tracing as many generations as possible across time and, in some cases, across countries.

THE DAILY SCHOOL LIFE

Margaret's Opening Activities: Chronicling School Life

During each morning session (i.e., kindergarten, first/second-grade, and second/third-grade periods), Margaret began with opening activities on the oval. At this time, more than any other, Margaret seemed to establish explicitly the themes and values that governed her classroom. Margaret and the children might share stories about the previous evening's happenings, adjust the calendar, play rhythm and rhyming games, make announcements about special school activities, and share a professional author's book. Margaret was the children's guide through time and place; she linked their activities to those of earlier classes and to their own future activities as class members, and she worked as well to link their out-of-school and in-school worlds. The intentions and values guiding her own behavior were most explicit in the opening days of the school year, when she welcomed a new kindergarten to the school. Thus, those days receive special emphasis in the discussion to follow.

Documenting the Passage of Time.   As illustrated in the anecdote that opens this chapter, Margaret brought her memories of former students into her present classroom. She used previous years' journals to demonstrate to the new kindergarten class the open-ended nature of the journal activity; that is, that different children do very different things. She reffered to children who had done particularly memorable projects. And she spoke of potential problems that "you" might have, the "you's" acting to unite present class members with past ones. For example, she explained a problem that had arisen when children had taken their journals home: "It sort of makes it difficult when you forget to bring them back, because then I'm afraid they will disappear into the something-or-other. . . . At the end of the year, you will get all of your journals except one. I keep one as a representative to show next year's kindergarteners."

Margaret frequently referred to individual children by name, implying that their individual history would also figure into the class's history. For example, Margaret explained to the new kindergarten class that they, too, would have their paintings hung on the wall. Individual creations would be dated and displayed, and in that way personal history and community history would be interwoven: "These are some people who have painted, and last night I was here long enough to make a name tag for every single person in the school. And I'm going to get—see those nails that are in there on top of the wall there? I hang paintings of everybody in the school up there. André knows 'cause he's been there and seen them." (André had visited the school in the past with his older brother, Joshua.) "Right, André?"

Not only paintings, but all creations, including journals, were dated. Numbers were important markers for keeping track of time, and they were often referred to: How many days until the school walkathon, somebody's birthday, a field trip to the park? What number journal are you on, 1? 2? 3? How many books have you had somebody read to you or read yourself? The following excerpt shows how Margaret explained "book reports" to her new kindergarten class.

MARGARET: You're the author of your journal, and you're the illustrator of your journal. [In doing book reports,] you have to write the author of the book you check out, and the illustrator of the book. And then the next question [on the book report form] says, "Who read the book to me?" Well, some of you may be able to read, and if you do, you put your name down; but, if you aren't able to read, you put down, "Mom wrote—or read it to me." Or, if Joshua should read it to you, André, you can put "Joshua" down; or, if you had an aunt or an uncle, or a grandpa or a grandma or a cousin, or just a friend.

CHILD: I have a cousin.

MARGARET: Whoever reads the book, you put there. Then the next word—

BRANDON: I have two cousins.

MARGARET: Oh. Well, maybe they'll read it to you sometime. When you have read 10 books, then Margaret will give you your choice of books from that big red box over there that says "Our Box." Now, that box is

full of books, and you can go through there after
you've done 10 book reports and pick out your own
[book]. I'll give it to you, and you get to keep it
forever.

. . .

Last year, Loan did 100 books, or something like
that.
CHILD: Phew, 100 books!
CHILD: Woa boy!

So, just as the older children have moved through the year, so will
you, Margaret seemed to be saying. And "you" are both an individual and
part of a larger "you," a member of the community we are building. We
will keep track of the accumulation of our days and our individual and
collective projects, by dating, counting, and remembering.

Linking Through Cooperation, Not Competition.   While Margaret did
refer to individual children's accomplishments and to the accumulation
of those accomplishments (e.g., number of journals completed), she
stressed cooperation, not competition, among children. For example,
Margaret downplayed differences in ability in her comments to the class
about book reports, by noting matter-of-factly that some children would
read the books themselves and others would be read to. Similarly, in the
kindergarten, she noted that some children wrote entries themselves in
addition to dictating, and some did not. Margaret acknowledged but did
not praise the knowledge and skill the children came to school with, nor
did she discount these. Margaret's attitude seemed to be best articulated
by one of her students, Nathan. Early in the kindergarten year, he explained to Margaret that he was capable of "overwriting" (writing over
words written by an adult), noting that "the reason I'm good at it is
because I've done this before." Those who were not particularly "good at
it" would learn.
Margaret did publicly acknowledge growth in each child's perceived
skill. For example, when Brandon first reread a story in his journal,
Margaret was clearly pleased: "Are you going to tell your mommy that
you read this story that was in your journal today? That would be very
nice. On the seventeenth of September of 1986, you read the first story to
me out of your journal."
In addition to deemphasizing competition among her students in
their knowledge and skill, Margaret worked to establish a general classroom climate that stressed negotiation and cooperation. She encouraged
the children to be mindful of the existence of the group, talking fre-

quently of "our" plans, routines, activities. If children brought special child-made objects to school, Margaret encouraged them to demonstrate to others how to make the objects; sometimes she arranged for a child to have a space during activity time, so that the child could teach others (e.g., showing others how to make a paper airplane). One day Chiel brought an "invisible object," which he showed to the class by doing a movement exercise his mother had learned at aerobics class. He, in turn, taught the movement to interested children during activity time. On another day, Cassie brought a math game. Margaret did not praise Cassie's math expertise but asked her, "How many people can play that game?" "Do you know it well enough to have people play with you?" "Would you like, when we have our choice [activity] time, to have about four or five people play the game with you?"

Margaret did not allow physical "competition" or fighting, although such fighting did happen occasionally. Early in the kindergarten year, Margaret acted out with the children a potential "fight" scene, in order to emphasize talking as an alternative to hitting.

MARGARET: We're going to try something. Nate, come over here. (begins to pretend to punch Nate) What do you say when you want someone to stop something?
NATE: Stop.
MARGARET: . . . Stop it. What's my name?
NATE: Margaret.
MARGARET: OK. Would you look at me and say, Stop it, Margaret?
NATE: Stop, Margaret!
MARGARET: That's right. Because when somebody does something that you don't like—and now, uh, Nate, would you tell me what I was doing that you don't like?
NATE: You were punching me.
MARGARET: I was punching him. Tell me, Nate, do you like to be punched? Say no. Well, tell me, I don't like to be punched.
NATE: I don't like to be punched.
MARGARET: OK. Now, this is one of the things that we do at our school. Uh, when somebody does something that we don't like, what do you think we're supposed to do?

As this example clearly illustrates, Margaret expected the children to refer to her by her first name, just as she referred to them by their first names. And, as will be evident throughout the exchanges between Margaret and her children, she emphasized cooperation and mutual respect in her interactions with them; the children were urged to express their feelings and opinions in ways considered clear but polite. In fact, the school program was dependent upon children's willingness to tell the teacher what activity they wished to do or, within a writing activity, what special topic they wished to write about.

Margaret certainly did establish rules and regulations, and, as will be illustrated in Chapter 3, the children themselves viewed Margaret as an authority figure, as one who was responsible for enforcing rules and keeping order. Nonetheless, her relationship with the children seemed to be built less on authority than those described as typical of most U.S. classrooms (Cazden, 1986). The children initiated interactions with Margaret, and she most frequently responded to her students as if they were interesting individuals who were very good company. The following exchange with Chiel, for example, seems more an exchange between friends than between teacher and child.

> CHIEL: Margaret.
> MARGARET: Yes, Chiel.
> CHIEL: I'm staying for lunch.
> MARGARET: You are? Then we can walk up to the lunchroom together.

Further, Margaret did not present herself as the definitive source of all knowledge. She frequently turned to the dictionary and the encyclopedia to answer children's questions and at times said she simply did not know the answer to a question. Moreover, she asked the children more genuine questions than testing questions (the latter being questions to which she already knew the answer). She wondered about the experiences they commented upon, the objects from their homes they brought to display, their activity preferences and book choices. Indeed, during a practice session for the end-of-the-year achievement tests, Maggie, then a kindergartener, questioned Margaret's knowledge of a matching task. Margaret asked the children if they could find the picture in the row that went with the one in the first box. "Can you do it?" Margaret asked the class. "Can *you* do it, Margaret?" Maggie replied.

Linking Home and School, the Social and the Academic. In the opening activities, Margaret often discussed her own problems and joys. She presented herself as a person with a life outside the classroom, but one whose school life meshed with her home life. For example, she often told them that she had taken their journals or other products home with

her or that she was sleepy because there had been a late meeting at the
school the evening before. In the following interaction, Margaret inter-
twined her personal experiences with those of Jamie and Nate, and, in the
process, both Margaret and the children attempted to refine each other's
understanding, each other's words.

> MARGARET: Now, Jamie had a bloody nose last night. That's
> some more bad news, but the good news is that she
> did not have another one this morning.
>
> CHILD: How do you get a bloody nose?
>
> MARGARET: Well, she occasionally has them. One of my sons
> used to do that. No reason at all, and all of a sudden
> blood would be spurting out of his nose. And it
> would scare me to death, and the doctor would say
> there's really nothing to worry about.
>
> JAMIE: But it was this morning I had a bloody nose.
>
> MARGARET: You had a bloody nose. Uh huh. But your mom said
> there's really nothing to be concerned about. Yes.
>
> NATE: You know when I'm on a trip, you know what
> happens? Just about all day my nose is bloody.
>
> MARGARET: Did you hit it? Or does this happen with you occa-
> sionally?
>
> NATE: Not usually.
>
> MARGARET: It just happened that one time, huh?

Margaret not only talked with the children about their home lives;
she invited children's parents into the room to help the children during
journal time and, more relevant to the point here, to give the parents the
opportunity to share their experiences and expertise. Brandon's mother
demonstrated her rug weaving and Sonia's her expertise with calligraphy.
On another occasion, a visit by Rencho's father may have helped the children understand not just the father but Rencho himself more clearly.
Rencho was a curiosity to some of them. Despite his intermittent displays
of battle-scene and vehicular sound effects (an exclusively male style in
this classroom), his slight frame and long braided hair gave him the
appearance of a little girl. Rencho's father also had a long braid, but he
was quite clearly a man—a large, muscular man. During his visit, he
talked about many Native American customs, including the length of his
and Rencho's hair.

Perhaps more important than this sharing by the children's parents,
Margaret made connections between what might be considered academic

tasks (e.g., those having to do with literacy and arithmetic) and the children's interests and experiences. In the following examples, Margaret responded to the children's interest in being "older" and then to their enthusiasm for Great America, an amusement park. In both cases, Margaret attempted to extend the children's interests through the use of numbers and language, both helpful tools.

CASSIE: Who's the oldest kid?

MARGARET: Uh, the oldest kid? You see, we'll have to wait until we get all the birthdays. We'll start on birthdays next week.

CHILD: What does that mean?

MARGARET: That means that will be your homework—that you have to memorize your birthday.

KIM: We are (   ). Then we goin' to go, to Great America

MARGARET: Oh. Is this your birthday or something?

KIM: No.

MARGARET: It's just a special day when your're going to celebrate? I like celebrating Thursdays, too. Uh, Bumi?

BUMI: I've gone to Great America.

CHILDREN: (mumbled announcements of their own trips to Great America)

MARGARET: Yeah. Let's see the hands of everybody in here who's been to Great America. One, two, three, four, five. I've never been to Great America. I've got that exciting thing to do yet.

NATE: There is, uh, there is a ride at Great America. And it does—you go around a loop that that that you go upside down the loop three times.

MARGARET: That sounds exciting. You could write about that in your journal.

Choice Time: Journals

In the kindergarten class, following the opening activities, children could choose what to do next, and one of the "choices" was journal writing. As noted already, the journal activity was the cornerstone of the school's literacy program. It was meant as a way for children to express their own experiences and feelings within the school. Since their own written thoughts would be read, the journal activity was viewed by the school faculty as both a reading and a writing activity and as one that would be meaningful to children from a variety of backgrounds. This philosophy was stated from the very founding of the shool:

> One of the major reasons for the students falling further behind as they progress through the grades is the instruction and learning environment which is provided for them in the earlier grades. . . . This project will provide a rich, responsive learning environment and instruction which will build on the strengths and interests of the students. . . . Specific activities are scheduled for teachers, aides and parents to work with children on oral and written expression. One method of creating relevant "readers" is through recording of direct experiences and feelings into personal books [journals] throughout the year including photographs and drawings to accompany and stimulate verbal expression. [Continuation Application for Urban Magnet Program in the Arts and Humanities, 1974]

This school's language arts program, then, was shaped before the emphasis on young children's writing that arose in the late 1970s. It was thus most influenced by the older "language experience" approach, which bases initial literacy programs on children's own developing language (Veatch, Sawicki, Elliott, Barnette, & Blakey, 1973).

Margaret herself felt that the children's lives would be enriched by writing, just as her own was. Through writing, she "kept track of her life" and "sorted out her feelings," especially in her diary. She wrote letters to her mother, who lived in Nebraska, and she wrote telegrams to government officials whose decisions alarmed her. She sometimes read to the children those telegrams or poems she had written.

Margaret viewed the children's journal writing as an avenue for their feelings, experiences, and imaginings, a way for them to become "open to expressing themselves." She intended, first of all, to help the children view written language as one of the expressive arts and, second, to help them learn written language conventions.

Because of the perceived importance of journal time, Margaret monitored the kindergarteners' participation in this activity. She kept a record of how many times the children had chosen particular activities (painting, the home center, puzzles and games); if they had not worked in their journal for a couple of days, she asked them to do so. Some days, especially when there were parent visitors in the room and thus extra adults to help, she had all the children work in their journals. In the first/ second- and second/third-grade classes, all children first worked in their journals and then were able to choose an activity. Margaret also kept track of the centers in which the older children participated. If a child had not had an opportunity for several weeks to engage in an alternative activity, especially painting, Margaret would offer the child the time to do so.

Before actually beginning to write in their journals, the kindergarteners often engaged in whole-class projects focused on words, especially their names, and letters. They read their own and each other's names when Margaret had papers to pass out, they found each other's names on their mailboxes or small wooden cubbies, and they discussed the alphabet books each child was creating.

The first, second, and third graders talked about punctuation and capitalization, sometimes studying sentences Margaret put on the board. They discussed word categories, like synonyms, antonyms, and homonyms. They brainstormed descriptive words and thought of alternative ways of beginning a story or of describing an object or person.

Sometimes Margaret read a professional author's book to the children before they actually began writing. Often she read from the children's earlier journal work or had individual children read their own journals. For both professional and child-produced literature, Margaret talked about the kind of story she had read. She emphasized that there were many kinds of stories—true, not true, adventure, funny, historical, imaginative. There were ones with descriptive language that painted "word pictures"; ones with many details; and ones with clear beginnings, middles, and ends.

The length of talk about journal writing varied, from none at all to taking up most of the period. Eventually, though, the children lined up before the journal box to search through the alphabetically arranged folders, each looking for the one with her or his own name, containing her or his own journal.

Aiming for Children's Self-Expression.   Margaret had begun her career teaching high school students, some of whom could not read or write and who did not seem to have made the connection between their spoken ideas and the printed word. She wanted her kindergarteners to be "immediately aware that these little marks on the paper have to do with the things that come out of their mouths," that is, with their expressive language. She thus asked the kindergarteners to dictate "stories" to accompany their drawn pictures.

As the children dictated, Margaret talked with them about their stories, often asking questions to encourage them to elaborate on their ideas. As noted earlier, Margaret emphasized that stories could come from anywhere, from personal experiences at home or at school or from imagi-

nary tales heard or made up. Indeed, *story* was a general term for whatever the child formed on his or her paper. But, as will be discussed in
Chapter 4, the kindergarteners especially tended to describe their pictures
through their dictations; and Margaret, too, relied on pictures for elicit-
ing text from children who seemed to have little understanding of this
notion of dictating a story and, at times, for children who were having
trouble coming up with an idea. The following vignette is a case in point.

> Jeremy has dictated, "Once upon a time. I couldn't think of any-
> thing else." Margaret finds this text very funny. After laughing
> heartily, she focuses Jeremy's attention on his picture.
>
> MARGARET: Who are these people that you have here?
>   JEREMY: This is my—this is my daddy. This is my mama.
>   And this is my little brother.
> MARGARET: OK. Let's put that down. This, is, my, daddy. You
>   see. All you had to do was talk about your picture.
>   This is my daddy. D-A-D-D-Y.
>   . . .
>   Now, see? Once upon a time you could think of
>   something.

Margaret also called attention to the orientation and layout of print
on the page, the names of letters, and terms like *sentence, word,* and
letter. After taking dictation, Margaret first reread the piece, often encouraging a child to read with her. As is commonly recommended in language experience approaches to beginning literacy, the child was to
"overwrite" the first line of the dictation and, when his or her pencil
movements were more sure, "underwrite" or copy the first line (Veatch,
1978). Margaret expected that, throughout the year, some kindergarteners
would begin to write their own entries. Those children, though, would
still continue with the guided practice of dictating some of their stories.

Margaret did not discourage, although she did not formally encourage, the kindergarten children's independent exploring of print. Paper
and pencil were freely available, and all case-study kindergarteners did do
some independent writing. Children sometimes wrote each other's
names, occasionally exchanging names and phone numbers, sometimes
making presents or cards for each other or for Margaret (a present or card
most often consisted of a picture and the recipient's name). Margaret
displayed all pictures and writing that she received, including writing
that no one but the child could read. The children wrote letters, names,
and the word *love* on the covers of their journals and, early in the year, on

their pictures. This behavior in the journal itself lessened as the year went on, perhaps because the children's notions of what it meant to "write" their stories was narrowing; that is, a particular kind of writing in a particular kind of place was growing in importance. Throughout the year, however, all the children did write cards for holidays, and the circulating of names and cards continued.

The following two exchanges, the first with Brandon and the second with Rena, illustrate Margaret's interactional style during the kindergarten journal time. Rena's piece is unusual in that it is about her personal experiences, but Margaret's style is typical.

MARGARET: Now, OK, Brandon, tell me your story, hun.

BRANDON: (in deliberately paced "dictating" voice) Look at the mailboxes and look at the houses.

MARGARET: Look at the mailboxes and look at the houses?

BRANDON: Yeah. That's part of the mailbox. That's where you get the newspaper. (in conventional tone, pointing at his picture)

MARGARET: The apartment mailbox? Wait 'til I write that down. At the mailbox. Look at the mailbox. (rereading) Look, L-O-O-K. (writing) See, that word spells *look*. Look, at, the, houses? Is that what you said?

BRANDON: Houses and the mailbox and, um, the apartment.

MARGARET: Uh. That's the mailbox? Uh, there's the mailbox that you get your newspaper?

BRANDON: Mmm huh.

MARGARET: (examining Rena's bandaged finger) What did you do to your finger?

RENA: I got caught in the door.

MARGARET: You got caught in the door? Did it bleed?

RENA: Yup. But it didn't—it didn't, um, it didn't break my finger.

MARGARET: Why don't you do a picture of that? And say you caught your finger in the door, and it bled. But it didn't break.

RENA: I have some good news and some bad news. [This is how Margaret often began her own reporting of recent events or pertinent announcements to the class.] And that's the—and the good news—that was the bad news, and the good news, and—

MARGARET: Well, you could say that. I have some good news, and some bad news. Want me to write that, and you can do the picture?

. . .

(begins writing as Rena dictates) And some bad news. I caught, C-A-U-G-H-T, caught, my, finger, in, the, door.

RENA: And it hurt. We were going to, uh, a nurse's house.

MARGARET: And, and it—

RENA: And her name was—

MARGARET: You were going to a nurse's house? We, were, going,

RENA: And her name was my mom's friend.

MARGARET: to, a nurse's, house. Her name was my mom's friend?

RENA: Was my mom's—(giggles)

MARGARET: (giggles) Her name was my mom's friend.

RENA: Sheila! Sheila!

MARGARET: Sheila. OK. My, finger, bled. My finger bled, but it didn't break, right?

RENA: No-o. (Margaret is checking the accuracy of her wording, but Rena responds to the accuracy of the words' meaning.)

MARGARET: Bled—

RENA: Bled? You call it bled? I call it bleed.

MARGARET: Oh, it bleed? Oh. I'm sorry. I'll change that, then. My finger bleed, but it didn't break.

The first, second, and third graders wrote things out by themselves. Although some children's journal entries were initially shorter when independent writing (rather than dictation) began, the children did not produce one-word stories, as teachers have reported their first graders doing (Newkirk & Atwell, 1982). This was no doubt because an expectation of the sort of extended language that belonged in the journal was well established by first grade.

In her first/second- and second/third-grade classes, Margaret spent much of her time with children who were stalled in their writing—that is, having difficulty coming up with or developing an idea—and those who needed assistance with spelling. She stressed that journal entries had to make sense, and particularly problematic were partial, incomplete sentences. This was something Jesse frequently did, as exemplified by his line, "The spaceship blew up and it." Margaret had the children complete such entries. In addition, she asked for elaborations of ideas; she aimed to have those ideas come from the child's conversational talk. Finally, she had the children proofread their work for punctuation and spelling. The following example illustrates Margaret's interactional style.

> Jake has just completed his written story. He now begins drawing his accompanying illustration. In addition to the vehicles mentioned in his story, he draws a dune buggy and then begins to elaborate orally upon the dune buggy's adventures. Margaret is by his work table, and Jake calls out to her.

JAKE: Margaret. This buggy—see? He's digging in the dirt. It's brown. It's going ( ) the earth. Then it will get out of there and the ( ) will blow up the whole thing.

MARGARET: Oh, wow. I wish I had read that in that story.

JAKE: Yeah. I could put it in.

MARGARET: You could. Good idea.

JAKE: (begins to add "but I see a dune buggy" to his story)

JOSHUA: (to Margaret) Blew up. (wants to know how to spell "blew up")

MARGARET: Where is your dictionary? (referring to the home-made dictionaries where she puts frequently requested words)

JAKE: I'll spell it for him. Wait. Uh. B-L-O-W-U-P.

MARGARET: How would you make it *blew*?

JESSE: Green.

JAKE: B-U-E.

MARGARET: /l/ /l/.

JAKE: Blew. (looks at his own story) That's *blew* (pointing to *blow*)

MARGARET: You change that *o* to—

JAKE: *e*.

MARGARET: B-L—

JAKE: E-W

Respecting, Celebrating, Sharing. As is evident in the examples just given, Margaret intended that the children should consider the journals their own. Margaret made suggestions, but the children were the final authority. Note, for example, that Margaret expanded Brandon's text by interpreting his conversational "That's where you get the newspaper" as though it were dictation, even though it was spoken without the deliberate articulation that most kindergarteners begin to use for dictating. (See

Sulzby, 1982, for a study of children's adaptation of dictation to written language.) But she continually referred to Brandon as the final authority of his text's meaning. Note, too, that Margaret accepted without hesitation Rena's correction of *bled* to read *bleed*, and that Jake felt comfortable assuming responsibility for spelling *blew up* for Joshua, and that Margaret accepted his desire to spell the word.

Margaret's emphasis on individual children's ownership of their journals was particularly evident during the formal sharing of individual children's journals. After children had completed a journal, they were to pick three stories to read to the class. Margaret generally had the children read the stories themselves, although, early in the kindergarten year and always when requested, she would read the stories herself as the child stood beside her. While Margaret may have pressed for sense and elaboration during writing, during sharing the emphasis was on appreciating the child's journal. Margaret praised particularly well detailed or colorful drawings. She stressed that each child has his or her own vision of what objects looked like or how they should be described, and she discouraged the sort of criticism that was often present when the children worked on their own (as will be illustrated in Chapter 3).

> NATE: (in response to another child's picture) Alligators
>   don't look like that. That looks more like a snake.
> MARGARET: Some of us have different conceptions of alligators.

Margaret noted stories that were well formed (i.e., had beginnings, middles, and ends), used particularly descriptive words (painted word pictures), or displayed relatively sophisticated writing techniques (e.g., used story titles, chapters). In recognition of each child's completion of a journal, Margaret presented the author with a homemade certificate telling the child to "write on."

THE CHILDREN'S KNOWLEDGE OF CLASSROOM STRUCTURE

As illustrated in the preceding sections, Margaret established a structure within which a community of children could grow, a community where children were tied to each other and to the children who had, in past years, progressed through the school. While not specifically encouraged to "help each other write," the children were urged to be interested and thoughtful of each other. They were told to speak up, to take pride in their collective and individual accomplishments, and to be responsible for completing expected tasks. And, while they were encouraged to express themselves in print, the more comfortable media of pictures and speech were ever-present, supportive tools.

In this nurturing environment, the children themselves began to assume more responsibility for carrying out classroom rules and procedures. This developing knowledge was particularly evident when parents visited the kindergarten and children explained to them "how we do" various activities in the room. Indeed, in the children's world, competence—know-how—was important, and part of being competent was knowing what they were supposed to do, as the following anecdote shows.

> Margaret has just explained to a small group of kindergarteners that they are not to bring "Garbage Pail Kids" to school. ("Garbage Pail Kids" refers to cards, similar in construction to bubble-gum baseball cards, that depict broad-faced children engaged in grotesque acts.)
> NATE: I know some people with Garbage Pail Kids.
> RENA: I already knew that.
> NATE: [Child's name] has Garbage Pail Kids.
> RENA: I know. Don't tell me that.
> Chiel laughs and explains the importance of "don't tell me that" to his father, who is visiting on that day:
> CHIEL: That's what we do at clean-up time when we work with the big blocks. When we know it's clean-up time, right? People are always coming up to tell us it's clean-up time, and whenever someone comes up and says that—"Don't tell us it's clean-up time. We know!"
> RENA: Yep. I did it.

Knowledge of the journal activity was also becoming part of the class-member knowledge valued by the children. *Look-it,* a phrase used to call a peer's attention to one's drawing, was a regular part of classroom talk during journal time. And being able to spell one's own entry, without the teacher, was an important mark of independence, of knowing.

By spring of the kindergarten year, the children not only had an understanding of school rules and procedures, they had their own social world, a world that was not identical to the school world they shared with Margaret. In their world, Margaret was an important force, but she was not the center of attention. In the human classroom she so influenced, the children attended most closely to each other. Brought together by their common age and situation, they sought companionship and recognition in the peer group. The social energy thus generated first manifested itself in the children's talk, including their talk about their drawings. But, in time, that energy fueled the development of writing itself. In the next chapter, then, I move deeper inside the children's world.

3

The Children's Social World: Unintentional Helping

In the previous chapter, we saw how Margaret shared her classroom with the children, allowing the children's interest in each other to become a part of the official academic world. In time, the children formed their own social world, a world that was influenced by but not fully accessible to teachers, who, like parents, both protect and threaten children's social order. Listen, for example, to the following journal-time conversation, in which the children playfully acknowledge the importance of the journal activity in the adult world and their own capacity as "kids" to act in opposition to that world.

JAKE: Wanna put some cotton in here after every paper and make it a fat book and make it look like it's finished?

MANUEL: Yeah.

JAKE: And stick some cotton in it, and then we'll be finished with our thing. And make our mom and dad think we did lots of pages.

HAWKEYE: And then your mom and dad will say, "Hey! You skipped pages, you little kid."

In this exchange we sense the spirit of children together, reacting to and clearly influenced by the official school world, but also defining

Much of this chapter is based on A. Hass Dyson. (1988). Unintentional helping in the primary grades: Writing in the children's world. In B. A. Rafoth & D. L. Rubin (Eds.), *The social construction of written communication* (pp. 218–248). Norwood, NJ: Ablex. The material was adapted by permission of the publisher.

themselves as a group whose goals and purposes are not identical to that official world.

This potentially "oppositional" nature of children's social lives has been discussed primarily in the literature on inner-city adolescents (Labov, 1982; Ogbu, 1985). But, as the students in Margaret's classroom so vividly illustrate, young children are also intensely interested in each other. School literacy can even become a negative unifying force for young children, particularly for urban minority children, just as it can for older children and adolescents. That is, children may join together in their discomfort with or, more strongly, their rejection of academic demands. Among those aspects of school life most often cited as divisive are those that touch on children's relationships with each other—on the "I" and the "we"—children having to work silently, to value adults more than themselves and their peers' approval, and to compete with friends for that adult approval (Gilbert & Gay, 1985; Gillmore, 1983; Labov, 1982; Philips, 1972; Tharp et al., 1984).

But, as illustrated in the previous chapter, Margaret did not expect silence. She encouraged the children to take pride in their own and each other's work, and, in general, she did not offer approval or disapproval based on competition among students. Indeed, her goal was cooperation. Thus, in Margaret's classroom, the social energy of the peer group—the children's desire both to link themselves to each other and to distinguish themselves among their friends—actually infused the official curriculum, fueling the children's growth as language users, including their growth as writers. This mutually supportive situation was created without explicit attempts by Margaret to have the children help each other write. Just by "being kids," the children unintentionally helped each other become literate.

As a participant observer in this classroom, I had no official authority over the children, and, at the same time, I offered little protective assistance. For example, I did not intervene during routine child skirmishes over drawing markers and seating arrangements. Being far less central to their lives than Margaret and having no teaching responsibilities, I was able to sit and observe the children's chatting, arguing, and playing as their classroom life together unfolded. This chapter, which relies most heavily on data collected on the first and second graders, focuses on the children's collective social life and, particularly, the evolving role of writing in that life. The central themes are the children's perception of themselves as a group of "kids" who were different from "adults"; the children's strong interest in each other and each other's activity; and the potential of that interest to result in the children unintentionally helping each other learn to write. That is, as the children responded socially, and often playfully, to each other's strengths and shortcomings, they unintentionally and interactively accomplished critical and demanding intellectual tasks (Dyson, 1987b, 1988b).

THE CHILD COLLECTIVE

Margaret's children displayed a sense of being "kids" in school together in varied ways. First, they frequently joined together to engage in collective action, sometimes spontaneously doing group activities previously initiated by Margaret. For example, they spontaneously sang "Happy Birthday" when Margaret announced that it was her birthday, just as they regularly sang to the "birthday child." At the work tables, when one child began reciting a television commercial jingle or singing a pop song, others joined in. (The Bruce Springsteen rock song, "Born in the USA," was especially popular.) Sometimes the group was called to action by a spokesperson. One day Margaret announced that Rebecca, another teacher, would be retiring at the end of the school year. Jake immediately stood up and loudly claimed: "Many people don't want Rebecca to leave 'cause she's got all those puzzles and stuff. How many people don't want Rebecca to leave?" All of the children raised their hands, apparently wanting to have their say in the matter. Margaret assured them that the puzzles and games belonged to the school, not to the retiring teacher.

A second way of expressing their identity as "kids together" was to activate a group memory. Some memories were of projects or interests the children shared outside of school, such as television shows, popular singers, and baseball and football teams. Many, however, were of shared school experiences: "Remember when" a child got in trouble, or they made "fruit" in art class, or they played in the sand on the playground during a rainstorm? Jake considered a vehicle he had "invented" (i.e., one that he had drawn in his journal) to be a significant event his peers should recall, although this belief did not go uncontested.

JAKE: Who made up the bubble cars?
RUBEN: My brother have a bubble car.
JAKE: WHO MADE UP THE BUBBLE CARS?
SONIA: Your dad, for one thing.
JAKE: *I* made up the bubble cars.
SONIA: Well, how in the world could Ruben have one?!
. . .
JAKE: I was the creator of the bubble car.
SONIA: You're not a famous inventor.

On another day, Sonia acknowledged that Jake might indeed become famous for his invention, perhaps even by the time he was 10. As if to support this prediction, when Jake stood before the class to share a completed journal, several children shouted, "Bubble cars!"

As a third mechanism for expressing the collective, the children joined together to react or respond to school procedures and activities. Who was the substitute teacher? Was she mean? Would she know where to find the special game they were supposed to play? And, like workers in any organization, they wondered if they were being treated fairly.

SONIA: Finally, I get free time.
JAKE: I should get free time. I should get extra credit, because I finished two journals and I'm gonna finish my story. I should get some credit. She doesn't give me credit. [Margaret never talked about giving children "credit."]
JESSE: I know. She never gives you credit.
JAKE: She doesn't give *me* credit, that's for sure.
JESSE: She never gives me credit, for sure.

This interaction illustrates two characteristics of the children's talk about school procedures: the use of "school jargon" and the emphasis on the teacher's authority. In addition to *credit*, the children used the terms *flunk* and *pass* or *get promoted*, although, again, I never observed Margaret using these terms. They also discussed older children who had been *expelled* or *suspended*. They even talked about an elementary school near many of their homes, a school where children were supposedly quite "bad"; the school was in a naturally integrated, working-class neighborhood close to, in Jake's words, the "middle, the crazy part" of the city. The "you" in the following discussion is clearly kids.

JESSE: They be bad all the time there. People come home crying. People come home crying.
JAKE: Yeah?
JESSE: Yeah.
JAKE: I'd sure like to go to that school, then. Do they bench you or anything [i.e., do teachers make kids sit on a bench during recess if they get in trouble]?
JESSE: Uhhhhhhhhhhhh—
JAKE: Suspend you?
JESSE: Uh, probably not that much.

This example also illustrates the children's interest in authority. In their own classroom, from my viewpoint as observer, Margaret was a rather low-key authority figure. She expected the children to follow the rules, but she quietly and respectfully pointed out these rules when there was a need. To the children, however, Margaret seemed to be another "superhero," one with powers to be feared, depended upon, or defied. For example, on one occasion Jesse had used the Scotch tape to shape a boat in his journal, an inappropriate use of Scotch tape in this classroom. Jake scolded him: "You might have gotten busted by Margaret. You shouldn't have taken such a chance, because she will bust." Another time, Ruben and his brother Pedro claimed that they would stand up to Margaret's power.

PEDRO: Ruben! One more page is all I have to do (referring to his journal). But I'm not going to share it.
JESSE: You have to.
PEDRO: I'm—Nobody's gonna make me.
JESSE: Margaret's gonna make you. (laughs) O-o-o-o-o-o-oh! [As in, "You're gonna be in trouble!"]
RUBEN: Nobody's gonna make him, not even Margaret.

A fourth way in which the children expressed the child collective was to identify and share their common problems as "kids." Certainly their problems included concerns shared with adults, including the AIDS epidemic, starvation in Africa, terrorists in airports, the Challenger space tragedy, and the possibility of a war between the United States and the Soviet Union. In fact, Sonia, Jesse, and Jake once discussed their desire to wait to grow up "'til everybody dies, . . . and there wouldn't be anybody but us." This was wise, explained Jake, as "there might be a Vietnam again."

JAKE: They're going to ship out machine guns and, everybody, even the kids—They'll give them to every single kid in the United States.
JESSE: Except for babies.
JAKE: Kids would be wild. Kids would be the best.
JESSE: I know. They just die first, Man. I know why. Kids are small.
JAKE: The kids are small. The kids are mean.
JESSE: I know.
JAKE: I'm the slyest. I'm the—I'm sly.

Perhaps Jake saw himself as surviving such a horrible but, for a child captivated by war stories, exciting prospect.

Among the more frequently discussed and more modest problems were losing teeth (having "The Great Gap" in the front, as they called it); whether or not there was a Santa Claus; getting, keeping, and losing friends and pets; riding a bike without training wheels; just getting a bike; completing a journal; figuring out a word's spelling; and finding a black marker that actually wrote. Jake considered writing itself to be a problem kids confronted, as the following vignette shows.

> Jake has stopped writing and begun drawing. His journal entry does not seem finished to me, so I ask him if he is finished writing. His answer is philosophical:
>
> JAKE: I think so. When I was in kindergarten I learned, I liked to write. When you get older you don't like to write.
>
> DYSON: Why?
>
> JAKE: That's just the way with kids, some kids.
>
> DYSON: Oh. What happens to those kids?
>
> JAKE: Um. They like to write and write and write. So they just write, because they love to write.
>
> DYSON: And then what happens to those kids?
>
> JAKE: And then (large sigh), some kids just stop writing for awhile.
>
> DYSON: Why?
>
> JAKE: I don't know. That's what's happening to me. That's why I like to draw more than I like to work. [Note that writing, not drawing, is "work."]
>
> DYSON: Mmmmmmmmmm.

So Jake appeared to admit indirectly that his story was not quite up to his usual standard. As he explained it, though, what was happening to him was just the way some kids are—it's a common problem, just a stage; not to worry.

SOCIAL CONCERNS DURING JOURNAL TIME: NETWORKING

The previous section presented ways in which the children proclaimed themselves to be a group—"kids"—facing common challenges; creating a collective memory; and capable, albeit in a modest sense, of taking collective action. In illustrating the child collective, I have not placed in a separate section those examples that pertain to writing, because they did not occur in a "separate section" of classroom life. Written language was interwoven with the child collective.

This section pushes further inside the collective itself, describing the social themes or intentions that seemed to underlie the children's interactions or "networking" within the group. That is, the focus will not be on the children's distinctive relationship to the adult world, but on their relationships with each other as reflected in their talk. That talk reflected a desire to be not only a competent part of the group—a competent kid— but also to be a special, distinctive member, worthy of esteem.

Managing Resources

As previously noted, the children did not use their own pencils and marking pens, but selected these valued commodities each day from the common stores. One social concern or intention, then, was to manage these tools: "This is my eraser." "I need a blue." "Which is the darkest green?" "Who needs purple?" In addition, the children selected their own space, also a valued commodity: "Don't squish me." "Get your book off mine." "Don't bump me."

As with any valued commodity, materials and space could be used to establish positive or negative links with others. Ruben, for example, frequently offered his markers to other boys: "You wanta use mine? You can use mine." Jesse consistently turned down Ruben's offers, as he wanted to use Jake's markers. Jake, on the other hand, had a colored pencil feud with Kenji that lasted an entire semester. Jake and Kenji "ripped each other off" by taking the "whole tin can" of colored pencils when the other was not looking, made "straight deals" about who would get to use the pencils on a particular day, and warned each other that, if they weren't careful, they might "get busted" by their teacher for failing to share.

Not only pencils and markers, but the products of those tools were also valued. The children noted how many pages they had left before their current journal would be completed and how many journals they had already completed. Speed and quantity were in fact valued in many activities. For example, Jake, Jesse, and Ruben valued these qualities in baseball among other areas: A "helluva good baseball player" throws fast and makes many home runs. Sonia valued them in name writing; one day she even brought a watch with a second hand and timed all the kids at her table to see who was fastest. And, while just being a "little kid" could be a rationale for one's lack of ability in a particular area, all of the children participated in conversations in which more "years old" was clearly better. Seven-year-old Jake even bragged to six-year-old Jesse, "You'll always be behind me."

Displaying and Monitoring Competence

Like most of us, the children expressed clear desires to be competent at the things people their age should be able to do. The appropriate age was sometimes disputed, though, and there were mediating circumstances, such as opportunity for practice. Writing, particularly spelling, appeared to be an important "competency," just as was bike riding. To illustrate, compare the following discussions, the first about bicycling, the second about spelling.

JAKE: I just rode my [new] bike up and down my hill three times—two or three times.

SONIA: (impressed) I can't even ride it once up and down the hill!

JAKE: Why?

SONIA: (irritated) 'Cause (very softly) I don't know how to ride, yet.

JAKE: You still have training wheels? (politely)

SONIA: I'm learning how to ride on a two-wheeler.

REGINA: (squeals)

MAGGIE: I still have training wheels.

REGINA: ⌈My training wheels was took off when I was six.

JAKE: ⌊I saw a seven-year-old—
I saw a seven-year-old with training wheels.

SONIA: I still have training wheels.

REGINA: By the time you're six, the training wheels should be off.

MARCOS: I don't get to ride my bike that much. That's why I have to have training wheels.

Regina, a first grader, has just heard Wesley, a second grader, ask for the spelling for *candy*, which Regina can in fact spell.

REGINA: That is a shame.

SONIA: I don't know how to spell *candy*.

REGINA: It's easy.

SONIA: How?

REGINA: It's easy.

JAKE: C-A-N-D.

REGINA: Uh-huh.

SONIA: Maybe my mom didn't teach me or I don't need to.
Regina states again that "that's a shame" and claims also to be
able to spell *Mississippi*. However, she cannot spell it, and then
Wesley spells it correctly! Regina just grins and gets back to her
story. Later in the day, Regina does not know that "the kitchen
sink" is a kind of ice cream, and Sonia retaliates, "You should
know that by the time you're five years old."

As these conversations indicate, some of the children were more tolerant
of shortcomings than others, but all were interested in sharing their own
and hearing about others' accomplishments. The following are some
further examples of both kinds of behaviors.

Displaying Competence: "Look What I'm Doing!".   The children at
times announced their knowledge or skill: "I know" how to spell a
particular word, my phone number, my address, a funny story; "I can"
draw a jet, throw a fastball. Most of the time, however, the children called
attention to their ongoing work. In the beginning of the study, these calls
of "Look what I'm doing" generally had to do with how many pages or
journals they had completed, or with their ongoing drawing. The following exchange occurred when Regina had just drawn a picture of a candy
house, which she thought was quite nice.

REGINA: Sonia, do you like this picture [her previous picture of
          a dentist's office] or that one [the candy house]?
SONIA: That one [the candy house].
REGINA: Me, too, because it's gonna be looking real pretty. Better
          than the first picture.
SONIA: Can I see the first picture in your journal?
REGINA: Sure. That was my first picture.

                              . . .

          This one says, "I went to the dentist. I had to stay in
          the line for a three minutes because he was not here." I
          had to stay in there for an, for three or four minutes,
          and I thought that I would be there for my whole life.

It is noteworthy that Regina also spontaneously displayed her story
for a peer. As the case studies (Chapters 5 through 8) will illustrate, the
sharing of written texts emerged later than the sharing of drawings. The
children were generally willing listeners, though not always enthusiastic:

> SONIA: Want me to read this to you, Marcos?
> MARCOS: OK. From the starting? (worried)
> SONIA: YES!

In the sharing of their feats, be they drawing or writing or a nonliterary accomplishment, the children were aware of their own progress. For example, Jake noted, "This is the longest story I ever wrote"; on another day, he commented on his new "fresh *A*," claiming, "This is fresher than my other A." Commenting on one of her drawings, Regina noted, "Shoot, I never made an Indian before." Manuel observed, while displaying his journal, "I used to ask for every word," meaning that he no longer had to get all his spellings from others.

Monitoring Competence: "What Are You Doing?".   As is evident in the foregoing examples, the children were clearly interested in each other's work. Drawing was easier to monitor than writing because it was more clearly displayed (i.e., one did not have to lean over and decipher a code). When the children asked for spellings or reread their stories, however, the spellings and the stories were made available and were commented on by others.

Beyond simply expressing curiosity in each other's activities, the children's responses implied both positive and negative evaluations of others' efforts. Imitation is the sincerest form of flattery, as the saying goes, and indeed the children did pick up on each other's behaviors. Those behaviors ranged from producing appealing rhymes and phrases to using particular visual and artistic devices. For example, Jesse was particularly observant of Manuel and Jake. He attempted, as did several other children, to imitate the visual effects Manuel created with careful shadings and color mixings.

> JESSE: How do you make that with—Oh yeah. There's that orange. Is this the right color?
>   . . .
> MANUEL: Over here it's a little lighter.
> JESSE: Oh, we did like this. Right?
> MANUEL: No, I think I need something a little darker but not too strong.
>   . . .
> You need a long pencil to do this.

In the area of verbal style, Jesse picked up not only Jake's "tough talk" ("getting busted" or "ripped off") but also his concern with periods. During writing, Jake consistently asked adults if he "had any sentences yet" or if he needed any periods. Jesse began asking similar questions, even though he had less grasp of the sentence concept. For example, one day Jesse bragged to the group that he only needed "two dots" (periods) in his whole story, as though that were a real accomplishment.

Not all the children's responses to others' efforts were positive. Noting others' errors or need for help often gave children opportunities to display their own skill. This was particularly true for spelling. In this classroom, the observed children often asked adults, rather than other children, for spellings, perhaps because adults—who are supposed to spell better than children—were available for such requests. Hearing another child express a need for a spelling nonetheless consistently gave rise to offers of help from peers, which requests were not always accepted graciously. Jake, for example, did not like to have a first grader offer him help; in the face of such offers, he would attempt the word himself. The children also engaged in spelling duels, in which they would try to trip each other up on spellings. The following excerpts illustrate these behaviors.

JESSE: (to group in general) How do you spell *sun?*
JAKE: Which kind? [That day the children had been discussing homonyms.]
SONIA: Oh, it's easy, U-S-A. No, not USA.
JESSE: (laughs)
SONIA: It's U-N-A.
JAKE: S-U-N, U-N. No. Sun.
MANUEL: Yeah, S-U-N.
JAKE: That's your son?
MANUEL: No, it's a sun sun, not his son.
JESSE: (finds the word in his dictionary) Watch. This is gonna be easy. I'm not gonna look at it once. I'm not gonna look at it once. S-U-N. (to Sonia) You wrote U.S.A. (laughs) I was BORN in the U.S.A. (singing) Hey, Jake! Remember that song we were singing? We were, BORN in the U.S.A. (singing)
CHILDREN: (singing) We were, BORN in San Jose, in the U.S.A.

Regina has just written "Home Sweet Home" in her drawing and is quite pleased with herself.
REGINA: Joshua, do you know how to spell *sweet?*
JOSHUA: S-E—

CHRIS: Uh-uh. S-W.
REGINA: S-W-E-T. [She apparently doesn't notice she's spelled it
          incorrectly this time.] How do you spell *home*?

Joshua can in fact spell *home*. He does so; then he tests Regina by
asking her to spell *pig*, which she does. He then asks her to spell
seat.

REGINA: S-E-E—
JOSHUA: No.
REGINA: Oh. I don't know.
JOSHUA: Give up?
REGINA: I don't want to know.
JOSHUA: I want you to know.

Soon Jake and Jesse enter into the spelling duel, which continues
off and on throughout the remainder of journal time. Regina tries
to draw Maggie in, but she can't quite get into the spirit.

REGINA: (to Maggie) Do you know how to spell *sweet*?
MAGGIE: I don't care if I don't.
REGINA: Just spell it.
MAGGIE: OK. S-W-E-T.
REGINA: No, S-W-E-E-T.
MAGGIE: Well, I was close but no cigar.

Proclamations of what "I can spell" were more common than spelling duels in the kindergarten. But, on one occasion, Nate and Cassie
demonstrated the sophisticated social reasoning involved in the emergence and mastery of these duels. In this instance Nate wanted to dictate a
journal entry; as Margaret was busy, he asked me to serve as scribe.

NATE: This is, a cat. This, is, a cat. (using deliberate dictat-
          ing intonation) I'm gonna write down the word *cat*,
          OK? (faster paced)
DYSON: OK. (Nate writes *cat*.)

                              . . .

CASSIE: I know how to spell *cat*. I know how to spell *cat*.
NATE: How?
CASSIE: C, C-A-T.
NATE: You said, "C-C-C-A-T."
CASSIE: No, C-A-T.

                              . . .

NATE: Margaret, Margaret, Margaret, Margaret. I wrote this
          part of my story down. I wrote that down on my
          story. I wrote down *cat*.

MARGARET: What is it?

NATE: I wrote down *cat* on this story.

MARGARET: How do you spell it?

NATE: Mmm. C-A-T.

MARGARET: Oh! Boy!

CASSIE: I told him that.

NATE: No no no you didn't! I always knew. I knew it before.

CASSIE: (looks skeptical)

NATE: I knew it before.

. . .

CASSIE: Yeah. I TOLD you because you ASKED. You said, "How do you spell *cat*?" You were probably just kidding, right?

NATE: Yeah, I wanted to see if you knew! But but but but I always knew, so I wanted to see if you knew how to. But you didn't have to tell me. In fact, since—I've always knew how to spell *cat*, since I've been to school, since I've been four I knew how to. When I was four I knew how to spell *cat*.

Asking questions when you already know the answer seems, to Cassie, a strange thing to do, at least an odd thing for a peer to do, hence her reply, "You were probably just kidding, right?" Nate's testing her was an interactional game that seemed very familiar to the first and second graders. Indeed, all first- and second-grade focal children engaged in spelling duels with a gamelike spirit. Gloating about one's spelling skill, as Regina did, was not acceptable. For example, when Ruben persisted in asking Jesse how to spell words the latter did not know, Jesse retorted, "Hey, just tell me another word what I can spell!" Jake consistently reprimanded children who gloated (including Jesse, Ruben, and Regina): "You didn't know how to spell *house* in the first place, so you shouldn't be talking."

The children critiqued not only others' mechanics, but also the content of their imaginary worlds, as revealed by their talk, pictures, or texts. They questioned the logic of others' efforts by referring to the internal consistency of the told or written story; Jesse, for example, asked Jake how the "fastest jet in the world" could get captured by the bad guys. The children also questioned whether objects or characters in the story operated consistently with the way the world worked; to illustrate, Jake told Regina, "Brownies do not wear pink," as he noted her pink-shirted girl wearing a Brownie cap. In addition, they commented on written language itself, its clarity or grammaticality; for example, Maggie, when Jake had just written about "shooting them," asked him, "Who's the *them*?" Regina noted that Jake's "There is sharks" needed the word *are* instead of *is*.

In this critiquing, the children were often forced to wrestle with the distinction between the experienced and the imaginary worlds. They marked their own and others' stories as "real" or "not real." Mitzi even accused Jake of "lying in your story," which suggests a concern with how real "not real" has to be. Manuel came closest to explicitly stating the intellectual issue; during a dispute about whether or not a bomb could result in a volcano, he noted, "Well, anyway, it's a pretend story. In real life, it may [not] be true." That is, the criteria for literary truth are different from those for "real-life" truth. The children's operational definitions of these criteria were suggested and opened to discussion as they moved between imaginary and "real-life" worlds.

In judging the content of another's drawing or text, the children were not engaging in behavior specific just to the journal activity. They regularly commented on any peer statement that did not square with their perceptions of the experienced world, including ideas about how rain and snow operate, how dogs age, how young a mother can be ("My mother was a teenage mother."), how and whether being "a little bit chubby" is essential to the body's functioning, how bad "junk food" is, how probable World War IV is ("Did they already have World War III?"), whether or not everyone was indeed "born in the USA," and on and on. Their mental wrestling seems well captured by Tizard and Hughes's term, "passages of intellectual search" (1984, p. 114). While Tizard and Hughes apply this concept to mothers and their preschoolers, these early school-age children's eagerness to explore verbally—to puzzle through—confusions and contradictions certainly merits the term as well.

To this point, then, we have looked at the children spontaneously displaying their own and monitoring others' competence. In these interactions, they were not working toward any clearly specified educational objective, nor were they playing out the rules of any specific language arts activity. They were simply being kids together in their own classroom. Next, we turn briefly to an interesting and contrasting situation—the weekly spelling quiz.

Gauging Competence Through Grading: "What'd You Get?".   In February of year 2 of the study, Margaret initiated weekly spelling tests. She would give the children 10 words each Monday, telling the second graders to learn all of them and the first graders to learn 5 of them, for quizzes to be held on Friday. Margaret graded the quizzes by putting the number correct on the top of each paper. She did not mark papers as "passing" or "failing"; she commented directly to individual children, remarking that they had done well or should study harder.

Despite Margaret's low-key approach to this language arts activity, the children themselves seemed intensely aware of Margaret's evaluation of their performance. And that evaluation was clearly different from the flexible evaluation provided by peers. During their own informal spelling duels, a child could always point out to a peer something else she or he knew, dismiss a particular word as unimportant, bide time until an easier word came up, or find a word an overly confident peer couldn't spell—gloating peers would usually receive their due. Performance in the spelling quiz, on the other hand, was inflexible and defined by the teacher's written score. One could not say, "Ask me another word what I can spell" to the teacher, nor could one dismiss the necessity of the chosen words ("Maybe I don't need to [know how to spell it].").

Faced with these fixed scores, the children had to find other ways of ameliorating the evaluations and the institutionalized comparisons and gloating made possible by the scores' existence. For example, in one event I observed, Jake first admired and then, egged on by Jesse, put down Sonia for her good performance on a quiz.

> Margaret is passing back their spelling papers, as the children sit working in their journals. The children immediately begin displaying their own scores (their "number right") and monitoring those of others.
>
> SONIA: I got nine right. I got 'em all right.
> JAKE: She got almost—she got 'em all right.
>   (looks at his own paper) Five right. (neutral tone)
> JESSIE: (laughs at Jake but does not reveal his own score)
> MANUEL: Seven. I only got one wrong.
> SONIA: Uh-uh.
> JESSIE: (to Jake, referring to Jake's paper) Cross that out and put um eight right.
> JAKE: No. (irritated)
> JESSIE: Oh yeah, put one right. (laughs)
> JAKE: No, I'll put—(sounds devious)
> JESSIE: Zero right. (laughs)
> JAKE: Yeah. (Jake scratches out the number five and puts the paper away.)

Later in the morning, when Sonia shows her paper to me, Jake
intervenes.

JAKE: Give it here. (grabs paper)
SONIA: No.
JESSIE: Oh, yeah. Give it here.
SONIA: No-ooo. Give it to me, Jesse.

Margaret comes over to the table and retrieves Sonia's paper.
Sonia, looking frustrated and close to tears, folds up her paper
and stuffs it into her pocket.

JAKE: (giggles) We got her.
JESSE: Yeah.

In previous examples, Jake and Sonia displayed their friendship;
they were consistently interested in and supportive of each other's efforts.
Recall, for instance, that Jake did not tease Sonia over her inability to ride
a two-wheeler. Both children defended others whose competence was
under attack by peers, as has also been seen in previous examples. Yet, in
this example, they are set apart from each other because Sonia performed
well and Jake not so well on a spelling test. Jake and Jesse resorted to
peer-group play to "get" the child who had done so well, and Sonia
received a vivid demonstration of how performing well in school can
isolate one from one's friends.

Ironically enough, all of the children valued the ability to spell; in
fact, both Jake and Jesse were better spellers than Sonia in the children's
spelling duels. And, while certainly their appreciation of good spelling
was related to its value in the adult world, including the world of school,
the children had discussed spellings and engaged in spelling duels before
Margaret began the quizzes; in fact, they had done so the previous year
when there were no quizzes. It was the teacher's evaluation of performance on the spelling test that caused the tension.

In Margaret's room, such evaluation through fixed scores was a rare
occurrence; nonetheless, the children's response to it seems significant. It
illustrates the possible consequences of language arts programs that place
all of the children's language use under the evaluative authority of the
teacher. One sees here a possible preview of a conflict between, on the one
hand, the way school may work to single out the achieving individual
and, on the other, the way the peer group may serve to allow children to
collaborate in working out flexible, face-saving, and, at times, playful
ways of displaying and acknowledging competence. Given a different
classroom structure, one in which children's performance is regularly
evaluated both publicly and comparatively, the children's social and

academic interactions with each other might not in fact be so cooperative. Rather than serving to intertwine their social and academic lives, their interactions might help to alienate these aspects, one from the other.

Being Special

The children aspired not only to be competent, but to be special. "Special" here refers to being distinctive in some way, to rising above the crowd. The observed children were aware of the concept of "famous," as noted earlier. Pop singers Michael Jackson and Boy George, for example, were cited as "famous." Being famous did not involve being particularly competent on writing conventions, like spelling or punctuating; rather, it seemed most associated with being recognized for one's ability to create particular, powerful or meaningful objects or acts, as the following dialogue illustrates.

MANUEL: I want to be famous.
SONIA: Go on "Kids Incorporated" [a children's television show]. A whole bunch of famous kids—
JESSE: Yeah.

. . .

SONIA: You have to be a good singer I mean, like Boy George.
JESSE: No, no. Michael Jackson.

. . .

MANUEL: I want to be in a movie (   ). I also want to be a famous artist or singer.
SONIA: I think you would be better at the artist.
MANUEL: Still, I have a good voice. I wouldn't sing rock stuff.
SONIA: O-o-o-o-o-h. Gross.

Manuel, as it happened, was recognized by the group as being especially artistic; indeed, they called him an "artist." Jake even drew a picture of Manuel at the paint easel. Jake himself was considered by at least some children to be a potentially "famous inventor by the age of 10," because of his invention of the bubble car.

While not all of the children aspired to be famous, they all on at least one occasion remarked about a peer's particularly "neat" production or commented on their own "neatness." For example, Manuel, having invented a "magic word" in his story, observed, "God, I don't know how I made up those words. Never heard of them before." Maggie, on having written a story about a circus made of yarn, remarked, "I can't believe what I'm writing. This is so funny." And Sonia, on having drawn and written an entry on a sunset, commented, "Isn't this a good picture? I'm gonna put this story in a tape. It's real good."

Of course, one can also be special by defying convention; the children, for example, were very aware of who had been expelled or suspended from school. And one can be special by associating with people perceived as special. Jesse seemed to seek such specialness by associating with Jake. He even explicitly commented to me, "I have to do the same what Jake does." This points up a dilemma: To what extent can one borrow another's "specialness"? Although the children watched and mirrored peers' behaviors, for most, particularly for the second graders, there was a clear qualitative distinction between adopting a peer's technique or procedure and copying, line by line, a written story or a drawn picture. Writing conventions, such as letter formations, spellings, and punctuation marks, could be copied, as could particular literary techniques (e.g., ending parts of stories with "to be continued"). The exact and whole structure of a story or a picture, however, was the individual's, part of what made that person special. Even a particular story element (i.e., a character or action) could achieve almost "patent" status and thus could not be copied.

This was a particular problem for Jesse. He attempted to imitate both Jake and Manuel, whose journals he admired; both of these older boys drew and wrote better than Jesse did. Jake had no patience with this behavior. Once, when Jesse made a bubble car (Jake's "invention"), Jake was so upset that he would not let Jesse sit by him the next day. Manuel was more tolerant: He would let Jesse copy, but he made it clear that Jesse's story and picture should somehow be different, as seen in the following vignette.

> Jesse has been trying to make his picture just like Manuel's. He seems to think that Manuel should be pleased by this, as he asks, "Like it, Manuel?" He repeatedly questions Manuel about how to get particular effects. Manuel thinks this copying behavior is all right, up to a point.
>
> MANUEL: Just don't make exactly the same picture.
>
>   JESSE: Except not with the garbage can. (Jesse has noted earlier that he doesn't make garbage cans.) Same story?
>
> MANUEL: No.
>
>   JESSE: I'll make a different story.
>
> MANUEL: I don't want people to think I copied off you.
>
>   JESSE: Yeah, or I copied off you. I—
>
> MANUEL: I know because we'll both get bad reputations.

JESSE: Yeah. And we don't want that. Right?
MANUEL: No.

Being with One's Friends

Beyond managing resources and collaboratively acknowledging competence and specialness, the children simply enjoyed being with each other, sharing past experiences, and, often through play, creating new ones together. In many of the previous examples, the children shared their common experiences in the "real" world. In the following examples, the children play in imaginary worlds. To use Garvey's (1977) definition of play, the children are shown participating in spontaneous, nonliteral, pleasurable, and engaging activity that is its own reward. Their play sometimes involved writing tools, as when pencils became swords, but more often it simply used language itself.

MAX: How much old are you?
JESSE: Six.
MAX: Me too. So we're sixth grade.
JAKE: I'm seventh grade.
JESSE: I'm one-hundredth grade.
JAKE: You're not even 100.

Sometimes the children engaged in dramatic narrative play, in which elaborate stories would be collaboratively spun. Oral stories could evolve as an accompaniment to and in support of a child's drawing and writing; however, in these instances the desire for a unique and special content was clear: The author had the final say in whether or not an idea was incorporated into the narrative.

As will be illustrated in his case study (Chapter 6), Jake's narrative play was particularly interesting, as he consistently engaged in a great deal of such play during journal time, and because the nature of his play changed over the two years of observation. During the first grade, Jake's narrative stories evolved during drawing as he interacted playfully with his friends. He consistently drew and talked about the actions of powerful vehicles, especially jets, and adventurous men. His peers' amused laughter and comments supported his construction of elaborate plots. Yet, despite his dynamic oral narratives, Jake's actual written stories were descriptions of his pictures and contained no movement through time. During second grade, he started to use lively narrative play as he wrote, and only then did this element begin to appear as well in his written text.

Dramatic narrative play once again confronted the children with the distinction between the real and the imaginary, but in play surrounding journal production the distinction became more complicated. There was the wider experienced "real" world of people, places, objects, and events; and there was the ongoing social world; and, finally, there was the imaginative, symbolic world of living, three-dimensional players, of two-dimensional graphics, and of linear strings of printed words. The following episode illustrates these interwoven issues.

> In his written story, Jake has Manuel meet Buck Rogers. Then Jake tells Manuel to be careful, because, if he doesn't do what Buck Rogers says, he will get blown to pieces when Manuel and Buck take on the bad guys. Then, he tells Marcos (Manuel's brother), "You wouldn't see your brother again, Marcos. You would never see him in a story again."
>
> MANUEL: Oh God. Oh, well. It's been fun having adventures with you. Um, but I'm gonna get blown to pieces.
>
> . . .
>
> JAKE: You might get your butt saved by Buck Rogers. You want your butt saved by Buck Rogers?
>
> MANUEL: What I want is my body saved. I don't wanna die. I don't wanna—
>
> . . .
>
> JAKE: You want your whole body saved by Buck Rogers?

> Eventually, in Jake's written story, Buck does teach Manuel how to take on the bad guys—his existence in the imaginary text world is secured.

In a similar event, Maggie announced that she was going to erase her "running princess," a drawn figure that turned out rather poorly. Sonia objected: "Sonia means princess . . . I am a princess who runs. Maggie! You're going to kill me." Alas, the two-dimensional player died, but the three-dimensional one just laughed.

CONCLUSION

As detailed in Chapter 2, Margaret had established a classroom structure that centered on the children and their own activity. Within this supportive structure, the children's social energy became the major fuel for writing growth. Through their interactions with each other, the children established a social network that both bound them all together as a group and also allowed each to seek recognition as competent but unique individuals. The children's social networking included displays and admiration of competence, critiques of self and others, and interactional efforts aimed at both rising above the crowd and enjoying each other's company. Written language was a part of the knowledge and skill valued by the children, as well as a social tool that helped them to connect with and distinguish themselves among their peers.

The children's verbal attention to their own and each other's efforts helped highlight first their drawings and later their text worlds as interesting objects to attend to and talk about. Moreover, as members of the peer social group, they called attention to themselves as legitimate audiences for and critics of each other's efforts. Their critiques of those efforts—those symbolic worlds—often led them to consider the wider world of people, objects, and events, the world that must somehow be reconciled comfortably with the imaginary world. Thus the children began verbally to outline for themselves and each other the embedded worlds within which authors work: the symbolic world of the text, the ongoing social world, and the wider experienced world. In time, as will be illustrated in the case studies, these worlds began to blend together, as the children's texts became the sites of both social interaction and individual reflection, that is, as the children themselves learned to negotiate simultaneously among multiple worlds.

To this point, I have considered the children as a group, but each child was also a complete story, with distinctive ways of interacting with symbolic materials and with peers, and thus with distinctive ways of coming to negotiate among these varied worlds. In the next chapter, I highlight the nature of the differences among the children.

4

The Case Studies:
Discovering Similarities
and Differences

As discussed in Chapter 1, writing as a symbolic and social tool grows directly out of children's experiences with other tools—such as gesture, speech, dramatic play, and drawing—and their relationships with other people. The story of each child's growth as a writer, then, is influenced by that child's symbolic intentions and social life, by his or her ways of interacting with materials and people. Children who find their written voices, written homes, bring their individual stances toward the world into their written words. And then those words become avenues for expressing, reflecting upon, and interacting with others about life experiences. In Geertz's (1983, p. 99) words, works of art are "casts of mind"; that is, they are the visible imprints of how people experience the world.

In this chapter, I begin to outline distinctive faces in the child collective in Margaret's classroom. As authors, all the children faced the challenge of learning to coordinate multiple symbolic and social worlds. But they had different styles as symbolizers and socializers. Understanding these differences makes more sensible the children's varied developmental histories as writers.

THE NATURE OF STYLISTIC DIFFERENCES

Each of the observed children left unique impressions on the collected drawings, audiotapes, and recorded observations. Yet, in order to gain some insight into how their styles influenced their growth as writers, I needed an organizational scheme for describing the nature of those differences. The one that I developed, which seems most helpful and theoretically most salient, is based on the metaphor of children negotiating multiple worlds, worlds with differing dimensions of time and space. As presented earlier in Figure 1.3, the imaginary world, formed from varied media, is nestled within an ongoing social world, which itself is a part of a wider world—the child's experienced world of people, places, objects, and events. As they develop as writers, children confront and attempt to resolve the tensions among these worlds; that is, they learn to blend them more skillfully.

Initially, differences in children's ways of coordinating these realms were more apparent during drawing than during dictating or writing. As will be illustrated, many of the children's early writing efforts were governed by their prior drawing and talking. Thus, a primary focus is on differences in how the children began to manage their symbolic and social borders during drawing: What role did talking and drawing play in the forming of symbolic and social worlds? What role did other people play?

Crossing Symbolic Borders

Given a blank sheet of paper and an invitation to write, many young children will respond by weaving together talk, pictures, and text. The journal activity in Margaret's classroom, however, distanced the drawing from the writing, via the use of separate paper—blank for drawing and lined for writing. Margaret also started her students with an order of production—first drawing, then writing. Despite this uniform structure, the children's behaviors during the journal activity were far from uniform, in part because their styles as symbolizers were so different.

Style refers, not to knowledge about a particular symbol system, but, rather, to a way of using symbols, a preferred way of responding to, organizing, and communicating about experiences. Nurtured by the complex interplay of their individual makeup and social experience, individuals reach out in particular ways to make sense of new experiences. Their differences are not easily defined; I reveal them primarily in comparative terms ("Maggie, unlike Jesse . . . " or, "Jake, unlike Manual . . .").

Many descriptions of differences in symbolic styles begin by referring to the nature of symbol-making itself (Werner & Kaplan, 1963). Any symbolic act—talking, drawing, or writing—involves some sort of mapping skill, the ability to use culturally agreed-upon conventions (e.g., verbal names or labels) for representing objects, attributes, and experienced structures or patterns. And, at the same time, symbol use involves capturing personal experiences so that they can be shared with another.

Children may ease their way into complex symbol-producing processes by emphasizing one aspect of symbolizing over another (Bussis et al., 1985; Dyson, 1986a, 1987a; Wolf & Gardner, 1979). For example, when first learning to talk, some children may initially use oral language primarily in a referential mode, to talk about objects and actions; whereas others may use it mainly in an expressive mode, to communicate desires or feelings as they engage in activities with others. In Nelson's (1985) words, some children tend to talk "about activity," others to talk "in activity" (p. 99).

Similar differences can be seen in other kinds of symbol use. When drawing, some children focus relatively more on the physical aspects of a figure to be represented, creating a picture "about" the object world. Others may use graphic symbols as props in a told story, where the drawing is part of a larger activity (Gardner, Wolf, & Smith, 1982; Wolf & Gardner, 1979). To illustrate further, while reading, some children may initially focus on the accurate decoding of words; their self-directed talk (oral reading) may reflect their deliberate attempts to figure out individual words. Other children may focus relatively more on keeping the message flowing smoothly; their self-directed talk reveals the orally reconstructed story (Bussis et al., 1985).

As the preceding discussion suggests, descriptions of early symbolic activity other than talk itself still refer to or at least imply the importance of talk. Children's talk may be primarily analytic, an adjunct to activity, a way of monitoring their own construction behavior; or, it may be primarily expressive, an integral part of the symbolic activity itself.

In Margaret's classroom, talk was the primary window for understanding the children's approaches to symbolizing experiences. Both the functions and the topics of their talk revealed their stances toward symbolic worlds. (See Appendix B for details of coding procedures and analysis.) When drawing, some children's talk suggested that the child artists were on the outside of the imaginary worlds being formed on their papers. For these children, task-involved talk focused on *their own feelings or actions* and served to direct—to plan and organize—and to evaluate their worlds ("I'm gonna make . . ." or "Let's see now . . ." or, "There. That looks good."). They talked about their activity. The children often seemed to have some inner vision they were working toward; after all, even imaginary figures have to meet certain visual conventions.

The talk of other children indicated that they were inside their evolving worlds. Their talk was not only a tool for directing the act of drawing; it also served with drawing to represent meaning. These children crossed symbolic borders, interweaving talk and drawing and sometimes gesture, to construct an imaginary realm. They commented upon and, at times, dramatized *the feelings or actions of the figures and events in their worlds* ("And she's [a mother bird] looking at her egg, and waiting, waiting, waiting for it to open." or, for the sound effects of a bomb explosion, "1-2-3, Keplooooooh!"). Sometimes children's narrated and dramatized worlds stayed within the confines of the "momentary" picture frame; that is, their depicted figures did not move through time. Sometimes, though, children's worlds were dynamic, and their dramatic talk led to lines and swirls that piled upon each other, resulting in an action-filled product decipherable only by the artist.

As the children grew as independent written-language composers, similar differences were observable in how they used talk during writing. Symbolic borders between talking and writing might be blurred, as the artist used both media to narrate and dramatize an evolving realm. On the other hand, another child might use talk primarily as a tool for carefully organizing a written world.

Ultimately, to grow as composers, children must differentiate the symbolic worlds of drawing, talking, and writing so that they can more deliberately manipulate them. For example, to form the sort of coordinated drawn and written worlds evident in picture books, authors must be aware of the distinctive powers and limitations of each symbolic form. They must also consciously assume the stances or roles of the distant organizer or director and the more involved narrator or actor. It is by so doing that authors both organize characters and actions and become those characters, understanding the feelings and motivations shaping the unfolding events.

Crossing Social Borders

Authors move not only among symbolic worlds, they cross social borders as well. While children who use language "in activity" have been referred to as more socially oriented (Wolf & Gardner, 1979), this is not necessarily true (Nelson, 1985). Margaret's children were all interested in their peers, yet they varied in how they interacted with others during journal time, and these differences became more pronounced as their relationships with each other grew.

Here, too, the concept of crossing borders is helpful. Children sometimes collaborated with their peers as fellow actors. The borders between their own activity and that of their friends—between the symbolic, imaginary world and the ongoing social world—faded as their peers entered into their symbolic world. These artists at times extended their symbolic activity to incorporate peer responses; indeed, peer dialogues could be transformed into parts of pictures or texts.

Conversely, children sometimes kept fairly firm boundaries between their own and others' activity, with their peers thus serving more as the audience for, rather than collaborators in, their activity ("Do you like my picture of a girl?" or, "That's not what a lion looks like."). As discussed in Chapter 3, the children's critiques of each other's stories and pictures often led to a concern about the relationship between the imaginary and the wider experienced worlds, as they tried to reconcile discrepancies between the two.

As with boundaries between symbol systems, children must come to differentiate between and deliberately manage their own activity and that of their peers. Indeed, constructing imaginary worlds can be a way of both taking social action and engaging in social interaction, of being both a director of and an actor with others. For example, professional authors worry about striking a balance between providing enough information to guide (direct) readers' understanding and leaving enough space to allow readers to enter in and compose (enact) the story with them (Barthes, 1974; Bruner, 1986). Further, while their created worlds may be imaginary, they must also have their own internal logic and be consistent in some way with how the "real" world works, or readers may refuse to live within them (Bruner, 1986).

Stylistic Differences Among the Case Study Children

Within the classroom, all of the observed children had similar sources of support, including various symbolic media and a community of other people. As noted, however, their ways of interacting with symbolic and social materials varied. They differed in the ways and in how extensively they crossed both symbolic and social boundaries, as they encoded meanings (e.g., actors, actions, time) and involved other people in their own activities.

In a discussion of individual differences in oral language development, Wells (1986) cautions that such stylistic distinctions may be too simplistic. Indeed, as will become evident, they are simply helpful heuristics for beginning to understand the variation in observed child behavior. After reviewing the research in this area, Nelson (1981) stresses that most children no doubt fall between the extremes of a stylistic continuum; moreover, children may alter their styles to suit particular situations. Nelson also notes, though, that studying children who use various ways of approaching materials and people can be extremely revealing. Such children may alternately emphasize one or another of the aspects of the system to be learned, thus taking on different challenges and drawing in different ways upon available resources. Watching these children work helps to illuminate the complex and varied aspects of the language system, the diverse challenges the system thus poses for learners, and the many ways children may use available resources to meet those challenges.

The eight focal children in my study were chosen precisely because they seemed to have very different ways of working, which I initially identified by noticing their ways of using talk during drawing. Certainly the children did not vary only in style. As the case studies will show, their knowledge about written language differed as well. Some encoded words more easily than others, and some seemed to draw upon a store of literary figures and events, while others displayed no such knowledge.[1] However, closely studying each individual child over a two-year period revealed a distinctive personality—a distinctive way of interacting with people and with symbolic materials.

THE KINDERGARTENERS: BEGINNING PORTRAITS

In this and the following section on the first graders, I describe each case study child as a symbolizer and a socializer, as evident in the early months of 1985, year 1 of the project. The descriptions here are synchronic; that is, they are frozen in time and are designed to capture each child's typical behaviors as she or he sat drawing, talking, and writing. In this way, the pictures differ from the diachronic case studies presented in the chapters to follow, which detail how each child's ways of composing changed over time. As the children's unique portraits are drawn, the stylistic characteristics described in the previous section will serve both as thematic threads and as the means for highlighting similarities and differences among the children. While brief, these initial sketches will illustrate how the children's stylistic differences led to differences in the precise nature of their initial challenges as writers.

Jesse: Composing Dynamic Multimedia Worlds

Jesse was a small, wiry child who seldom sat perfectly still. During journal time, he was active and noisy, given to teasing and physical play. He was quick to enter into the imaginary play of a peer—especially a boy—or to involve a peer in his own imaginary play. He often engaged

---

[1]The kindergarteners' understanding of the alphabetic system was assessed using techniques adapted from Clay (1979) and Ferreiro and Teberosky (1982). Appendix C summarizes the results of these assessments.

classmates in pencil "sword fights" or "bombings," and he enjoyed pure language play as well. Jesse particularly admired older boys whom he perceived as tough, as evidenced in this description of his "friend": "[He's] bigger than everybody, in this class. And that class [Rebecca's], and that class [Bob's]. That's everybody. . . . He's in this school. He can beat everybody in this class. Everybody. Everybody gets him? [What happens if anybody is physically aggressive toward him?] One two poof. One two poof." (These sounds were accompanied by fist punches to accent each word.)

Jesse himself, though, was not so tough. He occasionally exploded when angered, crying and screaming, sometimes crumpling, ragdoll fashion to the floor. More often, he crawled onto Margaret's lap, wanting a hug.

Despite his very social nature, in kindergarten Jesse did not tend to link with others through his own world-making during journal time. (This pattern would change dramatically in the first grade.) There were suggestions, however, that he was discovering the power of the content of pictured worlds to yield social consequences.

> ANGELA: Now I'm gonna put a little girl right here.
>   JESSE: Do a little boy. (laughs)
> REGINA: Jesse, it's not funny. It's not funny.
> Regina seems to think that Jesse is making fun of Angela's paper.
> She tells Angela not to pay any attention to him, and then she
> retaliates for Angela.
> REGINA: When you were born, you were funny.
>   JESSE: I do not.
> REGINA: You looked just like a Ewok when you were born.
>   JESSE: No, I wasn't.
> REGINA: You shouldn't be laughing at her picture.
>   . . .
>   A girl, that's not funny. A boy is funny.
>   JESSE: Ah-huh! O-o-oh o-o-oh! (about Regina's text) You have
>   two o's in here, and you have two. You're suppose to
>   have one (   ).

Jesse, apparently sensing an opportunity to tease Angela, had commented that she—a little girl—should draw a little boy. That would indeed be an odd occurrence in this classroom! After Regina misinterpreted his teasing and retaliated with a personal insult, he counterattacked by focusing on the mechanics of her text.

Drawing.   When Jesse was involved with his own drawing, he used speech to enter into an imaginary world woven with talk and pictures, a world of destructive monsters, explosions, battles, and other displays of power and motion. The edges of his paper framed a moving picture. With representational language, he labeled objects and reported, narrated, and dramatized actions in the present tense. Actors, if mentioned, were most often identified by pronouns without lexical referents. His dramatized actions, often with accompanying sound effects, conveyed sensorimotor qualities, such as volume, force, speed, and emotional tone; indeed, the sound effects often served to define what those actions were (e.g., explosions, gunfire, zooming airplanes).

Jesse's drawings typically contained a central object of interest— usually the place that the action centered around (e.g., a castle)—and conveyed the result of the action (e.g., the castle was covered with lines and squiggles, signifying that it had been "destructed"). Although he was capable of drawing basic forms for people, vehicles, and houses, he seldom did so. He had no time for the visual details, for real-world accuracy, when creating a fast-paced story. He depended on talk to carry the meaning of his curved lines, dots, and splotches of color. The following excerpt illustrates Jesse's symbol-weaving style while he was actually drawing. In this instance he was in the process of producing the picture shown in Figure 4.1.

Jesse begins by making a small mark on his paper, which he says is a time bomb. He then writes numbers on his paper, accidentally making two ones. As he writes, he pronounces the numbers with a slow, deliberately paced rhythm, elongating each word. Ian, who is sitting across the table from Jesse, is curious about Jesse's activity; Jesse, though, does not look up from his paper.

JESSE: Ten, nine, eight, seven, six—
  IAN: What are you doing?
JESSE: Five, four—
  IAN: What are you trying to do?
JESSE: Three, uh, three—
  IAN: Two-one (quickly)
JESSE: Two, one. (deliberate pace) No, I don't need that one.
       (erases the extra one) ZERO, KERPLOOOH! (makes a
       burst of sound that fades, signifying an explosion)
Jesse now starts making dots all over his paper. In the following section of the event, Jesse *does* respond to and build on the questions of his peers.

ALEX: What are you drawing?

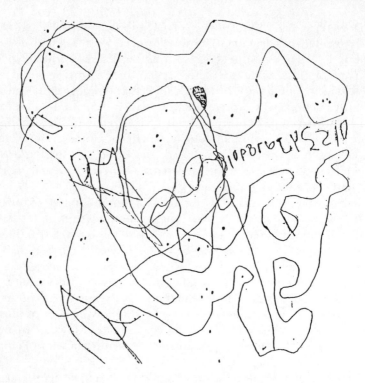

Figure 4.1. Jesse's "movie": The time bomb on the moon.

JESSE: The moon blew up.

 IAN: Tiny dots of moon, so you can't even see it.

JESSE: Let me see how many moons. (making dots) Now look how many moons are around the moon. Around the time bomb.

 IAN: Because there was a time bomb on the moon. You got to say, "HOT DOG!"

JESSE: Now the time bomb blowed up. Now the time bomb came out of there.

Jesse then connects the dots, making an airplane sound that captures the smooth, sweeping motion of his crayon. Ian returns to his own work and begins to produce his own sound effects. He is drawing monsters being attacked with laser beams. Ian tries once again to question Jesse, "What are you doing? What are you doing, Jess?" But Jesse does not reply.

Dictating.   Jesse's dictated texts generally maintained the gist, the central actions, of the experience talked, acted, and drawn about, using lexical referents for previously unidentified pronouns. Major meaning elements, however, sometimes were changed or left out. For the "time bomb" event, for example, his dictation went as follows:

This is a time bomb.
The time bomb is on a light.
And it blowed up a light.

It thus contained the major action, the destruction, but the "moon" became a "light" and there was no mention of the tiny moons. Jesse also began in the present tense, not the past tense commonly used in stories, most likely because he started by describing his picture. In telling the dramatized adventure, however, he switched to past tense and condensed the tale into a single summary statement.

In sum, Jesse enjoyed engaging in action-filled play with others, and there was at least some evidence that he could cross social boundaries to use symbolic drawn or dramatized play to interact with others. While drawing, Jesse crossed symbolic boundaries as he wove dynamic worlds that often centered on fast-paced action. He highlighted his actions' varied qualities—the rhythmic pacing of a countdown, the roaring and twisting of a racing motorcycle, the point-counterpoint of a battle. Jesse did not refer to the perceived real world as he worked, and he did not evaluate the accuracy or logic of his own or others' worlds. His written texts simply provided the bare bones of his drawn and narrated experiences. His efforts illustrate clearly the challenge children face as they move from the rich symbolic tool of speech—which simultaneously uses words, tone, pitch, volume, and other nuances of the human voice—to that of letter graphics strung together somehow to capture blasts and zooms.

Regina: Composing Static Multimedia Worlds

Regina had a sturdy physical build; her short, curly hair was styled with camphor oil to lie flat away from her face. In Margaret's view, Regina often seemed to be in her own world, and so it seemed to me as well. She often brought little toys (animals, dolls) to school; during the morning rug activity, she would talk to these little companions, at least until Margaret called her back to the task at hand. During journal time, while she talked about her imaginary worlds, it was to no one in particular. Yet, as was suggested above, in the excerpt involving her defense of Angela and insulting of Jesse, she valued her relationships with her girlfriends. As a matter of fact, she frequently asked girls for their approval (e.g., "Are you my friend?"). The children sometimes failed to answer her, but usually they responded positively to her inquiries. Maggie was particularly reliable.

REGINA: Does it look like my hair got cut?
DYSON: Yeah. It does.
MAGGIE: It looks nice.
REGINA: 'Cause my mama cut it.

Drawing.   Regina not only sought peer approval directly for herself, she courted it indirectly through her pictures, such as by asking, of her drawing of a girl, "Is she pretty?" She generally did not comment on others' work. Unlike Jesse, then, she seemed to make deliberate use of her peers as audience for, if not as potential collaborators in, her drawing efforts. While she occasionally reread her accompanying texts, she never discussed these texts with others, nor did she seek her friends' approval for them.

Like Jesse, though, Regina was a symbol weaver. She used talk to enter into and create imaginary worlds. As she drew her little girls, suns, flowers, and small animals, she spoke about each one. Using representational language, she described the figure's characteristics, reported its ongoing actions, and at times explained its motivations. One figure was not necessarily connected to the others. While Jesse's talk had dominated his drawing, propelling his imaginary world forward in time, Regina's drawing controlled her speech and centered her imaginary world within the time frame of her picture. Thus, any past actions were reported in the past tense and any potential future actions in future tense. The present was static. Regina's drawing was a slide,[2] rather than a movie.

Regina's greater concern with drawing was reflected in the care she bestowed on her "girls." As she talked and drew their hair and colored their clothing, one might think she was dressing her dolls, rather than drawing her girls. At times, she referred to a real-world referent for a drawn detail; for example, one little girl might have black, curly hair because Regina herself did. At other times she reported on home experiences or conveyed personal opinions that did not seem thematically

---

[2]I thank Judith Lindfors for this metaphor.

Figure 4.2.   Regina's "slide": The girls, the sun, and the Cabbage Patch Kid.

related to her ongoing work. The following transcript excerpt, which illustrates Regina's style, accompanied her production of the picture in Figure 4.2.

> Regina has drawn four little girls. One has turned out to have a rather strange shape, and one is unusually tiny. Regina asks her peer Anna if she likes her picture, but does not wait for her to answer.
>
> REGINA: She (noting the girl with the distorted body) looks stupid.
>
>   ANNA: She does look a little funny.
>
> REGINA: Yeah. The little girl she's the baddest one.
>
>   SARA: Does she steal cookies all the time?
>
> Sara misinterprets Regina's comment—and enters into Regina's imaginary world. Anna and Sara, however, soon turn their attention to Jesse, who is aggravating them by blowing his nose very

loudly, and Regina herself returns to her evolving scene, starting to "talk to her work" (Carini, 1985).

REGINA: Mine's got—all of my girls—two girls have red high heel shoes on. This girl has the long hair, the longest hair. (drawing hair) She has the longest hair. Her hair goes all the way through her barrette. Look how long her hair is. [The long hair reminds her of two popular singers.] Crystal Gayle—the only one who wears wigs was Crystal Gayle and Diana Ross. Those are the only ones who wear long wigs.

MAGGIE: (responding to Regina's remarks, which are not addressed to anyone in particular) Yeah. And they buy the long wigs all up. Once I was looking for a long wig, and I couldn't find it. They buy them all up.

REGINA: Yes, and they never leave some for someone ELSE.

MAGGIE: I know that. It isn't—it isn't fair.

REGINA: I know. (turning back to her drawing, adding a sun) And look-it. He [the sun] has his mouth full of raspberries—I mean jelly beans. He's up there: Mm-mm-mm-mm-mm. He's eating all the raspberries. And now I'm gonna make a Cabbage Patch Kid. And this is the bird that's flying him to the hospital. . . . (continuing to describe her characters) And this little girl, she's gonna jump out of the balloon and try to land on the red heart. And if she gets on it, she wins a surprise.

And so on Regina went, drawing and talking and, in the process, bringing to the foreground "background" figures such as the sun and the birds, and details such as the nature of the girl's hair or shoes.

   Dictating. In her own words, Regina's texts, like Jesse's, represented only a small portion of the "much, much, much" that was going on in her pictures. For the picture just described, Regina dictated the following:

These little girls are standing.
One little girl is going to school.
The other girl is playing with her longer hair.
One little girl in the balloon is going to land on the heart.

While Jesse's time bomb text was a narrative summary, Regina's was a description of her picture in present tense. While Jesse had created a movie, violating the expectation that a picture frames a point in time, Regina honored this convention. Organizing her "much, much, much" into one written story was a clear challenge. Indeed, Regina sometimes began her dictations with a fast-paced effort to describe all her characters in detail. But, when the inevitable "Wait a minute" came from the adult scribe, she relied on the most visually dominant figures, in this case, the girls. Any information about the past or future that had figured into her oral story was chopped out of her text frame.

In sum, Regina did not cross social boundaries, but she did seek her friends' opinions of her pictures, clearly hoping to please them. Like Jesse, Regina also crossed symbolic boundaries, but her stories centered on characters, rather than actions. Indeed, she had many potential written stories about the diverse characters in her pictures. While Jesse highlighted the tensions between talking and writing, Regina struggled with the shift between drawing and writing, for her talk honored the conventional time frame of a picture. To write or tell a conventional story, composers must be free to move beyond a picture frame and through time and space, as characters grow and plots thicken. A picture must become an illustration, not the whole story, for the space and time dimensions of pictures and discursive narratives are not the same.

Maggie: Composing Visual Displays

With her peasant skirts and long ash blond hair, Maggie had a fragile, waiflike appearance. She was a sincere, sensitive, often serious child. It was Maggie, for example, who promptly responded to Regina's query about her hair and who also somberly discussed the difficulty of obtaining long wigs. She did not like teasing, did not find teasers funny, and would say so, although she could also be quite playful. She sometimes giggled uncontrollably about a silly comment she had made; she had a ringing falsetto voice she used especially for those occasions.

Drawing.   Maggie was often quiet during journal time, but, consistent with her sociable style, she seemed attentive to her peers' talk and drawing. She sometimes offered unsolicited questions or comments in response to their talk about their pictures:

SARA: (noting her drawn frog) He's sitting down.
MAGGIE: Where?
SARA: On a log.

She was straightforward, expressing both criticism and approval in a soft-spoken but clear manner. She thus took on the role of audience for others' efforts, and, like many kindergarteners, borrowed appealing visual effects from them. Her motivation for this did not seem to be primarily social (i.e., "I like you so I will do what you do.") but artistic (i.e., "I like what you are doing, so I will do it, too.").

Maggie seemed to be an audience for her own work as well. Unlike Jesse and Regina, Maggie seldom wove together talk and pictures to construct her worlds. Her pictures were initially of hearts and flowers but expanded to include scenes with her mother, an occasional princess, and depictions of nature. Her humor was evidenced visually—a bird standing on a princess's head, she and her mother balancing cups on their heads. (Recall that it was the image of Maggie and her "thinking cap"—a chain of markers balanced on her head—with which I began this book.)

While Jesse's and Regina's worlds appeared to evolve in the doing, Maggie seemed to have a clear plan: Line, color, and shape were her major tools during drawing, not sound and word. Her talk about her own symbolic worlds served primarily as a tool for directing and evaluating her actions in constructing her visual displays. Although the following excerpt does not fully capture Maggie's stylistic differences from Jesse and Regina, simply because it is an excerpt of her talk rather than her silence, it is illustrative. It occured while she was creating the drawing shown in Figure 4.3.

> Maggie has been silently drawing a girl, who looks as if she might be a princess, standing among flowers. She has been working quietly, but then is interrupted by a classmate.
>
> SARA: Is that a big teenager?
>
> MAGGIE: No.
>
> SARA: Is that a teenager?
>
> MAGGIE: No.
>
> SARA: . . .
> It couldn't be a teenager, 'cause it's almost the same size as a rabbit.
>
> MAGGIE: Plus his head would be up to the sun.
>
>   . . .
> (attending to Sara's picture, commenting on the sun Sara has drawn) I'm gonna make the same size—Do you know what I'm gonna make? I'm gonna make the same kind of sun, only I'm not going to make the line on the sun.
>
> SARA: That was a mistake. (laughs) I just messed up.

Figure 4.3. Maggie's visual display: The little girl amidst the flowers.

MAGGIE: That's good enough. [Note that Maggie does not
          contradict Sara's statement but she does make a polite,
          socially appropriate comment.]
Sara's sun has a mouth with a crack in it, and she seems to think
Maggie's sun should also have one.
   SARA: This [your sun] doesn't have a little crack in it.
MAGGIE: I don't wanna—It isn't going to be EXACTLY like
          yours.
   SARA: The crack is the mouth. She's smiling like that.
MAGGIE: MMMM. That's nice.

Maggie's attentiveness to visual sense and style suggests that what she
means by this is, "That's a nice way to make a mouth," rather than, "That's
nice that the sun is smiling." She appropriated visual ideas that appealed to
her on their own merit, not because they came from people she liked.

Dictating.   Maggie's dictations seemed deceptively similar to Regina's, as they were primarily present-tense descriptions of her pictures. For example, for Figure 4.3, she dictated:

> This is a girl. She's playing in her garden and picking some flowers. And she's about to pick one more. That one more is the only tulip. The end.

Yet, Maggie's composing activity was distinct from both Jesse's and Regina's. For the latter two children, drawing had been at least in part a language experience. When dictating, they faced challenges in moving from spoken and drawn meanings to written words. Since language was only a peripheral part of Maggie's drawing process, she could not lean on experiences verbalized during drawing when dictating. She had only the picture. Her peer Christopher, who, as noted in Table 1.2 was initially a kindergarten case study, had a similar style during journal time. For his dictations, he described his picture or set the pictured characters and objects into situations recalled from television or the movies.

In sum, Maggie was an often quiet but nonetheless socially attentive child who willingly adopted the role as audience for others' drawing efforts. She was concerned as well with the visual sense and appeal of her own drawings, which became increasingly more elaborate over time. As an artist, she did not tend to cross symbolic boundaries. For Maggie, drawing, talking, and dictating were fairly discrete activities. Thus, drawing and talking provided both fewer challenges and fewer resources; that is, there was less verbal and symbolic material that could be transformed into written text. When Maggie no longer viewed picture descriptions as satisfactory "stories," planning those stories became problematic.

Ruben: Composing Visual Dramas

Ruben had a commanding physical appearance—taller than the other children, large-boned, and very solid. In the kindergarten, he had a strong social presence as well. Ruben often initiated conversations with his male peers about his own daily experiences and expressed interest in theirs. He was seldom silly and did not often engage in verbal play. He did sometimes tease the boys, and he was often teased in return, which did not appear to upset him—unless the remarks centered on his work.

Drawing.   While working in his journal, Ruben, like Maggie, was not a symbol weaver, and he did not use talk to carry part of the meaning of his drawn world. Unlike Maggie, however, he never spoke about his ongoing journal efforts. Ruben talked with his peers about his out-of-school experiences and seemed to be very sensitive about his in-school work. Despite his interest in talking about his experiences, he never responded to his peers' questions about the *content* of his journal activity. While he would discuss what number journal he was working on, he seemed purposely to isolate both his picture and his text content from his social talk with his peers. Indeed, he would sometimes cover up his journal with his arms and head if others began to express interest in his work.

Ruben's approach to the journal activity is illustrated in the following transcript excerpt, which occurred while he was drawing in his journal.

RUBEN: Guess what? I'm going to live in Mexico. (Ruben periodically went with his family to visit with his grandmother in Mexico.)

. . .

They kill a pig over there in Mexico.

CHRIS: Why did they want to kill a pig? To eat it?

RUBEN: They eat pig. They're some, um, they make some pig meat. Then the ear. They're good. They cook 'em.

. . .

Did you see the "Wizard of Oz" [on TV] Friday? I did. The "Wizard of Oz."

CHRIS: I saw it.

ANGELA: I saw it too.

RUBEN: I saw the whole thing.

ANGELA: So did I.

RUBEN: I like the um one of—

CHRIS: The lion?

RUBEN: No. When um when they throw some water to the witch.

Ruben has now begun dictating, and Chris teases him by repeating his sentences and playing with the pronunciation of the words. (Chris has been teasing children in this manner during the entire period.)

RUBEN: And all the friends came out. (dictating)

CHRIS: And all the bends came out.

. . .

RUBEN: I will rip your picture.

CHRIS: 'Kay. I'll rip your picture.

Dictating.   Ruben's drawings included nonrepresentational swirls and shapes, similar to Jesse's. But Ruben's drawings were not made sensible by his talk during the process. During dictation, Ruben seemed to study his pictures in order to discover their meaning. Such efforts by children to discover meaning in their already completed drawings are called "romancing." As discussed by Golumb (1974), when pressed by an adult to account for their pictures, children may develop interpretations, but they use the pictures only as starting points for those stories, which develop independently.

Ruben often treated his nonrepresentational figures as characters by referring to them by color name, thus enabling him to describe their actions (e.g., "The purple was going to the orange."). The event in which the drawing in Figure 4.4 was produced is illustrative of Ruben's process. On that day, Margaret had suggested that the children draw fish, as she had just read them a book about fish. Such a suggestion was rare in Margaret's classroom, for she usually expected the children to select their own topics. Indeed, many children ignored her prompt, but Ruben began drawing a fish. He worked silently, forming the basic shape of the fish, coloring it orange, and then deliberately and symmetrically adding purple lines, first on top of the fish's face, next on the bottom, and then on the back tail. Finally, Ruben went over his entire picture with the purple color. As he worked, Alex tried repeatedly to find out what he was doing, but Ruben offered no response:

ALEX: What are you making?
RUBEN: [no response]
        (continues working, then pauses and talks to Alex)
        Guess what? Guess what? My grandma have a gold
        watch.

When Ruben was finished, he dictated his text, and since Margaret was not available, I acted as scribe at his request. Ruben studied his picture before and during dictating, retracing the visual drama that took place as he drew:

The fish was in the water and swimming in the water. And all the fire came in to shoot him. The purple stopped the fire so they can't shoot the fish.

As was typical for Ruben, during the dictation process, he interpreted questions intended to clarify the *words* he wished to record as instead

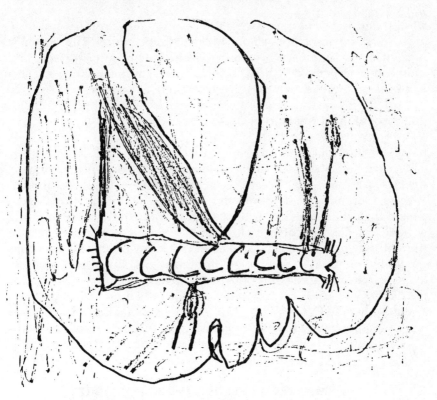

Figure 4.4. Ruben's visual drama: The fish and the colors.

being about his content. Indeed, his exact words changed during dictation, although his meaning remained the same:

RUBEN: (dictating) The fire came in. The purple stopped the fire
so they can't shoot the fish.
DYSON: And, all, the, fire, ⌈came (writing)
RUBEN: ⌊came, and, the purple the
purple, um, stopped the fire, and the fire was not shoot-
ing the fish.
DYSON: And the fire was not shooting the fish?
RUBEN: No, not anymore.

In brief, for Ruben, drawing seemed to be primarily a visual event—
he did not tend to use talk to help him represent or even shape his drawn

worlds. Further, he did not use talk to involve others in his world or to draw others' attention as potential audience for his efforts. Ruben seemed to be primarily interested in creating visual designs in his journal, but, unlike other children who drew in similar ways, he did not dictate "This is a design," but, rather, turned his colors into characters.

Summary of the Kindergarten Cases

Jesse, Regina, Maggie, and Ruben were classmates from kindergarten through first grade. In their journals they constructed symbolic worlds, each relying in different ways and to different degrees on lines, shapes, color, movement, sound, and words. These various ways of composing their drawings had distinct strategic consequences for dictating written text. The children each faced a different set of challenges in transforming their drawn and spoken worlds into written texts, problems created by variations in their use of the dimensions of time and space and by the unidimensional nature of written language, which demands words for qualities of voice, gesture, line, and shape. Further, the children's symbolic worlds figured into their social lives in different ways—as worlds to participate in with a friend, as worlds to be viewed and hopefully appreciated by friends, or even as worlds to be kept from them.

THE FIRST GRADERS: BEGINNING PORTRAITS

Jake: Collaborating in Dynamic Multimedia Worlds

In his overalls and red bandana, talkative, sociable Jake seemed to fit perfectly the message boldly printed on his red sweater: "The Kid." During journal time he often told stories about his out-of-school experiences and reacted with relevant comments and questions to the stories of others. Jake was interested in rockets, jets, and superheroes, and the sound and rhythm of language. His talk was enlivened with unusual phrases, like "flying earthling," "demonstration earthling holder," and "hovering teacher" (used when Margaret was watching over a child's shoulder). Jake sometimes turned straightforward conversations into opportunities for language play or imaginative adventures, as in this excerpt where Johnny was helping Sonia make a unicorn.

> JAKE: That's a unicorn-y?! That's a unicorn?
> JOHNNY: (to Sonia) That's a good start.
> JAKE: Yeah, it's a good unihorn. (teasing)

JOHNNY: Uni*c*orn. (seriously)

JAKE: Uni*h*orn—They're like leprechauns. [Note that the
rhythms of the words are similar.]

Drawing.   Jake's playfulness and sociability were evident during
journal time, particularly during drawing, when he crossed both social
and symbolic borders. His intention appeared to be to create an imaginative adventure. While Jake did act as an audience for others' drawing
efforts, he also involved others as collaborators in his own symbolic
worlds, drawn and spoken. Most often, Jake was inside an imaginative
world, narrating and dramatizing an adventure about powerful vehicles
and adventurous men. His raised voice suggested that he was performing
with language for his peers; they laughed and, at times, entered into his
story with him, leading Jake to elaborate and extend his plots. In this
sense, his friends, as well as his own drawing and talk, served as support
for his evolving story. Jake's style is illustrated in the following excerpts
from the event in which Figure 4.5 was produced.

JAKE: (having just drawn the ground and the sky) Now I'm
gonna make a mechanical man.

MANUEL: (sensible and calm, seeks some clarification) A mechanical man? You mean a robot man?

JAKE: You got it, Manuel. (elaborating) Here's a bomb head.
(draws two lines extending from the robot's head) It's
gonna explode. It hasn't even exploded yet. When it
does—

MANUEL: (a bit concerned) I hope it explodes in the next century.

JOHNNY: It's not going to be for real.

MANUEL: Well, in the future it is.

JAKE: Yeah, in the future it is.

MANUEL: I just don't like the whole journal to blast.

JAKE: Huh?

Manuel's comment initially makes no sense, until he explains that
he is treating Jake's imaginary and pictorial world in a literal
way.

MANUEL: I think this picture might blast, because his mechanical
man has a bomb head.

. . .

JAKE: Here comes the bomb explosion! There is the fire, a
little smoke. (makes quick back-and-forth motions with
his marker)

Jake's talk suggests that the explosion is beginning, but his subse-

Figure 4.5. Jake's frame: The robot man and the flying earthling.

quent remarks postpone that explosion, suggesting the influence of Manuel's talk on the evolving world.

JAKE: It's gonna explode in the next few days.

SONIA: What?

MANUEL: I hope it happens on the weekend, and then I won't be around. (again taking a playful but literal stance toward Jake's world)

JAKE: (playing along with Manuel) Not for long this school will be around.

. . .

SONIA: You're crazy.

JAKE: (adds another figure) I'm gonna make a flying earthling!

Writing.   Jake's mingling of media and his peers, present in his drawing activity, did not occur during writing. When he began to write, he focused on encoding, not message content. Graves (1982) also reports that the early primary-grade students he observed focused on encoding during writing. Jake's talk thus did not serve to represent—to elaborate, narrate, or dramatize—a world. Rather, his talk with both self and others served to help him encode his message. He spelled words himself and asked his peers and available adults for help. Jake's struggle with encoding is illustrated in Table 4.1, which presents an analysis of his writing and talking during the "robot-and-flying-earthling" event.

In order to hang onto his message through this demanding encoding process, Jake appeared to depend upon his drawing. As he said, "I copy offa the picture." Jake had told an adventure story during drawing, but his pictures represented particular objects in one moment in time, like frames taken from a movie. So, although he told a story with narrative movement, and although in reciting a story he was planning to write he sometimes created a story with narrative movement, his dependence on his pictures, which were stuck in time, led to stories that were stuck in time. His texts seemed bare and static, stripped of the lively and imaginative spoken ideas. For example, his struggle with the preceding picture resulted in the following text (after some spelling help from Margaret):

Once upon a time there were two men. One man was flying up in to the clouds. The other man was staying on the ground. The and.

Like kindergarteners Jesse and Regina, Jake highlighted the symbolic tensions among talking, drawing, and writing—the spoken dramas were often filtered through a picture frame before they were transformed into texts. In the process, he lost the lively interplay between his social and symbolic worlds, so evident during drawing. Jake himself did not enter into his written symbolic world; he concentrated on encoding.

Manuel: Reasoning Through Visual and Written Worlds

Manuel was a slender child with a shy smile. He had an attentive, questioning, but respectful manner with both adults and peers. Manuel was a peacemaker, occasionally comforting children who were upset or offering compromises during disputes. And, although Manuel could be quite playful, he did demand that people be truthful and reasonable. For example, in the preceding description of Jake, Manuel was seen playfully entering into Jake's dramas about an exploding robot man. Yet, in another interaction with Jake, Manuel pressed his friend about the definition of another sort of adventurous man, a ninja, which Jake had just announced he was going to make.

TABLE 4.1. Jake's "Robot-and-Flying Earthling" Event:
Writing and Talking

Jake's Text	Composing Code	Talk during Writing/Comment
once	S	Jake copies once from his personal dictionary.
	OV	Jake: Once a, a
		...
	R	Jake turns to the p page in his dictionary, looking for a pond.
pepperoni	OV	Jake: P-E-P-P-E-R-O-N-I. He is copying the wrong word.
	RR	Jake: Once... a Once... a pon a time Once... a pon a Once... a pon a He is rereading his text.
	OV	Jake: time
	IS-P	(to Mitzi) You don't know how to do times tables. Either does Jessica [Jess]. These remarks may have been triggered by the word time.
		Jess: I know. [I know I don't know.]
		Mitzi: I do.
		Jake: I do. I do. I know what 5 times 5 is.
		Peer: What?
		Jake: Five. ... Man, that's weird. One times 1 is 1.
	OV	Jake: Once upon a time, time.
	IS-A	Jake: I need time.

KEY: Dialogue: IS-P--Interruption Solicited from Peer; IS-A--
Interruption Solicited from Adult; IU-P--Interruption
Unsolicited from Peer; IU-A--Interruption Unsolicited
from Adult. Monologue: OV--Overt Language; RR--Reread;
PR--Proofread (make a change in text). Other: S--Silence;
P--Pause; R--Resource use; DR--Drawing; ///--Erasing (form
adapted from Graves, 1973).

MANUEL: What's a ninja?

· · ·

JAKE: OK. A ninja is a person who knows karate and knows acrobats.
MANUEL: This guy is a ninja. (referring to the figure of Mighty Mouse he is drawing)
JAKE: No.
MANUEL: I thought you said he knew acrobats.
JAKE: I did. I don't think he's a ninja.
MANUEL: Well.

· · ·

Robin's a ninja. And Batman, and Robin, and— Robin's a ninja.
JAKE: No, he isn't.
MANUEL: Well, he acrobats a little.
JAKE: Uh-uh. He isn't a ninja.
MANUEL: He knows karate.
JAKE: He does not.
MANUEL: Well—
JAKE: He knows how to destroy people, but he—
MANUEL: Well, maybe he's half a ninja and half Supergirl.

Drawing.   Manuel's sense of order and structure were evident in his own journal activity. Unlike Jake, Manuel did not tend to cross symbolic boundaries while drawing; rather, his talk was a tool for directing, reasoning about, and evaluating his efforts, not a part of the world being formed. That is, Manuel did not dramatize or narrate stories as he drew; he focused on the visual image he was creating. And although he did enter into ongoing conversations with his peers, he was often silent for long stretches of time. Thus, he did not involve others as active collaborators in his evolving world.

As an example of Manuel's visual artistry, consider the process he went through in creating the drawing shown in Figure 4.6. As he began, he said, "I'm making Mighty Mouse." Sometime later, as he focused his efforts on making the Earth in the background of his picture, he commented, "I think in a real Earth there's more water than that." He considered adding stars to his picture but decided against them, as they would not show up against his black "night": "Forget the stars. If I make stars, I'm probably gonna have black. Oh, I can't have black, either. It'll match this [the night].

Manuel thus reasoned his way to a typically well-detailed and visually pleasing drawing: A flying Mighty Mouse, complete with cape and bulging arm muscles, is set against a night sky; in the distance, so to speak, are the moon and the Earth.

   Writing.   Unlike Jake, when Manuel began to write, he did not have an already formulated story. Thus, he had to plan his story while writing. In composing it, Manuel appeared to lean on his knowledge of the expected behavior of his drawn characters: "I'm gonna write something about Superman and so on and so on." He occasionally talked about the whole story he was trying to create or a particular event he was grappling with. He appeared to make decisions regularly about which words would make a good story (e.g., "I think that sounds good. A nice little adventure story.").

   Manuel's talk thus served to plan, reason about, or evaluate the event to be represented in the text *or* the text itself. His talk did not share in the

Figure 4.6.   Manuel's visual display: Mighty Mouse.

representational burden of the written story (in contrast, for example, to Jake's talk during drawing, which did carry some of the representational burden of the evolving world). During both drawing and writing, Manuel's talk suggested that he worked outside of the worlds he was creating; he talked about those worlds, tinkering with words as he had tinkered with color and line. Manuel's reflectiveness is illustrated in Table 4.2, which analyzes an excerpt from the Mighty Mouse event.

Although Manuel appeared to focus primarily on his evolving story, the encoding of the text also took much effort. Like Jake, Manuel used talk to monitor the production of phrases, rereading them aloud in order to figure out the next word to be spelled, which he also often spelled aloud. Manuel consistently relied on others for spelling help and, gradually, on his own visual recall of frequently written words. Phonological analysis was problematic for him; he grappled with the whole process of matching voice and print. His encoding difficulties are illustrated in Table 4.3, which contains a second excerpt from the Mighty Mouse event.

For Manuel, then, the boundaries between drawing and writing, and between his own activity and that of his peers, were quite set. He produced visually complex pictures, working to make them as realistic as possible. In most events, however, his picture provided only minimum support for developing his story. This required him to plan his written story deliberately, choosing words with the same care with which he had chosen colors and strokes for his drawings. Like Maggie, he typically did not create a "story" in his picture (as he himself noted in the second grade); thus he found both less support and less tension in moving from drawing to writing. He often produced at least the beginning of a narrative adventure. For the Mighty Mouse event, he wrote,

> Once upon a time Mighty mouse was on a secret mission to find a bad guy. mighty mouse was flying when He felt something that did not feel good all of The sudden a ship came out of a clearing. The ship exploded.

Manuel seemed concerned about the logic of both his pictures and his texts, but he did not make explicit reference to potential audience reaction to the content of his journal entries. He did, however, occasionally make reference to the speed with which he worked. In the first grade, Manuel was known among his peers as an exceedingly slow worker—which he was. That judgment, however, would radically change in the second grade.

(text continued on p. 98)

TABLE 4.2. Manuel's "Mighty Mouse" Event: Planning During
          Writing

Manuel's Text	Composing Code	Talk During Writing/Comment
Once upon a time Mighty mouse was on a secret mission to find a bad guy.	OV	<u>Manuel</u>: I'm gonna write, "When something happened." <u>Manuel</u>: I don't know what to say. After a lengthy pause and a long unrelated conversation with his peers, Manuel writes another passage:
mighty mouse was flying when he felt something		
	IU-A	After another lengthy pause, I ask Manuel what he is thinking about. <u>Manuel</u>: Well, he felt something shooting him, but, "He felt like trouble" is what I'm going to write.
	OV	<u>Manuel</u>: Got to get some action in here. With much effort, as will be illustrated, Manuel writes a differently worded text that nonetheless captures his expressed idea:
that did not feel good		

KEY: IU-A--Interruption Unsolicited from Adult; OV--Overt
      Language (form adapted from Graves, 1973).

TABLE 4.3. Manuel's "Mighty Mouse" Event: Encoding During Writing

Manuel's Text	Composing Code	Talk During Writing/Comment
Once upon a time Mighty mouse was on a secret mission to find a bad guy. mighty mouse was flying when he felt something that		
	RR	<u>Manuel</u>: Once upon a time, Mighty Mouse was on a secret mission, a secret mission to find a bad guy. Mighty Mouse was flying, uh, when he felt something.
		Manuel has not been able to match voice and print accurately; he relies on memory to help him with this process.
		Manuel seems to think that the next word to be written is <u>that</u>, although the word <u>that</u> is in fact already on his paper:
	OV	<u>Manuel</u>: that, that, that, that, that, that, T-H
	IS-A	<u>Manuel</u>: (to me) Is it T-H? I think I've got two same words.
		<u>Dyson</u>: No, you've got <u>that</u>.
		<u>Manuel</u>: OK. That <u>that</u>'s over here, but I think I need <u>that</u> again. That. No, wait. I don't get this.
		Manuel then rereads and, realizing that the word he already has that begins with <u>th</u> must be the sole needed <u>that</u>, he writes the next word, <u>did</u>.

KEY: IS-A--Interruption Solicited from Adult; OV--Overt Language; RR--Reread (form adapted from Graves, 1973).

**Mitzi: Composing Visual and Written Worlds
Amidst Social Commentary**

Mitzi was a tall, thin child, with a low voice and a straightforward manner. Her talk centered around her family and a circle of close girl-friends. Mitzi took her relationships very seriously. Tears and hurt looks followed perceived injustices, such as a friend failing to sit next to her when the opportunity was clearly present. Mitzi, in turn, was very loyal to her friends. While very honest and direct in her dealings with children, Mitzi would defend her friends from the teasing or critical remarks of others. For example, during a heated discussion of "fatness" and "chubby" people (which Sonia initiated), Mitzi was quite blunt in point-ing out who was and was not overweight. When Jake somewhat sheep-ishly pointed out that Sonia herself was chubby, Mitzi retorted, "No, she isn't!"

Drawing.   While drawing, Mitzi concentrated on her designs and talked frequently with her friends, but the talk was not directly involved in her ongoing work. Most often, she drew little girls against a back-ground, but she did explore other possibilities. For example, sometimes she carefully crafted houses in three-dimensional perspective. She also experimented with different ways of using drawing instruments, such as manipulating several markers at once, producing a "fireworks" effect.

Mitzi's talk during journal time was about families and friends. For example, while drawing the little girl shown in Figure 4.7, she carried on several extensive discussions with her friends. In the following excerpt the children were concluding the discussion about "fatness" and whether or not everyone was a "little bit chubby," as Sonia had claimed.

> MITZI: You don't know about people, Sonia. Cause you ain't a
>   people—you ain't a person.
> JAKE: You're a person, not a people. You're not a people. You're
>   a person. (Mitzi and Sonia laugh.) [Note Jake's concern
>   with language.]
> MITZI: You're a people. (accusing Sonia)
> SONIA: No, I'm not, Mitzi. (defensively)
> JAKE: Yes, you are. (seriously)
> SONIA: (to Mitzi) You don't know. If you were that skinny, you
>   would die.

Writing.   Although Mitzi did not compose a verbal story during drawing, she did not concentrate on creating a story during writing,

Figure 4.7. Mitzi's visual display: The girl under the rainbow.

either. She did not appear to need to give much attention to a verbal message, given the repetitive nature of her texts. For Mitzi not only repeated certain themes, which was typical of most children, but she repeated the very structure of the writing itself. Her texts typically began with "Once there was," which served to label an object in her picture, often a female, a house, or a landscape feature, such as a rainbow or a tree. That line was followed by a statement, in present tense, of how she or "you" like, hate, might like, or might be liked by the object or figure; and finally came "The End." For the picture just shown, Mitzi wrote,

Once there was a girl. She might like You. She liveds under a rainbow. I LIke You. The End.

Mitzi produced her texts very quickly and appeared to concentrate on encoding. She silently wrote familiar words, stopped often to reread her text, and occasionally requested the spellings of words, but notably less often than her peers did. Further, she often volunteered spellings in response to their requests.

While Mitzi's writing process may have been less laborious because of her repetitive "I like" texts, these were not simply texts of convenience. They reflected her ongoing concern with relationships. As her rainbow piece illustrates, Mitzi would shift her stance as author from an observer of an imaginary world set in the past to a sociable actor in the present, bringing an unspecified "you" into her texts.

Mitzi thus falls between the extreme differences highlighted by her first-grade peers, Jake and Manuel. Like Manuel, Mitzi began with firm boundaries between visual and verbal art. She did not use talk extensively during the drawing process to create the depicted world, nor did she use her text to summarize the drawing/talking experience. The picture was on a topic, and she commented on that topic in her text. As a socializer, Mitzi, like all the case study children, would comment occasionally on others' drawings. Initially, her talk during writing did not involve others in her evolving story, but her texts did suggest a desire to connect her work with her ongoing relationships. In this sense, she seemed closer in style to Jake than to Manuel.

Sonia: Hesitating Between Drawn and Written Worlds

Round-faced and dark-haired, Sonia was a child for whom things were often not quite right. She occasionally got her foot stuck between the table and her chair ("I hate that."), and more than once she unexpectedly slid off her chair.

Sonia often discussed her own problems (her need for braces, her bout with chicken pox) with the children around her, and she listened attentively to their problems as well. Her talk often suggested a desire to be similar to others, a common part of the group. Many vigorous conversations were started by her insistence that her own qualities and behaviors were reflective of "everybody's." For example, the conversation on chubbiness, just excerpted in Mitzi's introduction, was initiated by Sonia's assertion that "everybody is a little bit chubby."

Despite this concern for common ground, Sonia also noted that not everybody has to possess certain skills. She defended others who were being criticized, admired others' accomplishments, and, on occasion, offered others advice, particularly about their pictures.

Of all eight case study children, Sonia was the most variable in her approach to the journal activity. Sometimes she used talk to elaborate upon her drawn world, but then she would not attempt to encode her talked-about experience into written words—it was just "too hard." Thus, Sonia had difficulty in deciding what to write. Most often, Sonia relied during drawing only on visual line and color; in these events, too, her writing would become stalled—"I don't know what to write." That is, she had no "story" to relay. To compound her difficulty, she had no consistent themes or patterns to her writing that might have eased her task.

Drawing.   Sonia was most concerned about producing a pleasing picture, often expressing her own pleasure or frustration with her product. And while she did not involve others in the imaginative world she was creating, she did at times ask others to help her draw certain figures. Sonia's approach is illustrated in the following transcript excerpt, which centered on her drawing a picture of an ice skating rink, shown in Figure 4.8.

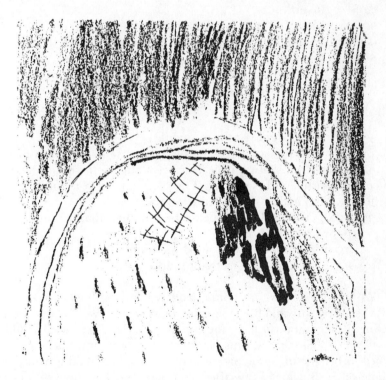

Figure 4.8.   Sonia's visual display: The skating rink.

As she works, Sonia remarks to Mitzi that her picture is not one of her dreams. (This remark seems to refer back to her discussion with Jake about drawing a dream, recounted in Chapter 1.) Mitzi's claim that her own picture is a dream, however, leads Sonia to consider the possibility of modifying her planned drawing so that it is more like Mitzi's: "Well, maybe some of it could be. I don't know." Mitzi then talks about how her name was changed from Emily to Mitzi, and Sonia responds.

SONIA: No one calls me Teresa.

MITZI: You changed your name now?

SONIA: Yeah. But I'm not telling my parents.

Next the conversation turns to the appropriateness of Sonia's picture. A classmate objects: "This is a winter picture. It's not winter in [our city]." [In other words, it does not get cold enough to have ice in this city.] Mitzi seems to come to Sonia's defense, although Sonia does not accept Mitzi's rationalization.

MITZI: Yes. 'Cause in [this city] there's San Jose, and in San Jose it snows.

SONIA: I know. This isn't San Jose.

MITZI: Well. There's—in San Jose it snows.

SONIA: I'm not writing about San Jose.

. . .

This is a ice-skating rink, but it's looking like, um, winter.

. . .

There's going to be a puddle.

By the end of the language arts period, Sonia has drawn a picture of a cracked ice-skating rink. Her peers offer both compliments and criticisms of this picture. The criticisms seem to sadden her.

JOHNNY: That's a nice picture, Sonia.

JOSHUA: You've drawn a better picture than that before.

SONIA: I know I have.

MITZI: You draw a very good picture.

SONIA: Not as good as that. (sadly)

Writing.   The next day Sonia struggled with both what to say about the ice-skating rink and how to get her message into words. She began by writing, "Once upon a time the ice skating rink," eventually adding, "was broken." Sonia had thus far encoded information that was clearly related to her picture—she had drawn a cracked ice-skating rink with a puddle on it. But here she stalled, complaining that she did not know

what to write. She finally wrote, "by [the] builder" and "The End."
When Margaret pressed her for more, Sonia expanded her text:

> Once upon a time the ice skating rink was broken by builder.
> The End of the ice skating rink and I hope you Like The rest of
> the journal.

In producing this text, Sonia had labored over each word, repeatedly
asking for help with spelling and rereading.

In sum, Sonia was variable in her approach to the symbolic boundaries between drawing and talk. Sometimes the two intermingled, but
more often there were clear boundaries between visual and verbal art,
leaving Sonia relatively unsupported when she began writing: "I don't
know what to write." She was, then, similar to Mitzi and Manuel in her
use of drawing and writing. Unlike Mitzi, though, she did not make use
of repetitive patterns to ease her writing task; and, unlike Manuel, she
seemed frustrated by the task of developing an extended text. As a socializer, Sonia was interested in others' activities, as were all the children. She
was self-critical about her own drawings and seemed concerned that
others would like her pictures, but the content of her symbolic worlds did
not seem to be a part of her relationships with others.

Summary of First-Grade Cases

Like their kindergarten peers, first graders Jake, Manuel, Mitzi, and
Sonia constructed symbolic worlds, relying in different ways and to
varying degrees on lines, shapes, color, movement, sound, and words.
And, for them too, these differences had particular strategic consequences
for composing, as the children faced various artistic tensions in moving
among drawing, talking, and writing. Just as important, the children
evidenced different ways of interacting with their friends during journal
time; friends could be playful collaborators or critical audiences; there
was even a hint, in Mitzi's case, of peers as potential characters in
symbolic worlds.

The first-grade cases, however, introduce new complexities. These
four children attempted to encode their own texts independently, which
allowed for the use of talk during text composing, as well as during
drawing. Relative to the four kindergarteners, these first graders engaged
in less self-directed talk and more extended interactions with peers about
the content of their *drawings* and about related topics. This greater

degree of interaction seems attributable to a number of causes, including the children's greater familiarity with each other and with the journal task, and their physically more compact seating arrangement. There was much less talk, however, about the content of *writing* than of drawing. The meaning of the written graphics themselves (the black-and-white squiggles) was not as accessible to peers as was the meaning of drawn pictures. Further, the complex writing task necessitated much self-directive speech, as the children used talk to assist them with the complex tasks of analyzing and encoding their messages.

As will be illustrated in the case study chapters to follow, the children's most dramatic changes as composers were evident in the nature of their talk during writing. As a group, the children found new ways of capturing their experiences in written text, as they more deliberately negotiated the boundaries between symbol systems. And they found ways, too, of interacting with their friends through their texts, and of anticipating and planning for that interaction, as they crossed between the symbolic written and social worlds. Further, this negotiation between the symbolic written world and the social world helped embed the children's text worlds more firmly within their experienced worlds, as the texts' logicalness and consistency with the real world became points of contention.

OBSERVATION AND REFLECTION:
UNDERSTANDING GROWTH

In this chapter, I have presented brief portraits of the eight focal children at work during the early months of the project. These sketches have highlighted the children's common resources, including their experiences with various media and their social relationships with other people. They have pointed out as well the differences in children's ways of making use of those resources, that is, their individual styles as symbolizers and socializers. The children revealed these differences in their ways of managing the boundaries between symbolic activities and between their own and others' activities in creating their imaginary worlds.

In Chapters 5 through 8, I present the case histories of four of the children, detailing changes in each child's composing behaviors over a two-year period. Since each child's development as a writer was linked to that of peers, all case study children appear throughout these chapters, although each chapter will depict writing and journal time from the perspective of a different child.

I selected the four central characters—Regina, Jake, Manuel, and Mitzi—in part because they consistently attended school during the first two years of the project. But I chose them primarily because they were strikingly different: Jake was the playful collaborator and weaver of symbols; Manuel was the reflective keeper of symbolic and social boundaries; Regina, another symbol weaver, was one who sought to cast others as audience for her efforts; and Mitzi was one who seldom crossed symbolic boundaries but whose texts seemed to reflect her social world. Each child's history highlighted different aspects of the process of learning to negotiate among multiple worlds and thus contributed in a substantial way to the theoretical perspective on writing development presented in this book.

In presenting the children's cases, I emphasize both the children's differences as symbolizers and socializers and the similarities in their resources and challenges as artists, authors, and friends. I focus particularly on the symbolic and social tensions that were evident in the children's efforts as a result of their developing realization of both the distinctiveness and functional power of the written medium. With individual styles, the children struggled to master writing and to effect its power for individual reflection and social exchange.

I present their cases as someone who is looking back and trying to make sense of their growth, not as someone who is attempting to predict their future. Studying the history of any one school child is similar, in this sense, to studying the history of life itself. As scientist Stephen Jay Gould (1987) explains:

> Life's history is massively contingent—crucially dependent upon odd particulars of history, quite unpredictable and unrepeatable themselves, that divert futures into new channels, shallow and adjacent to old pathways at first, but deepening and diverging with the passage of time. We can [at least attempt] to explain the actual pathways after they unroll, but we could not have predicted their course. . . . In this crucial sense, life's history does not work like the stereotype of a high-school physics experiment. Irreducible history is folded into the products of time. [p. 13]

What I offer in the chapters to follow are "the products of time," the records of the children's drawings, writing, and talk as shaped by my own efforts to understand the course of their development.

Regina

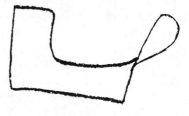

Figure 5.1.   Regina's two friends.

These girls are friends.
They go to the same school.
After school one girl is
going to the other one's house.

[September, Kindergarten]

This sample of Regina's writing, from early in her kindergarten year, displays the central theme of her journal entries: moments in the lives of little girls, who are often linked through friendship or sisterhood. These entries took form within Regina's own life at school, where friendships with little girls mattered very much to her.

In this chapter, I examine the changes in Regina's composing behaviors over two years of close observation. As with all the case study children, I focus on her gradual awareness of and attempts to reconcile the multiple symbolic and social worlds within which she, as a writer, worked.

The specific writing of interest here is Regina's daily classroom journal writing, which she did not seem to exploit deliberately as a social tool. But Regina did report using another kind of writing to take social action: "sign" or "note" writing. She explained to me that sometimes when she got mad at home, "when everything's going wrong, I just make a note that says NO . . . I make signs." Regina may have been introduced to this note-writing activity by her 8-year-old cousin.

> REGINA: [Her cousin] makes a note and it says yes and she puts
>   a little thing in it. She puts a special surprise in it.
> DYSON: What was it?
> REGINA: It was a thing that you put candy in it, to make me
>   happy cuz I was mad. I didn't know that she put it in
>   there and she put my name on it and so then she put
>   *surprise*. And so then I'll just write *yes*.

Journal writing in school was quite a different activity. The perceived goal was not to communicate feelings directly to others but, as Margaret encouraged, to make a "story." As illustrated in her introductory portrait in Chapter 4, Regina's written texts were initially governed by her pictures. In this chapter, then, I examine the symbolic and social tensions that contributed (1) to Regina's differentiation of her elaborate oral and drawn worlds from her written worlds and (2) to her growing awareness that making symbolic worlds, like writing notes, is a social act.

KINDERGARTEN: ELABORATING SPOKEN AND DRAWN WORLDS

As portrayed in Chapter 4, Regina was often a child apart, deep in her own imaginary worlds. Yet, during the kindergarten year, she was forging links with her classmates, especially the girls. She seemed sensi-

tive to the themes that permeated classroom and playground play—
threatening monsters, needy babies, and courageous fights. Nonetheless,
during language arts time, Regina concentrated primarily on the world
evolving in her own journal. She would bend low over the pictures,
talking softly, drawing steadily. When a peer or I paid attention to her,
"look-its" might appear in her talk, but she did not seem to require any
deliberate response to those requests. Occasionally she looked up from
her paper to talk about other matters that did not emanate directly from
her drawn world, as the following vignette shows.

> Regina is sitting at a table filled elbow-to-elbow with kindergar-
> teners. Kenji and Patrick are drawing monster battles, while Anna,
> Julia, Sara, and Regina are drawing scenes of little girls. Regina
> has just lost her eraser, and she looks quite perturbed. Then her
> mood suddenly changes. She turns to Anna and, in a dramatic
> voice, warns her of an impending tragedy.
>
> REGINA: (to Anna) A monster took it, and he's coming tonight
>   to get us. A monster. He's coming.
> ANNA: To kidnap my dolly?
> REGINA: He's gonna take you and your dolly.
> KENJI: He's not going to take anybody with me around.
> REGINA: He'll take Anna—he'll take Kenji too.
> KENJI: If we all fight him, he won't kidnap anybody.
>   EAUUUUGH!

As noted earlier, during her kindergarten year, Regina's self-directed
talk infused her drawn figures with history and motivation. She built
spoken worlds around them, alternately recalling the past, describing the
present, and anticipating the future. While her symbolic world took
form, she occasionally monitored the work of others, sometimes adopting
a drawing technique first used by her friends, like putting lipstick on her
girls and the sun. But Regina did not articulate these social influences,
nor did she deliberately seek others' participation in her imaginary
worlds. When she did pause in her work and seek peer approval, she
usually sought it only for the visual appeal of a figure in her picture, not
for the symbolic world of which it was a part.

Regina's early drawings contained a central figure or figures—such
as a house, a flower, or little girls—against a background including the
sun and the ground. Gradually, houses, flowers, and girls came to coexist
within one picture and grew increasingly detailed, as did her accompanying talk. By the end of the kindergarten year, Regina's talk elaborately
cushioned each figure. Indeed, Margaret worried about the slowness with

which Regina worked. Margaret's hectic classroom schedule allowed her ready access only to Regina's pictures and to the texts Regina dictated, and these did not fully capture Regina's imaginative creations.

In the event during which Figure 5.2 was produced, which occurred late in her kindergarten year, Regina made extensive use of self-directed, representational talk. She labeled her drawn figures, detailed their characteristics, reported their current actions, explained their motivations, and narrated their futures. She worked on this picture for three observation sessions. During the last, she attended primarily to the birds. As she talked about them, she maintained the time frame of her picture, correcting herself when she violated it. Regina's efforts to honor the time and space constraints of her picture are illustrated in Table 5.1, which reproduces her commentary on her drawing of a "mommy" bird and her egg. She had already used similar elaborating and narrating language for each

Figure 5.2.   Regina's mother bird and egg.

TABLE 5.1. Regina's "Bird-and Egg" Event: Functions of Talk

Regina's Talk	Function/Strategy*	Comment
I'm gonna make a bird in this nest.	Directive/planning	
...		Regina draws a bird. She has already drawn a "mommy" bird by the tree, but the bird in the nest soon becomes a mother bird, too.
You know what kind of nest he has?	Interactional	
He has a white nest--I mean a brown nest. And he have a egg.	Representational/ elaborating	Regina adds an egg to the nest.
And the egg popped up, 'cause the egg is popping up.	Representational/ reporting	Note how Regina appears to be to be correcting her verb tense here. This happens again.
...		
And she's looking at her egg and waiting, waiting, waiting for it to open.	Representational/ reporting	
She waits all day, and when she gets finished waiting,	Representational/ narrating	
know what she does?	Interactional	
She, um, takes the egg--I mean the baby, and she puts it to sleep.	Representational/ narrating	The inference here is that the bird has finished waiting --so now the baby is out of the shell.
(Dyson interjects: The mother bird puts the egg to sleep?)		

TABLE 5.1.   (continued)

Regina's Talk	Function/Strategy*	Comment
Uh-huh, 'cause the egg's getting ready to open.	Interactional-Representational/reasoning	
I'll make a crack.	Directive/planning	Regina draws a crack in the egg.
There's a crack.	Representational/labeling	
It's going to open. And [when] it opens, she's going to put it to sleep and feed it. First feed it.	Representational/narrating	Regina is narrating the actions of the bird in the future.

* The function / strategy codes are included here in order
  to clarify how Regina builds her symbolic worlds through
  talk.   These codes are fully defined in Appendix B.

girl in the scene and for one of the two butterflies, and she went on to do
the same for the sun and the cat (which looks like a unicorn). Regina
returned often, however, to the birds.

During the observation session in which she finished her picture,
Regina sat next to Maggie, who had straggled in late and, as Regina
herself noted, looked very sad. Maggie's attention seemed to be captured
by Regina's talk, and she became quite interested in Regina's drawing;
she was particularly amused when Regina drew little tongues—stuck
straight out—on one of her little girls, the mother bird, and the cat. And
Regina in turn complimented Maggie about her own drawing, which
was of a five-dollar bill ("That's very pretty, Maggie."); this was the first
time I observed Regina praise another's efforts.

Moreover, in the bird event, Regina seemed pleased with her imaginary world—her "story"—and anxious to share it fully with others. In the
following remarks, Regina moves between the word *story* and the word
picture; her talk suggests both her awareness of the elaborateness of her
symbolic world and her wish for her friend Julia and me to appreciate
this and not simply approve her picture.

REGINA: (to her friend, who is seated across the room) Julia.
         Julia. Come here. Did you know (   )? This is all about
         the birds. (to me) There's a lot of things happening in
         this picture.
DYSON: (confirming her) There *are* lots of things happening.
REGINA: It's all about the birds and the butterflies and the eggs.
         It's all about this much, this much, this much, and this
         much. (curving her arms in front of her in ever wider
         circles)

Despite this story "all about the birds," Regina's text, dictated a few
minutes after this exchange, focused on the visually dominant girls. She
mentioned the actions of the butterfly and the cat as well, but not that of
the birds:

**This little girl is watching the girl do her trick. And the butterfly
is looking at the rainbow. And the little cat was sticking his
tongue out. [May, Kindergarten]**

This dictation represents only a small portion of the "much, much,
much" that was going on in Regina's picture and talk, as is evident from
the preceding excerpts. To emphasize this point, three figures (the cat, a
girl, and the mother bird) were all sticking out their tongues (the act that
had so tickled Maggie during the event), but Regina's text refers only to
the cat's action. In dictating her text, Regina had placed that cat's action
in past tense. When she reread the passage, however, she used her picture
to help her recall her words, placing the action in present tense and
momentarily attributing it to the butterfly ("And the butterfly is sticking
his tongue out."). She immediately noted her butterfly error, stating that
she knew it was "not doing that!"

By the end of her kindergarten year, then, Regina's spoken worlds
had burst well beyond her picture frames, yet she continued to use her
pictures as bridges between the symbolic worlds she created during drawing and talking and those created during dictation. Her bulging spoken
and drawn worlds were filtered through her picture frames as Regina
leaned on those pictures to assist her in organizing and reading her texts.

Her kindergarten texts consistently reflected the central importance of
the pictures. The texts did not contain the aspects of Regina's worlds that
left no visible traces, such as the characters' internal motivations and their
pasts and futures. As a symbolic vehicle, a picture calls attention to objects
in the foreground—like the girls—not objects in the background—like the
sun, tree, and birds—and thus a picture cannot fully capture spoken words

like Regina's, where background objects were often central characters and indeed could each have given rise to a separate story.

Regina's texts contained linguistic indices of their origins within her picture frames. They were inextricably linked to the space and time structure of her pictures. I labeled texts like Regina's, "art notes": They pointed to the pictures with deictic expressions and/or progressive verbs ("This little girl is looking . . .").

In this way, Regina's texts were consistent with those of the other kindergarten case study children, as the majority (63%) of the kindergarteners' products were "art notes." Regina, like other child authors, seemed to assume the role of *commentator* on pictured worlds, rather than *observer* of worlds forming within texts themselves (a role indicated by a third-person stance in texts that were not art notes) or *actor* within those worlds (indicated by a first-person stance in non–art note texts).[1]

As would be expected in texts governed by picture frames, the majority of Regina's passages did not contain narrative movement, which is conveyed by two or more temporally ordered, independent clauses presenting a character's action or reaction (adapted from Labov & Waletsky, 1967). Yet, approximately one-third of her products *implied* movement and thus suggested the narrative tensions that existed within her composing act. To clarify this concept of implied movement, I refer again to the visual arts metaphors introduced in Chapter 4. A text with *no movement* through time is analogous to a *slide*; most of Regina's kindergarten texts were slides presenting a moment in time. A text with *accomplished movement*—a narrative—is like a *movie*; one action follows another, as characters move through time. A text with *implied movement* is analogous to a *frame* lifted from a movie. It has linguistic "sprockets"; most typically, these sprockets are tense shifts that imply accomplished or imminent movement.[2]

The following text illustrates this concept of implied movement: Actions are anticipated, just as they were in Regina's talk during drawing, but they are not accomplished:

> **These two girls are selling furniture and they have a dog. After they *are going to sell* the furniture, they are going to the beach and then they are going to a place where they *are going to eat*. [January, Kindergarten]**

---

[1]Coding categories for author stance are illustrated in Appendix D, which also provides coding procedures and case study percentages across the two years of observation.

[2]Coding procedures for movement within children's texts are also described in Appendix D.

In the first grade, as will be seen, Regina's texts began to assume some independence from her pictures, and, at the same time those pictures, and the spoken world within which they were embedded, began to assume a greater role in her social life. These developments unfolded both as Regina became more aware of the tensions that existed between the space and time dimensions of her spoken, drawn, and written worlds and as her peers became increasingly vocal critics and collaborators in her efforts.

FIRST GRADE: ARTICULATING SYMBOLIC AND SOCIAL TENSIONS

Regina was surprised and delighted to find, as she entered first grade, that her old kindergarten friends were part of her new classroom. Many of her second-grade schoolmates had familiar faces as well, for she had met them the previous year in schoolwide activities, including lunch and library periods and the two morning recesses. The following episode reveals the anxiety she had felt as the new school year approached.

Regina and Sonia are discussing the number of journals each has completed. Regina remarks that she was initially mixed up about the number of journals she had done, as she was thinking about the number completed the previous year in the kindergarten. This explanation triggers the following conversation.

REGINA: Last year [before school started in the fall] I thought I was gonna be in kindergarten, still in kindergarten. That's what I thought was gonna be.

SONIA: But you're really in first grade.

. . .

REGINA: And they say, "No you're not gonna be in kindergarten. You're gonna be in first grade." And I got so sad. 'Cause I didn't know who was gonna be my friend.

SONIA: Now are you glad you're in first grade?

REGINA: Uh-huh. You better believe it. (with conviction) Shoot, I was—I was spending, all my time thinking, Sunday, "What'm I gonna do? What'm I gonna do? Tomorrow's school!" That's when I was turned into a first grade. I say, "I want to go to my ol' school. I bet nobody's gonna be my friend."

SONIA: I just made the pink sprinkles [on your picture].

And on Sonia goes, being Regina's friend.

The comfort of reconnecting with "old" faces may have contributed to Regina's greater sociability in the first grade. As will be evident, she engaged in more extended conversations during language arts time, as her journal efforts became more effective avenues for social connections. Yet, despite this evident social ease, Regina's new first/second-grade classroom presented her with different demands, both symbolically and socially. As noted in previous chapters, the nature of the composing task had changed. In the first grade, the children were expected to compose their own stories independently, a demand that Regina met with relative ease.[3] Journal writing had become an activity in which all the children participated at the same time, and there were more children. The children had been together longer by now—the second graders for their third year—and, perhaps influenced by this familiarity, they were more vocal critics and collaborators. Margaret herself was more demanding; during the daily meetings on the rug, she often reminded the children that their stories had to "make sense," and children whose stories did not make sense would be sent back to try again.

In my initial observations of Regina as a first grader, I noticed several familiar behaviors, such as telling elaborate stories to accompany her drawings and seeking her peers' approval for those drawings. However, changes were also clearly in the making. The new emphasis on independent writing led to the proliferation of spelling duels, as described in Chapter 3, and Regina was quite good at these. (Readers may recall her remark, quoted in Chapter 3, that a second grader's inability to spell *candy* was "a shame.") In some ways, Regina's concern with spelling accuracy was comparable to her predominant concern in kindergarten with the pleasing nature of her drawing forms. That exclusive focus on form, however, would come under increasing pressure, from Margaret, from Regina's peers, and from her own more critical eye.

Coordinating Symbolic Worlds

Early in the observation phase of Regina's first-grade year, Margaret voiced her worries about this student—not only was she working very slowly, but her stories did not make much sense. Regina herself was quite keenly aware of this expectation that her stories make sense. The initial awkwardness of her texts arose in part from her increasingly deliberate struggle with the difficult transitions between drawing and talking, on the one hand, and writing on the other. Indeed, on the very first day of the

---

[3]See Appendix C for a description of Regina's performance on encoding/decoding tasks.

new observation phase, Regina articulated the previously inferred challenge of writing a single story about her multistoried picture. After
drawing and talking about a little girl, a chocolate "gold coin" candy,
and "the mom," Regina picked up her pencil to write and then announced, "This [pointing to the picture] is her mom. And this is the little
girl. I'm talking [going to write] about the little girl."

Regina's struggle with the space and time dimensions of pictures, on
the one hand, and texts, on the other, peaked in a subsequent journal
event, which focused on a little girl who had a mishap with mud.
Regina's own worries were also punctuated by comments from her peers,
so, as will be illustrated, Regina's increased deliberateness about her
symbolic efforts contributed to and was supported by the social life of
which she was a part.

During the first day she worked on the "girl-with-mud" entry, Regina was sitting at a table with Maggie on one side of her and Sonia on
the other. Sonia worried audibly during the entire session about her
text—she did not know what to write and, after each attempted beginning, announced, "This doesn't make sense." Maggie was quietly drawing a princess, but she stopped occasionally to observe Regina's efforts or
Sonia's frustration.

Regina began her own entry by drawing a tree, complete with roots,
a cloud, the sun, a dog, and a little girl (see Figure 5.3). Then she decided
to label each of these objects with a written word. As she explained, "This
is just a picture that has words on it." Jesse found this very funny, but
Maggie, the careful observer of others, objected to Regina's use of writing
in drawing.

> MAGGIE: Everybody knows what—about the sun, moon, and
> the clouds are. Why did you write those?
> REGINA: I just want to.
> MAGGIE: You don't have to write that.

"Everybody knows," as she said, calling Regina's attention to her audience and to the social world within which her symbolic world figured.
In other words, why write what is already so obvious in the drawing?
Regina did not respond immediately to Maggie's comments, but after a
few minutes erased her words. (Later she added *RYF* ["Ruff"] next to the
dog—a sensible, not obvious, addition.)

After erasing her words, Regina began to add details to her drawn
girl, entering into her imaginary world by using representational language to report on the external actions and internal reactions of her girl.
As she had in her kindergarten drawings, she developed her story by

Figure 5.3.   Regina's girl with mud.

branching out from a central point in her drawing, implying the past and considering the future. Having just drawn the girl lifting up the hem of her dress with her hands, she said, "She's holding up her dress, like this. . . . Because she has some stuff on her shoes, and she doesn't want her dress to get all dirty—that stuff on her dress. I mean, she has some stuff on her stockings." Another first grader, Julia, came over to the table and interrupted her: "Regina! Guess what I wrote in my journal. 'I love Bill'" [the teacher]. Regina responded, "Let me see," and paused to read Julia's text, the first time I had seen her give such attention to another's writing. Meanwhile, Luan, also a first grader, ran from table to table, whispering in girls' ears about Julia's bold text. Regina then called Julia's attention to her own picture and the girl in it: "She's going like this," dramatizing a girl lifting up her dress. "It's kind of different."

Regina was quite pleased in the end with her "kind of different" picture and the story surrounding it. Turning her attention to the text, she wrote, "This is a girl," then said to Sonia, "Look how she's holding up her dress. And you know what this stuff is? It's mud. 'Cause she fell into the mud puddle and then she's holding up her dress so her dress won't get on—so the mud won't get on her dress."

After her relatively easily encoded opening sentence, Regina concentrated intensely. Unlike her talk during drawing, Regina's talk during writing did not serve primarily representational functions, but, rather, served to help her direct and seek information for her encoding effort. She spelled most words herself, using visual memory, her dictionary, and phonological supports, although she often sought confirmation of her independent spellings ("Is this how you spell *ruff*: R-O-F-E?").

Regina's completed text was an art note:

This is a girl She has something on her leg's but she doesn't know that it was on her but she will know it. [February, First Grade]

It is in certain ways like her previous texts, in that it focuses on one figure and there are vacillations of time. There is a significant difference, however. Rather than describing the external actions of the figure, the text notes the internal feelings of the poor girl with the mud. In fact, in 9 of Regina's 16 first-grade entries, she included reference to characters' feelings. She was beginning to move away from stating in her texts what "everybody knows," in Maggie's words, toward revealing aspects of characters' internal lives not evidenced via drawing.

This effort to go beyond describing her drawing could cause problems, as Regina herself noted. When she reread her text, she became quite concerned. Just as Regina's dependence upon a picture had led to her self-correction while reading her bird-and-egg piece, so did it here: "It [the text] can't say that," she explained. The girl could not be unaware of the mud on her legs "because she's going like that" [holding up her dress]. Regina was here explicitly confronting the time problem caused by the coordination of picture and text, just as she had explicitly confronted the problem of focus in space with her comment, reported previously, "I'm talking about the little girl," not the little girl's mom. Her difficulty in coordinating the time frames of the picture and the written text led her to evaluate and then to revise that text. Regina adjusted her entry to read that the girl "know now that it was on her legs" (rather than "doesn't know") and that "she will not like it" (rather than "will know it"). With that, she was satisfied: "There. That's it right there."

While, for this event, her text was now all right, it was one of her last art notes. Her texts became less tied to her pictures, as she became increasingly attentive to the complex interplay of drawing, text, and talk.

Coordinating Imaginary and Experienced Worlds

In the girl-with-mud event, both Regina and Maggie attended to the sense of Regina's picture. In a subsequent event, Jake and Maggie, who were seated by her, led Regina to consider the relationship between her drawn and spoken world, on the one hand, and the wider experienced world, on the other.

Regina began by drawing a Brownie Scout, talking as she worked about the Brownie's characteristics and actions. Her talk was primarily centered within her imaginative world, except for her occasional request for feedback on the accuracy of her drawing ("Maggie, does this look like she has her hair in a rubber band?"). Jake, however, heard her talk and engineered the transformation of her self-directed, task-involved talk into conversational task-related talk.

As illustrated in Table 5.2, Jake's inquiries about Regina's symbolic world led to a sharing of experiences and joint pleasures—popcorn, cheese, and ice cream—and an exchange of opinions about the logical-ness of Regina's efforts. That is, talk about Regina's symbolic world led the pair to reflect about experiences in the wider world of people, places, and things. Through talk in the social world they shared, Regina's private symbolic world gained real-world relevance for both children.

When Regina returned again to her drawing, she not only talked about her depicted Brownie, but also made continual references to the nature of real-world Brownies. Her imaginary Brownie represented in certain ways real-world Brownies. This sort of talk suggested that Regina had achieved further distance from her drawing. She was explicitly rea-soning about why her depiction (accurately drawn or not) was appro-priate as a representative of a category of real-world figures or objects, thus apparently moving more deliberately between the imaginary and the real world.

One particularly lengthy monologue occurred after an unsolicited interruption from Maggie:

REGINA: (talking to self) These are her [the Brownie's] legs.
MAGGIE: Let me see your picture. You better make some knees on here—on her.
Regina works on this, drawing circles for knees, which seems to give rise to the notion of roller skates (which have circles for wheels):
REGINA: These are not her knees [they are wheels]. Her knees are off the ground. She's skating. *The Brownies have to skate.* She's skating because she's a Brownie. *And they*

TABLE 5.2. Regina's "Brownie" Event: Functions of Talk

Children's Talk	Function/Strategy (topic focus)*	Comment
Regina: This is a Brownie. ... She's a little girl. She has a brown dress. She's a Brownie.	Representational/ labeling, elaborating (task-involved; focused on depiction)	Regina is drawing a little girl wearing a pink shirt and a brown dress.
Jake: You're a Brownie. You're a Brownie. (teasing)		Jake, who enjoys language play and is himself of mixed Black/Anglo ethnicity, seems to be teasing Regina about her skin color. She does not understand and responds quite indignantly.
Regina: No, I'm a Girl Scout.	Representational/ labeling (task-related; focused on personal experiences)	
Jake: You're a Brownie. (teasing) Brownies do not wear pink. (in reference to Regina's drawing) Brownies deliver cookies.		
Regina: So do Girl Scouts.	Representational/ reporting (task-related; focused on real-world referent)	
Jake: You delivered any cookies?		
Regina: Next Sunday we're going to. ...	Representational/ reporting (task-related; focused on personal experiences.)	Regina continues to talk about what Brownies do and then returns again to her drawing.
She's wearing a pink shirt with	Representational/ reporting (task-	

TABLE 5.2.   (continued)

Children's Talk	Function Strategy (topic focus)*	Comment
stripes.	involved; focused on depiction)	
They [Brownies] have to wear the same thing.	Representational/ reporting (task-related; focused on real-world referent)	
<u>Jake</u>: They can't wear pink shirts.		
<u>Regina</u>: They can wear pink shirts with stripes. I was 4 and I always wore this stuff. We sold popcorn.	Representational/ reporting (task-related; focused on real-world referent and personal experience)	
<u>Jake</u>: Oooh. Popcorn is yummy.		
<u>Regina</u>: We had cheese and ice cream,		
<u>Jake</u>: Oooh.		
<u>Regina</u>: chocolate fudge and we had chicken. I had French fries.		

* The coding categories for the topics of the children's
  talk are included here in order to display more clearly
  Regina's movement among worlds. These codes, introduced
  in Chapter 1, are more fully defined in Appendix B.

*have to stay in one place. And if—and um. Now the
ball goes somewhere else, they have to stay. If the ball
goes somewhere else, they stay.* She's skating in one
place. (The underlined sections refer to talk about the
general concept of "Brownies.")

Regina's recollections about Brownies lead to her statement about
Brownies not being able to run after balls. Soon Regina adds a
ball to her picture.

As depicted in Figure 5.4, Regina's completed drawing seems rather
sparse, given the great amount of information about "her Brownie" and
Brownies in general that she had voiced. The Brownie is wearing skates
and "jumping" off the ground. She is outside. A bird is flying by, and a
ball is bouncing into the scene.

After completing her drawing, Regina was ready for her "story." As
in previous first-grade events, she needed to decide what parts of her
drawn and spoken world would find their way into print, a process she
articulated to some extent aloud. "She's just in the Brownies," she remarked, pointing at her drawn girl, "but I'm not gonna say that she's in
the Brownies." And so Regina turned to encoding her text about the little
girl, the unacknowledged Brownie:

Figure 5.4.   Regina's Brownie.

> The little girl was playing with The Bol and She was Satg [skat-
> ing] on The ground. She had two sisters. One was Named Eliza-
> beth and one was Named Diana. [March, First Grade]

This is primarily a description of Regina's picture, but it is in past tense, not present. Further, it provides information that was not foreshadowed by her drawing and talking—the existence of two sisters. Information that she had revealed in spoken or drawn form was not necessarily transformed into writing, and information not developed during drawing and talking appeared during the writing itself. Thus, not only was Regina moving more deliberately between the imaginary and the real world, she was moving as well between different symbolic renderings of her imaginary world.

Writing texts that moved beyond given (drawn) information and included characters' internal motivations and expectations helped Regina to write stories that were judged more sensible and more interesting by Margaret. One of Margaret's favorite stories accompanied a picture of a clown in the spotlight, surrounded by cheering fans (see Figure 5.5). Significantly, the clown was not mentioned in her story:

> The mom went to the show and had a good time but the little
> girl had to go to bed. [March, First Grade]

In later events, Regina's writing gained even greater independence and a more deliberate connection with her own experience—rather than her own drawings—as Regina herself became an actor within her written worlds.

Becoming an Experienced Actor in an Imagined World

Compared to her kindergarten work, Regina's drawn and spoken worlds had become more unified. Her drawn figures were not only united in a visual frame, her speech united them into a single world. Regina tended to talk elaborately about each new figure she added to a drawing, reinterpreting earlier characters so that they fit into her evolving story.

Regina may have been aided in achieving more control by her own greater involvement in her worlds. She herself stepped into her drawn worlds as actor—and, indeed, she stepped into her written worlds as actor, too, a talking actor. There were 16 products in all, in her first-grade collection; among the latter 8, Regina became an actor in 5 written texts, a role she had rarely adopted before.

In entering into her own imaginary worlds, Regina could rely more directly on her experiences in the real world to help her construct her

Figure 5.5.   Regina's clown show.

imaginary one; she knew what had happened—and thus what might happen—in such a scene. In the event to be described in this section, as in previous events, Regina's talked-through and drawn world expanded outward from her drawn objects (see Figure 5.6). She began by drawing a table and then added a "messed up" television and a "cake." The cake seemed to trigger thoughts of Santa, and then it became a remote-control device for the television and another table was drawn, complete with cookies and lemonade for Santa. Next came a fireplace and, hanging above it, a "Home Sweet Home" sign, which stimulated a long spelling duel initiated by Regina (see Chapter 3). Finally, she added herself under a table, her talk guiding her through this last addition.

Despite more than one interlude for spelling duels, Regina's speech during drawing focused primarily on her evolving scene. She used representational language to report on the objects existing in her picture and on her own present-tense actions as an actor. And, just as he had in the

Figure 5.6.   Regina's girl waiting for Santa.

Brownie event, Jake responded to her talk, calling her attention to both the imaginary world she was drawing and the experienced world she was transforming.

> REGINA: This is me under the table. And I am going to take a picture of Santa Claus when he comes down. He has to be careful.
>
> JAKE: For real? Did you see Santa Claus?
>
> REGINA: (switching to the "for-real" world) My grandma did.
>
> JAKE: For real?
>
> REGINA: She slept downstairs. 'Cause I looked in her room and she wasn't in her room. She was downstairs.

So, Regina was not the original person lying in wait, it was her grandmother! Jake, who was a year older than Regina, may have been finding this "for-real" discussion of Santa a bit beneath him. (On another occasion, he had announced that Santa was "your mom and dad.")

He teased Sonia about believing in Santa, which Regina did not find funny.

> JAKE: Guess what? Guess who said—Guess who said—
> REGINA: I have lots of toys.
> JAKE: Guess who says, "Santa Claus came down the chimney and leave this writing"? She left—Sonia said.
> REGINA: Santa Claus writes pretty.
> JAKE: Guess who wrote it? Her mom.

Thus, Jake invited Regina out of her imaginary world to discuss the nature of the real-world referents for her picture; the two children recalled "real" personal experiences as they considered Regina's interpretation of those referents (i.e., her belief that Santa was real). Yet, as in the Brownie event, Jake was not able to draw Regina into a playful stance about the world she perceived as real. Santa Claus, like the Brownies, her friends, her drawings, and Regina herself, was not to be taken lightly. Indeed, in one exchange, Jake tried to no avail to bring Regina into his own imaginary world.

> Jake has been writing stories about the space adventures of his friend Manuel and now is playfully threatening to bring other children into these dangerous exploits, including Ruben and his brother, Pedro:
>
> JAKE: After I finish my bubble car story, I'm gonna do the evil forces of Pedro.
> MANUEL: (laughs) The evil forces.
> JAKE: The evil forces of Pedroville—Pedro and Ruben—
>   . . .
> Then I'm going to make the evil forces of Reginaship. Of Regina. (glances at her with a teasing, triumphant look)
> REGINA: (very deadpan) So what's bad about that?
> JAKE: The evil forces of Reginaship.
> REGINA: So? You keep on saying you're making things, but you're not making nothing.
> JAKE: (trying again, in a teasing, playful voice) I like forces. Like the evil forces of REGINA!
> REGINA: Evil forces of Jake. (irritated and serious)

Regina's completed picture, as usual, only hints at the story bulging within its edges (refer to Figure 5.6). It includes, in addition to the items already mentioned, stockings hanging at the fireplace (the only clear indication of Christmas), and three pictures on the wall. Actually, it was only after writing her first three sentences of text that she returned to her picture to add a few details to her face and to put the third picture on the wall. She originally intended the picture to be of "me when I was a baby," but it turned out to be "my grandma's picture." She explained her reasoning about this to me, and, most significantly, explicitly referred for the first observed time to her audience:

REGINA: (talking as she draws) This is gonna be my grandma's picture. The reason I know it's my grandma's picture is this is her when she got married.

DYSON: (not having heard her final words) The reason you know it's your grandma's picture is what?

REGINA: I'm gonna keep that a secret, because everybody else is gonna know and they'll laugh.

Her written text did keep the "secret" about her grandma. This was different from those produced in the previously observed events. Regina entered into the scene and told it from her own perspective within that scene, the story revolving around her anticipation of the unpictured Santa. Further, she imposed written-language characteristics (past tense, dialogue) on her talked-about and drawn-through ideas:

Ho Ho Ho. Santa was comeing to see me. I was hiding under the chair to see santa. Santa was singing to himself. I had a camera in my hand. I said Mary Chrisms. [April, First Grade]

In striking contrast to her development of imaginary worlds during drawing and talking, when she alternately recalled the past and antici-pated the future, Regina seemed to develop this text linearly. Further, her adoption of a first-person stance and her use of characters' talk allowed her to convey movement through time: Santa must have been coming at least within hearing distance ("he was singing"), and then Regina re-sponded verbally to his arrival. Indeed, all four of Regina's first-grade *narratives*—that is, her texts containing movement through time—in-volved the use of dialogue, which allowed her to move forward in time without moving outside the space framed in the picture.[4] Her linear "what-next" strategy (Bereiter & Scardamalia, 1982) is generally consid-

---

[4]As Leondar (1977) discusses, a major developmental challenge facing preschool storytellers is to construct plots in which all the actions do not take place in one space.

ered young children's simplest technique for text construction (Graves, 1983; Harris & Wilkinson, 1986). Yet, developing a story linearly was, for Regina, a helpful way of moving through the space/time frame of a narrative.

Coordinating Action in the Imaginary, Ongoing Social, and Experienced Worlds

By the end of her first-grade year, Regina's writing had been liberated from simply describing her picture, as she made more deliberate manipulations of time and space. Yet she was still having difficulty coordinating her drawn and spoken world with her written one. Further, her written texts were not as elaborate as her spoken and drawn ones, nor were they as socially constructed, with her peers taking part spontaneously. There were hints, though, that Regina's texts were beginning to figure into her social life in the way that drawing first had—as objects useful for gaining social approval.

Both the social nature of Regina's drawing and the social potential of her writing were illustrated in the last event observed in her first-grade year. This occurred over the course of three days, two of which were spent drawing the "Candyland" picture that appears in Figure 5.7. Regina engaged in a great deal of task-involved and task-related talk during drawing, the latter unusual in that *Regina herself* initiated it, asking others questions about her drawn figures and simply calling others' attention to her work, of which she was quite proud.

Table 5.3 presents an analysis of portions of her talk. With her directive to those who had tasted a banana split, and Sonia's question about the ice cream called "kitchen sink," a long interactive episode began in which the children at the table posed questions about each other's tasting of varied kinds of ice cream. This was interwoven with spelling duels. As will be recalled from Chapter 3, Regina's critique of Wesley's difficulty in spelling *candy* led Sonia to put down Regina over her ignorance about ice cream.

SONIA: Did you taste the kitchen sink?
REGINA: No. YOU TASTE A KITCHEN SINK!?!
SONIA: YEAH. It's an ICE cream. You know, the kitchen sink ice cream.
REGINA: Oh. EEEECH. ⌈What's wrong with you?
SONIA: ⌊You don't know what the kitchen sink is.
REGINA: Y'all have to tell me.
SONIA: Gee you're dumb.

Figure 5.7. Regina's Candyland.

REGINA: I'm not dumb.
  SONIA: You should know that by the time you're five years old.
REGINA: I'm not five years old. I'm seven.

· · ·

            Well I tasted Mississippi Mud.
  JESSE: ⌈Eeuuuuuu.
  SONIA: ⌊Eeuuuuu.
REGINA: It's not mud. It's chocolate ice cream.

· · ·

   JAKE: Who's had sherbet ice cream?

· · ·

MANUEL: Who ever tasted chocolate-chip ice cream?

· · ·

   JAKE: Have you ever tasted ice cream—bubble car ice cream?

Jake returned soon after this to his bubble car drawing, which
Regina complimented ("Now *that's* a bubble car!"). She soon returned to

TABLE 5.3. Regina's "Candyland" Event: Functions of Talk

Regina's Talk	Function/Strategy	Comment
This is how big the whole place is. It's very tall.	Representational/ elaborating (task-involved; focused on depiction)	Regina has just drawn the structure of her candy house.
Let's see.	Directive/ monitoring	
For the grass it's gonna be ice cream. ...	Directive/ planning	
(to Sonia) I'm making a Candyland house.	Interactional-representational/ reporting (task-involved; focused on self)	
I been--I been at Candyland before. ...	(task-related; focused on personal experience)	
I'm gonna make a banana split.	Directive/ planning; representational/ reporting (task-involved; focused on self)	Regina has drawn her house and the ice cream grass and is starting a banana split on the ground.
Whoever tasted a banana split, raise your hand.	Interactional-directive/ requesting	
(Aarison says, "I have.")		

her imaginary world as well. As shown in Table 5.4, however, Regina's social talk with her peers about tasty foods was not only task-related; it also became task-involved and contained themes of the previous task-related talk about real-world ice cream. For, despite Sonia's obvious dislike of Regina's gloating, she did become very interested in Regina's evolving Candyland. Indeed, Sonia entered into Regina's drawing and talking, and with this, Regina's ongoing social world and her imaginary world came together. With her "Can I do that?", Sonia joined in with

Regina. She added pink sprinkles and green peppermint around Regina's Candyland house. And she directed Regina to "do something with the windows." Regina seemed both pleased with Sonia's interest and protective about her picture (No, spr— Not like that, like this.") Her efforts to gain positive responses from her friends through her drawings certainly were successful with Sonia. The completed product was indeed "neat" (refer to Figure 5.7).

In fact, when the Candyland picture was completed, Regina began to show Sonia other entries in her journal, and as Sonia showed continued interest, Regina began to read her accompanying texts to Sonia. The texts, though, had to be accompanied with talk in order to make sense. For example, Regina read, "This one says, 'I went to the dentist. I had to stay in the line for a 3 minutes because, he was not here.'" Then she added, "I had to stay in there for the um for 3 or 4 minutes, and I thought I—that I would be there for my whole life." This was the first observed event in which Regina spontaneously sought peer approval for her written text, rather than for her picture. And it was also the first observed event in which she elaborated to a peer on the meaning of her written story.

Regina had drawn and talked about Candyland for almost two full language arts periods, but her elaborate world of raining lemonade and chocolate sprinkles had yet to be transformed into a comparable written world. When she finally composed her text, neither her drawing nor her talk seemed to provide the substance of it. What it was about, though, was meeting and talking with friends, which certainly had happened in Regina's "real" world during this event:

> I found the Candy House where My Friends lived. It's us said them. Hi I said. Can I come in? Yes they said. Come in. We have three dogs. Wow wee I said. [May, First Grade]

During the production of this text, Regina concentrated on encoding. She was quite independent, asking for help with spelling only 2 of the 25 different words. As she worked, she paused between each sentence, which suggested that she was planning her text linearly, as the results seem to confirm.

As in all four of the narratives that she produced during the year, Regina went beyond the information given in either her talk or her drawing, and she used written language structures including dialogue, to help organize her material. (The short sentences of the dialogue here seem to have a "basal reader" style, but there is no indication in Regina's journals as a whole that basal readers were her text model.) As in the Santa event, the liberation of Regina's text from her drawing made that

(text continued on p. 134)

TABLE 5.4. Regina's "Candyland" Event: Functions of Talk
          with Peers

Children's Talk	Function/Strategy	Comment
Julia: What are you drawing?		Regina has now begun to draw lollipops next to her banana split.
Regina: Lollipops.	Representational/ reporting (task-involved; focused on self)	
Gosh!	Personal/evaluating others	Regina seems to be irritated with Julia's question.
Biggest lollipops you ever tasted!	Representational/ elaborating (task-involved; focused on depiction)	Aarison comes to the table to show the children his drawing of Heathcliff (a cartoon cat). All the children are impressed, including Regina ("Gosh, you sure can draw!") Regina then seeks some acknowledgement of her own drawing.
Regina: (to Sonia) Look-it. Like my lollipop?	Interactional-directive/ requesting	
Sonia: What?		
Regina: Hey! Look-it!	Interactional-directive	
Lollipop!	Representational/ labeling	
Know when you go to the fair?	Interactional	
Sonia: Yeah.		
Regina: They have those little swirl lollipops?	Representational/ elaborating (task-related; focused on real-world referent)	
Well, I was gonna get	Interactional Representational/	

132

TABLE 5.4. (continued)

Children's Talk	Function/Strategy	Comment
one one time. But I didn't get to. And--I taste it before though.	narrating, reporting (task-related; focused on personal experience)	
Sonia: They taste so sweet, and sugary.		Regina has been discussing eating varied delightful foods with her friends. That task-related talk now seems to feed into her talk about her actual drawing.
Regina: Yeah, that's right.	Interactional Personal/evaluating others;	
I got a good idea.	evaluating self	
I'm making lemonade drops.	Directive/ planning	
And when it rains, there's lemonade drops. And people like it.	Representational/ reporting, elaborating (task-involved; focused on depiction)	Regina here is narrating her story to Sonia, rather than to her work; Sonia is interested and soon joins in.
(to Sonia) See?	Directive-interactional	
When it rains, people are--they come outside. Some people on this side, um, that side, they want lemonade. On this side, they want chocolate sprinkles on this side.	Representational/ reporting, elaborating (task-involved; focused on depiction)	
Sonia: Yeah.		
Regina: Chocolate sprinkles on this side.		
Sonia: (to me, referring to Regina's drawing) Isn't this neat? ... Can I do that?		
Regina: Yeah!	Interactional	

picture seem to be an illustration (rather than the basis) for the text. While the bulk of her energy—and the social energy of her peer group—was directed toward her drawing rather than her writing, that writing was beginning to assume dominance.

SUMMARY

In the beginning of this project, Regina's journal-time talk suggested her deep involvement in the imaginary worlds she was drawing within her blank pages, worlds where little girls and small animals had, for the most part, pleasant experiences. While she would occasionally refer to real-life events related to her creations, the figures on her paper seemed to have a life of their own, as opposed to being representations of an imagined or real life. Thus, her little girl would be doing something, feeling something, or awaiting some happening, or perhaps she would have experienced something already. Regina's dictations described her pictures, thus failing to record the meanings that had been carried in her talk, including discussions about the internal feelings of her characters and those characters' past and future actions.

During the first grade, Regina explicitly confronted the space and time tensions that existed between her drawn and spoken worlds and her written ones, as she worked to coordinate her drawing and her writing. At the same time, her classmates became increasingly vocal about her spoken and drawn worlds. Their comments directed Regina's attention to the nature of her imaginary world as a set of objects, objects that could not only be lived in but also talked about and critiqued by others.

Thus, as a first grader, Regina began to comment on what aspects of her drawn and spoken worlds she was going to include in her written texts and which ones were not going to be included. In moving from drawing to writing, then, she acknowledged a distinction between a shaped symbolic world and that world's referent (e.g., "She's just in the Brownies, but I'm not gonna say that she's in the Brownies.").

Beyond Regina's explicit attempts to resolve space and time tensions between drawn and spoken worlds and written ones, she also began to use written language structures. These assisted her in moving beyond the space and time frames of her pictures. Most notably, she began to use past rather than present tense and to incorporate written dialogue into her worlds. The use of these conventions seemed to result in linearly structured text worlds, which were very different from the expanding circular worlds built during drawing and talking, worlds that stretched both backward and forward from a central, present time. All four of Regina's narratives based on actual (as opposed to anticipated or implied) movement through time depended upon dialogue and on new information beyond that included in the talk accompanying her drawing.

The use of the first-person perspective also seemed to assist Regina in creating dynamic worlds. In going inside her texts she could perhaps more easily move them along. Two of her narratives involved Regina herself as the fictive "I," and two involved the depicted character referring to self as "I" in dialogue. More detailed data on narrative movement and author stance evident in Regina's texts are presented in Table 5.5.

As stressed throughout this chapter, Regina's increasing differentiation between drawn and spoken worlds, on the one hand, and written worlds, on the other, took place amidst the critical attention of others. Margaret usually read Regina's texts and responded with acceptance, pleased laughter, or a request that Regina "read this and see if it makes sense." But Margaret had many children to attend to in a short span of time, so, as a present and interactive partner, she figured into Regina's composing only intermittently, when Regina took her a completed entry or when Margaret happened by. Regina's peers, on the other hand, were always present. They supported the *elaboration* of her spoken and drawn stories and her own *distancing* as artist from those stories. It was at the invitation of her peers that she left her task-involved talk and, within her ongoing social world, considered the real-world origins of her imaginary depictions.

In brief, through interaction with other symbolic materials and with other people, Regina was becoming a more sophisticated manipulator of written and drawn symbols, as well as a more active social participant in classroom life.

EPILOGUE

In kindergarten, Regina's journal-time activity seemed to be a time for private fantasy. She wandered off into her imaginary worlds, just as she often became lost in play with her small toys as she sat on the edge of the rug during class activities. She offered the surface structure of her drawn worlds to her peers for their approval: "Do you like this girl?" Gaining distance from her own imaginary worlds was supported both by her own interaction with her work and by the attention of her peers to that work, that is, by the embedding of her drawn and spoken worlds in the social life of her classroom. While drawing and talking, rather than

TABLE 5.5.   Movement and Stance in Regina's Written Products

	Kindergarten*		First Grade**	
	% of products	No. of products	% of products	No. of products
Movement				
No movement	64	9	50	8
Implied movement	36	5	25	4
Movement	0	0	25	4
Stance				
Art notes	93	13	13	2
Art notes/observer	7	1	13	2
Art notes/actor	0	0	6	1
Observer/actor	0	0	0	0
Observer	0	0	38	6
Actor	0	0	31	5

* $\underline{n}$ = 14.

** $\underline{n}$ = 16.

writing, garnered the most attention, there were hints that writing—and talking during writing—would soon gain a place.

And so it seemed to. During the spring semester of second grade, Regina was observed on seven occasions, twice very closely. She was seen engaging in representational and interactional talk cued by her own and others' text worlds. For example, in the first observation, Regina, along with Mitzi and Sonia, helped their friend Nicole construct a written text about Manuel—one that detailed his tendency to turn quite red when embarrassed or, as Manuel pointed out, when something was funny.

> NICOLE: (writing) OK. Let me see. When he starts laughing—
> No, um, when he's, um—

REGINA: When Manuel gets embarrassed—
NICOLE: When he's embarrassed.
SONIA: (suggesting a revision) You have to fix that sentence.
          You have to fix that sentence. Manuel can— Every time
          Manuel gets mad, he—his face turns red.
REGINA: I like that.
SONIA: That's embarrassed. (to Manuel) You're embarrassed.
NICOLE: Yeah, but when you're [Manuel] mad at me, your face
          goes (makes a face and giggles). It turns red.
REGINA: And he looks like a big tomato when he gets—
SONIA: When he gets embarrassed his face turns red, too.

In this event, Regina became quite upset when she felt Nicole would "never say anything I say" about Manuel, which was not true. Nicole was simply trying to negotiate among all the children who wanted to have their ideas included. As Regina saw her comments take form on the page, she was appeased. This was Nicole's final product (Regina's contributions are underlined):

Every time Manuel get's mad he looks like a red tomato. When Manuel gets embarrassed his face gets red his nose looks like a pickle. Marcos [Manuel's brother] looks like a clown with a bangle on his head.

Regina's own journal activity in second grade tended to begin with written stories, rather than with drawing, and her tales did not center on the experiences of generic little girls but were about real or imagined events in the lives of herself and her friends. Thus, like Regina herself, her texts seemed more firmly embedded in her ongoing social life and in her accumulating world of experiences. They did not contain the elaborate detail about characters' motivations and the historical context of characters' actions that were typical of her talk in kindergarten; indeed, this information still emerged primarily in her talk during drawing. But her writing was independent of her drawing. It revealed the life she shared with her friends, as in the following, which was written to accompany the portrait shown in Figure 5.8:

Nicole

Nicole had a slumber party and invited all her Friend's to it and they went to a drive-in movie and when they got home they had pizza and soda pop. [May, Second Grade]

Nicole really did not have a slumber party, but imaginary text worlds are also good places to play with one's friends.

I saw Regina for the last time in the spring of her third-grade year, when I returned to visit Margaret and the children. Having spent that academic year doing my own writing about a little girl named Regina and her peers, I didn't initially recognize her, she had grown so. I was taken aback as well by her writing and drawing. Gone were the brief descriptions of sweet little girls; in their stead were murder mysteries and horror stories. As Regina herself explained to me, she used to write "about girls going to the seashore and girls picking flowers and riding their bikes and about girls going to the candy store and girls getting ice cream bars and the ice cream falling off. . . . I changed this year because I didn't want to make stories about girls any more. I like stories about people and scary stories and more scary stories, like this one. It's called 'I'm Coming to Get You.'" As she talked, I remembered the "monster" who had taken her eraser in the kindergarten, an event that had captured the attention of her classmates.

Figure 5.8.   Regina's portrait of Nicole.

The ideas for Regina's scary stories came from books she had read or movies she had seen. She was currently working on a story based on the popular movie, *Jewel of the Nile*. Her recollection of this movie seemed amazingly detailed, a fact that concerned Margaret, who would have liked Regina to depend less upon these remembered details. And yet, having spent months studying her written descriptions of drawn characters, I was awed by the apparent ease with which Regina created her new characters' actions and made them chronologically sensible. Further, she had discovered new tools for crafting written stories—parentheses, exclamation points, "loud" or boldface words—which she learned, she said, by reading. There was continuity, too, in her efforts: Regina's insight into her characters' reactions and motivations was still conveyed primarily through the familiar technique of creating a chatty first-person dialogue. The following is a brief excerpt from her lengthy piece, which was accompanied by finely drawn illustrations of key scenes. To set the stage, the central characters, a married couple named Joan and Colton, have just arrived at a party:

> When they got there, one of Joan's Friends was rushing up to see Joan. (Joan did not see her). "Joan! Joan, over here." Joan turned around and smiled. "Oh Jessica I was just going to call you but time flies." When Joan said That Omar came and said "are you Joan Wyler?" "yes, I am." Said Joan. "then, come with me." said Omar. So, Joan said Goodbye to Colton and left. [April, Third Grade]

As I talked with Regina about her work, her good friend Marissa joined our conversation. I was pleased to learn that Regina had a close friend and that, as they both suggested, Regina's writing was very much a part of their friendship. When Regina told me about her story called "I'm Coming to Get You," Marissa said, "It's a good story." Regina acknowledged Marissa's contribution: "I got the story from her because she had a book." Marissa replied, "It was called *The Baby Sitter*, but she changed it." Not only did Marissa influence Regina's writing, Regina influenced Marissa's. On that same day, Marissa had written in her journal a "funny poem" that Regina's grandfather had taught Regina and that she, in turn, had taught Marissa:

> Once upon a time
> the monkey drank the wine.
> the goose played the fiddle
> on the sweet potato vine.

Regina's friendship with Marissa was supported by and supporting their shared interest in texts of varied types. Regina, the little kindergartener who had spent so much of her time in her own imaginary worlds, had become a third grader who shared at least some of those worlds with another.

Literacy's power for supporting friendships was also a central theme in the case study of the child who had early on involved Regina in social talk about her imaginary worlds—the spirited Jake, to whose history I turn in the next chapter.

6

Jake

Figure 6.1.   Jake's war in the jungle.

There is a War in the jungle and Nobody
is getting killed. They are friends.
They are only testing their weapons.
The eNd

[March, First Grade]

Jake's "war in the jungle" illustrates well both the theme and spirit of Jake's journal-time activity. Throughout the two years of observation, Jake filled his journals with action-packed pictures of male dramas. His drawn adventures were occasions for enacted adventures with his friends. As illustrated in his introductory portrait in Chapter 4, Jake interacted with his peers during drawing, talking through elaborate tales as his pictures evolved. Yet, as also noted earlier, Jake's writing activity was quite different. He struggled with encoding, and any interaction about writing focused primarily on spelling.

Jake himself was quite straightforward about his feelings toward drawing and writing. If a blank sheet for drawing was next in his journal, he proclaimed his good fortune to his friends *before* beginning his activity: "I'm lucky. I get to draw." Faced with the prospect of writing a text to accompany that drawing, Jake cheered only *after* the work was completed: "I'm done!"

Like Regina, Jake's stance toward writing and drawing changed dramatically over the two years of close observation. Writing gradually eclipsed drawing from its spotlight position. More so than Regina, Jake came to view writing, too, as a grand opportunity for playing with his friends. It is this process of change that is the focus of this chapter.

FIRST GRADE: DRAWING AS SOCIAL PLAY,
WRITING AS SOCIAL STRUGGLE

Jake viewed himself as a "normal kid," and, moreover, he forged links with other kids. He imagined with them the possibility of stuffing their journals with cotton to outwit parents and teachers and dreamed of living in the land of "cotton candy." His sense of language's rhythm and rhyme augmented his playful style with his peers: "You can skip" empty pages in your journal, he told a downhearted Sonia, who couldn't think of what to write. "You can skip and then be slick, Sonia." The following vignette illustrates his spirited approach.

Margaret has decided to have the children practice punctuating sentences before working on their journals. Jake and Sonia, lying side by side on the rug, are copying and correcting the sentences printed on the blackboard. At Jake's initiation, they enliven their work by reciting rhymes.

JAKE: Peter, Peter, pumpkin eater. Had a wife and couldn't keep her. Put her in a pumpkin shell.
SONIA: And he keeped her very well.

JAKE: Yep. I wish I were in the land of cotton.
SONIA: I wish I were in the land of ⌈ cotton candy.
JAKE: ⌊ cotton candy. That would
be much funner.
SONIA: Yeah. We wouldn't have to have moms and dads to tell us
what to eat.
JAKE: Yeah. We could just eat our bridge [in the land of cotton
candy].
SONIA: We could eat anything we wished.
JAKE: Gol! We could eat things made out of cotton and candy
and other candy.
SONIA: Yeah.
JAKE: We better get working—
SONIA: Instead of dreaming about cotton candy.

Jake's playful talk permeated his drawing, but not his writing. Like
Regina, he looked to his pictures for support when writing, so the oral
narratives that surrounded the creation of those pictures were not captured in his written texts. Indeed, 9 of Jake's 14 collected first-grade
journal entries (64%) did not contain any narrative movement, while 4
(29%) only implied movement. His texts tended to stay within the past or
present moment, as depicted in the picture, but those with implied
movement seemed to push against the picture's frame.

For example, in one event Jake drew and narrated a story about a
torpedo racing a rainbow (see Figure 6.2). Before he began writing, he
recited the story he planned to write: "Once there was a torpedo racing a
rainbow, and it was beating—the rainbow was beating the torpedo. And
the torpedo lost. And the end." Yet, as Jake wrote this story, its time frame
changed, so that it was no longer set in the past but rather anticipated the
future. Jake's stance as author also changed: His "Once there was,"
suggesting an observer of a past world, became "There is," indicating an
art note commentator:

There is a torpedo racing a rainbow. And the torpedo is winning
and the torpedo is going to the finishing line. the end [March,
First Grade]

Jake's difficulty in encoding his written texts was compounded by
his difficulty with reading. His friend Manuel, who also had trouble
reading, warned me one day, "He isn't gonna read that well" a point with
which Jake did not disagree. In fact, he voiced his own concerns about
reading.

Figure 6.2.   Jake's torpedo racing a rainbow.

JAKE: I'm not going to get left behind.
SONIA: How do you know?
JAKE: Because I gonna, in school ( ) I have to do some home-
work at my home. I have to learn how to read good.
I'm not learning good.

At least in part because of his reading difficulties, Jake often restated his already written sentences while composing his texts; that is, where other children might reread their work, Jake restated his. As Jake himself explained, "I memorized that. I wasn't really looking at the whole sentence." In the midst of all the printed graphics, he had to work hard to remember what he had written and to figure out what he should therefore write next.

The Text as Social Object

Perhaps because he was so focused on encoding during writing, Jake did not initiate talk about the meaning of his written texts with his friends nor did he comment on theirs. But, during the third month of observation, his peers began to critique his writing. It was Jake's very struggle with encoding that made his texts available for his peers, for, as just noted, he frequently had to state the sentence he was attempting to write as he progressed word by word through his story. While Jake himself was focused on remembering and encoding, his listening peers sometimes reacted to the sense of his texts.

As described in Chapter 3, the children assessed the internal logicalness of texts and their consistency with the way the external world works. Such activity often engaged the children in task-related talk about the nature of real-world referents. The children also sometimes responded to a text's clarity or grammaticalness, which could lead to metasymbolic talk about the nature of the written language system itself. In the following example, Jake's written language was called into question by Hawkeye.

> Jake has finished drawing and has been working hard on his text. He eeks out "There is a three" and then rereads, "There are three." He self-corrects, though, to the more accurate (if less grammatical) "There is a three." He proceeds and eventually writes, "There is a three designs in the sky and the." He backs up a couple of words, rereads, and attempts to sound out the next word: "And the /b/." He figures out the *b* and, with adult assistance, finishes *big*. He backs up once again and rereads: "The big one, the big one is, /i/i/" [*one* is not written]. Jake spells *is* and then rereads the whole line, perhaps to figure out what the next word should be: "This [there] is a—this is a three designs in the sky and the big one—" Jake realizes that he has not written *one*. He adds the word and once more rereads. To this point Jake's speech has been task-involved, focused primarily on directing the spelling of his text. Now, though, Jake's peer Hawkeye enters into Jake's writing process. Hawkeye attempts to change Jake's focus from encoding to a metasymbolic consideration of his text's syntax.
>
> JAKE: (rereading) There is a three—
> HAWKEYE: There is three.
> JAKE: There is a three—
> HAWKEYE: There is three ⌈ designs in the sky
> JAKE: ⌊ designs in the sky and the big one is—

Hawkeye's attempts to change Jake's focus have been unsuccessful. He now intervenes in a more direct way.

HAWKEYE: There is three designs in the sky. Erase that *a*.
JAKE: Why?
HAWKEYE: Because, "There is A three designs—"
JOHNNY: There IS three designs [Johnny's subsequent comment suggests that he is pointing out to Hawkeye that, indeed, Jake has drawn three designs and therefore should not be corrected.]
HAWKEYE: There is— Listen: There is a ⌈ three designs
JOHNNY: │ three designs
JAKE: ⌊ three designs in the sky.
HAWKEYE: That doesn't make sense.
JOHNNY: Yes it does. You don't know nothing.

Jake, however, erases the *a*.

In this event, as was typical for Jake, he worried about whether or not he was reading correctly what he had written. Thus, while rereading, he corrected his oral "There are three" to "There is three," which matched the text. Hawkeye was asking Jake to reread for a different purpose, to judge whether or not what he had written read correctly in another way, namely sensibly. Hawkeye was demonstrating for Jake that a text is a symbolic object, just as a picture is, and that, like a picture, its adequacy can be judged. While Jake did not orally indicate that he understood Hawkeye's objection, he did indeed change his text. His final text was a straightforward art note:

There is three designs in the sky and the big one is the Captain of the three designs. The And [March, First Grade]

In a later event, Jake's peers seemed to lead him to abandon his entire planned story. In this instance, Jake announced his intention to write the following text to accompany the picture shown in Figure 6.3: "One day I saw a tiger jet going over the desert, and it bombed the, the, the desert, and the desert made a volcano and the volcano erupted and the, all the people that lived on the um desert were DEAD from the volcano." Hawkeye was impressed with Jake's text and asked him to read it again, apparently not realizing that it was, in fact, not written. Whereas in the "three-designs" event, Hawkeye had focused Jake's attention on the grammaticalness of his text, here he disputed the logic of the text.

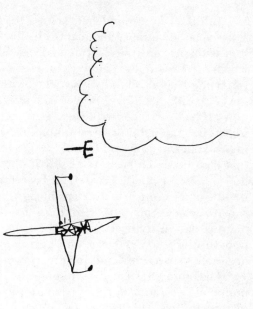

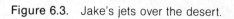

Figure 6.3. Jake's jets over the desert.

HAWKEYE: That can't happen! Volcanoes are made out of rock,
          not sand! Plus the lava in the volcano comes from the
          center of the earth. That [lava] doesn't come from that
          (referring to Jake's drawn desert). You have to draw a
          hole all the way down to the center of the earth.
          That'd make a volcano out of sand.

JAKE: Uh-huh. Look. You bomb something and you pull it
          out.

PETER: Uh-huh.

HAWKEYE: Yeah, but you can't make a volcano out of sand.

MANUEL: (trying to settle things) Well, anyway, it's a pretend
          story. In real life, it may be true.

Just as Jake himself had helped Regina consider the relationship between her imaginary and real worlds, so too did Jake's friends confront him with the multiple worlds within which he had to act and within which his written text had to exist. His *imaginary* world, set in the past, was being responded to by his friends within the context of the ongoing *social* world; his imaginary world affected others' behaviors toward him—it had social consequences. Further, his text was being questioned in part because it didn't seem compatible with his picture; that is, according to Hawkeye, a bomb would have to be drawn well into the earth so that it could touch lava. As he saw it, the differing *symbolic* worlds did not comfortably mesh. Finally, the basis for the argument was whether or not the imagined world was sensible, given their knowledge of the wider *experienced* world. The resolution to their argument, suggested by Manuel, lay in trying to figure out exactly how true "not-true" stories were supposed to be, that is, in figuring out how Jake as author should negotiate between real and imaginary worlds.

Jake himself seemed to resolve the argument by abandoning the notion of a volcano. He returned to his picture, adding more details to his two drawn jets. He labeled two attachments to one jet "graphohooks" and seemed very pleased when none of the children at his table knew what they were. Soon Jake was reporting and narrating a jet adventure, in which a large jet "needs big fire otherwise he'll get catched by the warriors [in the small jet]." Nonetheless, in his written text, Jake depended heavily upon the logic of his picture. He began the piece as an actor in a past world, but he ended by making present-tense comments on his picture. The small jet was described as trying to get away from the large jet, but, within the text itself, it cannot—it's stuck within the picture frame. Thus, movement is implied but not actually accomplished:

I saw a jet flying over the desert. And the little jet got away. But the little jet is trying to get away. [May, First Grade]

By the end of his first-grade year, Jake's struggle with encoding was somewhat eased, as he could depend more upon his own knowledge of sound/symbol correspondences and his visual memory. Lively interactive dramas, though, were still confined to the drawing phase of his writing events; indeed, in the last observed session of his first-grade year, Jake produced his most elaborate recorded oral drama, in which a spaceship meets its doom. An analysis of his talk during this imagined adventure is given in Table 6.1.

After discussing and completing his picture, Jake was "ready for my story." In writing the story, Jake's efforts were interrupted occasionally

TABLE 6.1. Jake's "Doomed Spaceship" Event: Functions of Talk

Jake's Talk	Function/Strategy	Comment
He's gonna shoot the sun.	Representational/ reporting	Jake is referring here to his drawn spaceship.
Do you want him to shoot the sun? ...	Interactional	This question seems to be directed to Johnny.
See he's shooting the sun. Fire's all coming up.	Representational/ narrating	
He better scat 'cause fire's all coming out. ...	Representational/ reasoning	
It only needs one more touch.	Representational/ narrating	Jake is drawing fire lines from the sun to the spaceship.
Look--Johnny-- how much is left, then dying.	Interactional	
Eehhhhhhhh	Representational/ dramatizing	
Closer, closer, closer, closer.	Representational/ narrating	
Look, what it's doing!	Interactional	
It's circling around it.	Representational/ reporting	Jake is drawing fire lines around the spaceship.
EEEEOOOOOOOH!	Representational/ dramatizing	
YUY!		
It touched already.	Representational/ narrating	Note that Jake has moved through time and now changes from present to past tense.
Its ship got burned up.		Jake puts red lines on the space ship.

for conversations with peers about nontask-involved topics, including a discussion about *Charlie and the Chocolate Factory* with Johnny, and a joke with the general peer group at his worktable ("Say 'do'. That means you're gonna get married."). Jake's text reflected the story he had dramatized during drawing, but reduced that story to one event clearly depicted in the picture:

One day I saw a jet. It shot the sun. [May, First Grade]

Jake may have added to this text on a following day, but his was the last day of my observations in first grade that year.

Interestingly, Mitzi overheard Jake read his text, and, like Hawkeye on a previous day, raised an objection. She not only disputed the verity of the text, she questioned the "truth value" of Jake as writer.

MITZI: You're lying. You're lying. That isn't a true story.
JAKE: After all, I did see a jet once. I saw a hundred jets once, 'cause I have—I got a jet collection.

Mitzi's expressed disapproval of Jake and his story may have been due in part to Jake's adoption of an actor stance, which was not his usual approach to imaginary worlds, and his lack of a "once-there-was" opening, which serves to let the audience know that what follows is "make-believe."

In the following year, as will be seen, Jake not only liberated his writing from drawing, he also found ways to negotiate more comfortably among his symbolic, social, and experienced worlds. He continued to "lie" in his imaginative worlds, but he learned how to bring his peers into his "lies" with him.

SECOND GRADE: WRITING AS SOCIAL INTERACTION

Jake continued to display his flair for the dramatic in the second grade, and he still evidenced great pleasure in words, but his language seemed tougher. Many of the terms seemed to come from some of the older boys in his neighborhood—in his words, a neighborhood in "the middle, the crazy part" of his city. "Getting busted" by the teacher and "ripped off totally" by a child who ran off with his markers were distinct possibilities, as were being able to "trick you out of your mind," make a "straight deal," and admire a "helluva fine fight" by wrestler "Hunk Hogan." Jake still seemed to adopt appealing words from school, too, and from me. One day he noticed something he had forgotten to make in his journal and remarked, "Oh-oh. I got to do some research."

As in the first grade, Jake involved his peers in his playful and imaginative narratives, which he could use to exert considerable social influence. In the midst of a serious peer discussion, he could introduce a "what-if" and change the whole nature of the talk. For example, one day Jake and some other children were discussing whether or not they would be able to go outside for recess (it was raining) and play in the sandbox. Jake started an elaborate, group-constructed story, in which the children built a hole in the playground and hid from the teachers. On another day, recounted as follows, Jake turned his peers' recollection of an explosive event into an occasion for play.

Jake is sitting with a group of children at the back work table, writing in his journal. Ruben is wearing a baseball cap today. The last time he wore that baseball cap in school, Jesse teased him by grabbing it off his head, and Ruben, uncharacteristically, covered his head and cried. On this day, Sonia and Jesse recall that earlier scene, perhaps because Ruben's reaction surprised them both. Sonia seems to have lingering guilt about the event; Jesse, a feeling of bravado.

JESSE: Hey, Ruben! (tries to grab his hat)

SONIA: Last time we made him cry, remember? (guiltily)

JESSE: Oh yeah. I made him cry. [With the "I," Jesse assumes responsibility—credit—for the crying.]

MAGGIE: You made him cry? That's not funny.

JESSE: On yeah, I made him cry.

SONIA: We gave it back to him. (still guiltily)

JESSE: (laughs and turns to Jake) We were having a— Guess what? I was fooling around, and grab hat. [Jesse sometimes swallows words when he's excited.]

SONIA: He was starting to cry, and I didn't like that. It was funny, the first part.

JESSE: We were playing "keep away from Ruben."

Jake then takes imaginative control of both the discourse and the drama. Fittingly, Jake's heroic actions are those of the good "superhero."

JAKE: Then, in I came and you went, "AY!" (dramatic playful tone)

JESSE: "YIY-YIY!" (adopting Jake's playful tone)

SONIA: "YIY YIY!" (adopting Jake's playful tone) Me, too.

JAKE: YOU GAVE 'EM THAT HAT AND I GAVE—

MARGARET: Jake!
JAKE: I know. Be quiet.

Margaret quite understandably expressed some concern about Jake's talkativeness. She worried that he was not actually writing, but rather "just talking." At the same time, she greatly enjoyed his sense of humor and, in addition, felt Jake, like all young children, needed to talk about his feelings and ideas. Nonetheless, loud talking and empty pages were not acceptable, as Jake himself knew ("I know. Be quiet.").

Jake's social and language finesse may have contributed to his role as a class leader. It was Jake, for example, who called Margaret's attention to the "people's" concern about Rebecca (another teacher) retiring and taking the puzzles and games with her. During teacher-led discussions, Jake at times piped up with comments to the group, rather than just to Margaret. During journal time, he offered advice to other children about efficient ways of completing journals and of using writing materials. As with his advice to Sonia about planning her stories, his suggestions were given in a friendly tone; he was helping others "be slick." Jake was particularly admired by Jesse, who often imitated his actions, as noted in Chapter 3.

Although Jake was achieving social success in the second grade, he continued to express some misgivings about his academic standing. He was particularly vocal about the spelling quizzes, which he found very hard. As illustrated in Chapter 3, Jake could use difficulty with school-work to establish common ground and support his alliances with his friends. Another case in point is his comment to Christopher on that child's first day at school after a long absence. During the opening group activities on the rug, Margaret explained to Christopher that the class had begun having spelling quizzes. Jake immediately spoke up: "You'll hate it, Christopher. It's harder than anything." Later Jake grinned and muttered jokingly to the children sitting around him: "I'm gonna cheat. I'm gonna cheat this time. That's how you do good in spelling." Jake, of course, did not cheat, but the notion of cheating—of tricking the teacher—was amusing to him and to his friends.

Despite his expressed dislike of spelling quizzes, Jake continued to write. And he found in writing an avenue for playful interaction with his peers and for their admiring recognition. This discovery came about as he began to negotiate among his symbolic, social, and experienced worlds in new ways, reflected in three significant changes in his journal entries. The first was the liberation of Jake's writing from his drawing, and the path to that freedom was forged by the bubble car.

Renegotiating the Writing/Drawing Relationship:
The Bubble-Car Period

During my initial observation of Jake in the second grade, he invented and drew pictures of a marvelous vehicle that was propelled by blowing giant bubbles (see Figure 6.4). Jake first named the vehicles "stir-crazy cars," but he changed his mind a few minutes later: "It's called a bubble car. It's blowing a bubble. For some reason, I just made a bubble car. Sounds fun. Bubble car."

While the text accompanying his first bubble car did not refer to this vehicle, by the second journal entry, the bubble car was a dominant force in both the drawing and the text. Indeed, the bubble car or its variation, the bubble jet, figured in 14 of the 20 entries Jake produced during this observation period. He developed the characteristics of these bubble cars

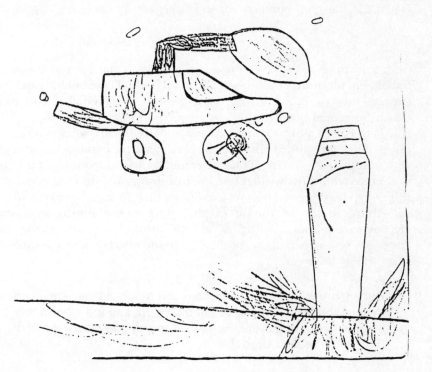

Figure 6.4. Jake's bubble car.

Figure 6.5. Jake's bubble cars and jet (also known as the "wierd" spaceship).

during drawing, as he used representational talk to narrate and dramatize bubble-car adventures for himself and his friends. These bubble cars were daring—they could fly in the air, blow up other vehicles, and meet disastrous results themselves.

Jake had begun to comment occasionally on his written message, rather than only on his spelling, in part, perhaps, because his struggle with encoding was easing. Once he explicitly voiced his intention to try to capture within his written text the just-drawn and dramatized adventure of two bubble cars and a jet (see Figure 6.5): "I'm gonna make all the col—things in it: road, run out of gas, gonna get shot down and crash." He was writing, not drawing, as he continued: "I'm really getting into 'keechew, keechew, peehew, oochew'" [sound effects]. Jake's completed entry was as follows:

> Once there was a wierd spaceship and a bublble car. Then two of the buubble cars is going to get blown up. and the other buble car is running out of gasline. But the jet is going to crasht the end [February, Second Grade]

This text was still clearly within his picture frame, although it was pushing against the edges. Note, for example, that he predicted the eventual blowing up of the bubble cars (which had, in fact, blown up in his talk before writing). But, while this text did not actually break through a picture frame, it did break through Jake's pattern of using one page and one picture per story. The text was quite lengthy, covering three lined pages. In Jake's words, "This is the longest story I've ever wrote." Its length meant that, after writing, Jake felt he had two additional pictures to draw, which he proceeded to do (see Figures 6.6 and 6.7). In them, he depicted the vehicles' actions over time. Figure 6.6 shows the "wierd spaceship" in flight, heading toward its doom, unbeknownst to the driver. Figure 6.7 illustrates the eventual demise of all the vehicles, as reflected in the last two sentences (final page) of Jake's text. The horrified spaceship driver is yelling "O no," as he sees the large rock looming in front of him.

This was a major turning point in Jake's development as a writer, because his text world began to assume dominance over his drawings.

Figure 6.6.   The "wierd" spaceship in flight.

Figure 6.7.   The doomed vehicles.

Because his text had preceded two of his drawings, Jake had used the pictures in a narrative or storylike way, to depict a series of related happenings.

Jake was clearly proud of his bubble-car creations and of his long story. "Who made up the bubble cars?" he quizzed his peers one day. And, when the answer was not forthcoming—"*I* made up the bubble cars." These stories of Jake's indeed gained the class's attention. One day when he stood before them to read his journal, shouts of "bubble cars" rang out. Sonia even suggested that Jake might be famous by the time he was 10 because of his marvelous invention. Jake agreed and speculated on how difficult life would be when people began hounding him to move to

Hollywood and draw bubble cars for the movies. He insisted that he would not leave his home.

So Jake's imaginary worlds were well received within his social world. And perhaps in part because of this, he kept them up; his bubble-car story became his script. Throughout February and March, he wrote 10 consecutive journal entries that were variations of "Once there was a bubble car that is going to be destroyed." For example, compare the first bubble-car text (entry #2 in his journal, quoted in the previous discussion) with the one produced next in his journal:

> Once there was a three head bubble car "an a jet that is running out of gasoline Then the bubble cAr is going to-crasht. But the jet is going to blow up because it is out of gasoline. the end

This repetition of basic text structure and words allowed Jake to attain greater writing fluency. He became quite fast at writing, a fact that he regularly pointed out to his peers. Repetition also made drawing before writing unnecessary: Since Jake knew what he was going to write, he no longer needed a picture to "copy offa." He explained to his classmates that writing before drawing was quicker. He even admonished Jesse, who continued to draw before writing: "Do you remember what I said? You should never draw before you write. Breaking my rule. You're breaking Rule One of mine."

Despite this new emphasis on writing, Jake's representational language during drawing continued to be his most information-rich symbolic medium, just as it was during his first-grade year. He used it to make elaborations upon his basic bubble-car script; for example, cars and jets crashed into rocks or doors, rather than simply "crasht." Other elaborations found their way into his texts during the post–bubble-car period, to be examined next. For example, dialogue—such as pilots yelling, "Oh no!"—was originally limited to talk during drawing and then incorporated into the drawings themselves via cartoonlike bubbles; indeed, such dialogue had necessitated adding drivers and pilots to the drawn bubble cars and jets. As will be illustrated, dialogue did eventually become an essential part of Jake's written texts. During the bubble-car period, however, most of Jake's elaborations remained in his talk during drawing.

While writing, Jake continued to focus on encoding; however, in contrast to his early-first-grade dependency on others for spellings, he was relatively independent in second grade. His requests for assistance often took the form of asking "Is this how you spell ————?" rather than, "How do you spell ————?" To encode, he relied on visual recall, phonological analysis, and his personal dictionary. He was increasingly attentive to the visual details of written text and consistently asked available adults to help him figure out the placement of periods. Hyphens, apostrophes, and other graphic marks, like fun-sounding words, seemed to appeal to his playful side. For example, one day he changed the spelling of *and* to "*an*. He used a quotation mark rather than an apostrophe, but he had the right idea: "That's ["] for right here. Cause I'm just gonna put an A-N."

Jake's dominant focus on encoding during writing, however, was soon to change, as his bubble cars and jets came under attack in the real, rather than the imaginary, world.

Relocating Dramatic Talk: The Manuel Adventures

Although Jake and his friends enjoyed the bubble-car adventures, his teacher, Margaret, was understandably becoming concerned. She asked him please to write about something else. She suggested that he think about things he had recently done, that he make a list of other topics he might write about, and that, for homework, he come up with an idea other than a bubble-car adventure. But Jake, also understandably, found coming up with another topic difficult, as he explained.

> JAKE: It's [writing] not as easy as you really think it is nowadays, 'cause you see, now I can't be writing about my bubble car all the time.
> MANUEL: Why?
> JAKE: 'Cause Margaret says so.
> MANUEL: She doesn't want any bubble-car stories?
> JAKE: Yeah.
> JESSE: She hates 'em.
> JAKE: No, she doesn't. She's getting tired of 'em. That's all. That's why they're not as easy as they used to be.

Jake, however, soon came up with a solution—Manuel stories. His selection of Manuel was surprising but sensible. Manuel was a friend of his and someone who was himself admired within the peer group. During the time that Jake was becoming famous for his bubble cars, Manuel was becoming famous for his "snowman" story, a beautifully illustrated story that took up his whole journal. So Jake announced his intention to take up his whole journal with Manuel. Following is the conversation within which this decision was apparently made.

> SONIA: That's good, Manuel. (admiring Manuel's entry)
> MANUEL: Thanks.
> SONIA: How long is that story? The whole book?
> JAKE: Yeah.
> MANUEL: It's gonna be the whole book.
> JAKE: I think I'm gonna write about Manuel in the whole book.
> JESSE: Yeah, I'm gonna—
> JAKE: I think I'm gonna write the rest of the book about this story, "Me and Manuel."

The incorporation of a peer into Jake's texts supported a second and third change in Jake's writing. The *first* change, the decreased domination of drawing over writing, had not released Jake's stories from their space and time constraints. Thus, while narrative movement was sometimes implied (e.g., "The jet is going to crasht."), it did not actually happen. With the adoption of the Manuel stories, the dramatic and narrative language that had been a part of Jake's drawing—including his dialogue with his peers—began to accompany his writing and, moreover, to be incorporated into his text. He used his writing, rather than only his drawings, to interact within his social world. As a result, his texts became true narratives, as they moved through time. This was the *second* major change in Jake's writing during his second-grade year.

To accomplish this movement, Jake used dialogue, just as Regina had. Unlike Regina's written texts, however, Jake's began to approach the elaborateness and socialness of his previous oral storytelling during drawing, perhaps because Jake as actor shared both his ongoing social world and his imaginary world with his fellow actor, Manuel. For example, in the following event, Jake threatened Manuel's existence within the imaginary world he was writing, just as in the first grade Jake had threatened Manuel's existence while drawing (see Chapter 4).

> JAKE: (to Manuel) I'm deadly. I am deadly. I'm gonna put your name in this story and you are gonna be dead too. I'm gonna make sure you get blown to pieces. (laughs)
> MANUEL: Blown to pieces. (softly and a bit awed)
> JAKE: Yes, sir. You won't be able to see your mommy ever again.

Jake writes, "Once there was a boy that is named Manuel."
Manuel looks pleased but cautious, and he intervenes in Jake's efforts.

MANUEL: What are you writing about?

JAKE: You. I'm gonna make it bad.

MANUEL: What do you know about me?

JAKE: I'm not gonna talk about you. I'm just gonna make sure you get blown to pieces.

MANUEL: Blown to pieces?

Manuel playfully retaliates, although he is not actually putting Jake into his story.

MANUEL: In my story you're going to meet a magician who's going to turn YOU into a snowman.

JAKE: Well, actually, guess wha—

MANUEL: And melt you flat.

JAKE: (seeming to back down) Actually, um, I, I'm, I—we're gonna, I'm writing about um us flying the fastest jet in the world. None of us—both of us are—isn't gonna get blown to pieces because it's the fastest jet—it can out-run any bullet.

MANUEL: Oh wow! I like that.

JAKE: And it's as bulletproof as it can get. (goes on writing) (but later, still writing) Watch out Manuel! (writes *blow up*)

MANUEL: Just at the very end when they're just so happy, it's almost—they're just so happy and they read the entire story and they loved it, I get blown up.

JAKE: Yeah.

MANUEL: And they cry and cry and cry and cry—it's so dramatic.

Later Jake read his story to Manuel:

Once there was a boy that is named Manuel. Manuel is going to fly the fastest jet and I am going to fly the jet too. But Manuel's headquarters is going to blow up But I am OK. But I don't know about Manuel but I am going to find Manuel. But when I find him I like him. But I think I see him. He is in the jet. Manuel are you OK? Yes I am OK. you are being attacked. I will shoot the bad guys out of the universe. OK yes shoot them now. The end. [April, Second Grade]

In this event, Jake used his written texts to interact within his ongoing social world in more deliberate ways than he had in the first grade. But his peers, specifically Manuel, were still assisting him, highlighting conflicts among multiple worlds. The imaginary world was separate from the real perceived world ("In my *story*," asserts Manuel, you shall have problems of your own); and it was separate as well from the social realm in which the piece would eventually be read ("Just at the very end when they're [the readers] just so happy . . . I get blown up."). Further, the example illustrates how the tensions between realms could be evident within the text; Jake tried to create a past imagined world, but then he found himself within the present world he was sharing with Manuel.

The preceding example also illustrates the *third* major change in Jake's journal entries. As in Regina's case history, Jake's inclusion of himself and/or a peer in his imaginary world as a character seemed to help him incorporate the internal worlds of his characters, their thoughts and feelings ("I am OK. But I don't know about Manuel."). In his story, Jake began as a third-person observer but soon became an actor. In a later event, Jake deliberately maintained more distance from his constructed world, reflecting on the nature of it and, further, announcing his decision to maintain an observer stance. An analysis of some of Jake's talk is given in Table 6.2.

During this involved event, Jake did attend to encoding, although, as noted previously, he was indeed a more independent and a faster writer now, which impressed both Jesse, his first-grade admirer ("Jake can go fast!"), and himself (I could finish my book faster than Christopher could."). That speed, however, may have contributed to Jake's periodic entanglement with syntax. Relative to his first-grade composing behavior, though, Jake was more attuned to whether or not his reading made sense, rather than simply to the accuracy of his reading. Indeed, he self-corrected omitted words (especially articles); he also consistently noticed awkward phrases (e.g., "figure out it" as opposed to "figure it out"), although he often needed adult help to untangle the words. In syntax as in story, then, Jake seemed a more distanced, more controlled manipulator of the written world.

In brief, as Jake began to manage more deliberately the boundaries between his imaginary world, the ongoing social world, and the experienced world, he also began to reflect spontaneously on the nature of his symbolic vehicle—on the clarity of his written language. He seemed to acknowledge implicitly that his story had an existence separate from the written symbols and that the ability of others to understand his story was dependent upon his skilled manipulation of those symbols. Indeed, in one event, Jake explicitly worried about what his readers would think if he didn't finish his "shark" story: "But people wouldn't know what happened to the sharks!"

During this period of the "Manuel adventures," drawing faded in importance. In the Buck Rogers event, for example, Jake engaged in little

(*text continued on p. 167*)

TABLE 6.2. Jake's "Manuel and Buck Rogers" Event: Functions
            of Talk

Jake's Talk	Function/Strategy	Comment
		During today's class meeting before writing, Jake had attended closely as Wesley read his stories, both of which had titles and both of which were about going "back in time" on spaceships. Now, sitting at a table beside Manuel, Jake seems to be planning to follow Wesley's example.
<u>Jake</u>: Now I'm gonna write a story about Manuel. This time he's gonna be alone [i.e., I will not be him]. It's gonna be an adventure story.	Directive/ planning; representational/ elaborating	Jake's talk here is task-involved and focused on the nature of his symbolic vehicle (i.e. the genre of his written language).
(to Manuel) You're going back in time.	Directive- representational/ reporting	Jake focuses on the figure to be depicted in his imaginary world, who is also his peer in his ongoing social world.
<u>Manuel</u>: OK.		
<u>Jake</u>: Manuel goes back in time.	Representational/ reporting	Jake's intonation suggests that this utterance is the title of the story. But Jake does not actually write this phrase.
...		At this point, Jake has written:

Once there was a jet and Manuel is going to fly the jet and Manuel is going to shoot them but then Manuel is goin in time and when he does |

TABLE 6.2.   (continued)

Jake's Talk	Function/Strategy	Comment
		he is going to the twenty-first century but Manuel
		Jake pauses to reread his story, and as he does so Maggie voices an objection:
<u>Maggie</u>: Who's the <u>them</u>? Who's the <u>them</u>?		Maggie is questioning the clause, "Manuel is going to shoot them."
<u>Jake</u>: The <u>them</u> is the bad guys.	Representational/ labeling	Jake's talk is task-involved and focused on the nature of his symbolic vehicle (i.e., its clarity).
<u>Manuel</u>: The bad guys?		
<u>Jake</u>: Yeah.	Interactional	
<u>Manuel</u>: The <u>them</u> is the bad guys? Who's the bad guys?		
<u>Jake</u>: The <u>them</u>.	Representational/ labeling	Jake's symbolic world is here under scrutiny in his ongoing social world. His reasoning may be a bit circular, but he is being forced to reconsider his text. The next time the "bad guys" are needed in the story, they are clearly referenced.
I'm gonna put in the old Buck.	Directive/ planning	Jake writes that Manuel is going to see Buck Rogers.
		The next day the story continues. As in the previous event, Jake teases Manuel with the possibility of being blown up. And, again as in the previous event, there

163

TABLE 6.2. (continued)

Jake's Talk	Function/Strategy	Comment
		will be a rescue. This time, however, Jake himself does not rescue Manuel-- Buck does.
Uh, Manuel,	Interactional	
you get to see Buck Rogers.	Representational/ reporting	Jake's talk is task-involved and focused both on the figure to be depicted in his imaginary world and on his peer in the ongoing social world.
Manuel: What?		
Jake: Buck Rogers.		
Manuel: Oh, oh. You mean in your story.		Manuel is here highlighting for Jake the boundaries between the imaginary and the experienced world. Later Jake himself makes such a distinction.
Jake: Yeah. Buck Rogers, twenty-first century person.		
Jesse: Oh yeah. I saw Buck Rogers before. ...		At this point, Jake has added to his text: [Manuel] is going to see Buck Rogers Buck is going to teach Manuel how to the bad
Jake: This time Manuel is deadly. He's gonna be deadly. Buck Rogers is teaching him how to do it-- shoot deadly. (laughs) You're deadly.	Representational/ reporting	Jake is again focused on the figure being depicted and on his peer. In the imaginary world itself, Manuel is going to be deadly (just as Jake previously was)--with the assistance of Buck. Note that Jake is moving between

TABLE 6.2.   (continued)

Jake's Talk	Function/Strategy	Comment
		present and anticipated action ("gonna be," "is teaching"), just as he had been doing in his representational, task-involved talk during drawing.
Manuel: That doesn't sound very appealing.		
Marcos: Jake is Buck Rogers.		Marcos, Manuel's brother, apparently senses as do I that Buck is somehow taking Jake's place in the imaginative world. But Jake denies this.
Jake: No, I'm—This guy's [Manuel's] going to get blown to pieces if he doesn't do what Buck Rogers says. 'Cause they're going to go against the real bad guys.	Representational/reasoning	Jake is again task-involved and meshing his imaginary and social worlds.
		Jake writes:
		[bad] guys and they are fighting the real
		Jake is about to write the "real bad guys," a descriptive phrase used in his earlier talk.
		He then remarks to Manuel that he [Manuel] is going to be blown up.
Marcos: And Manuel got blown		

165

TABLE 6.2.   (continued)

Jake's Talk	Function/Strategy	Comment
into nothing. The evil--		
Manuel: (laughs)		
<u>Jake</u>: I'm gonna-- you wouldn't see your brother again, Marcos. You would never see him in a story again.	Representational/ reporting	Jake's talk is task-involved and focused on possibilities in his imaginary depict-ion and in the on-going and future social world.
<u>Marcos</u>: I wouldn't?		
<u>Jake</u>: In my stories--uh-uh. 'Cause that would be the last. Eepoof! Nothing.	Representational/ reasoning	
<u>Manuel</u>: Oh God. Oh, well. It's been fun having adventures with you. Um, but I'm gonna get blown to pieces.		
<u>Jake</u>: Buck Rogers might save you. ... You might get your butt saved by Buck Rogers.	Representational/ reporting	Jake is again focused on possibilities in his imaginary and social worlds. To elaborate, peers might continue to find Manuel in his stories, his imaginary worlds. Here is Jake the the author as superhero, as controller of the imaginary and the social world.
You want your butt saved by Buck Rogers?	Interactional	
<u>Manuel</u>: What I want is my body saved. I don't wanna die. I don't wanna--		

TABLE 6.2.   (continued)

Jake's Talk	Function/Strategy	Comment
Jake: You want your butt saved by Buck--		
Manuel: What?		
Jake: You want your whole body saved by Buck Rogers? ...		
But the ending-- but the end of the jet is gonna blow. ...	Representational/ narrating	
You gonna be glidin', boy. You're gonna have some fun, boy. You're gonna be scared to death.		
Manuel: Well, can I have fun with you? Because if you're right where am, you can't make me blow up because you don't want to blow up.		And so Manuel invites Jake back into the story. But Jake does not come. Buck him-I self handles the situation.

representational (e.g., reporting or narrating) talk while drawing. Talk during writing, rather than talk during drawing, was now the most information-rich medium.

Moreover, through his writing and talking with his peers, Jake was developing a number of settings, actors, and actions, as well as interesting language phrases with which to capture the feelings and tone of the actors and actions. The latter included references to the twenty-fifth century, Buck Rogers, evil forces (a phrase first used by Manuel's brother, Marcos), seeing or not seeing a character, seeing "the last" of a character, and being "OK." In the following story, Jake used a number of these new elements, together with familiar ones developed through earlier dramatic play during drawing (most notably, bad guys, bubble cars, spaceships, shooting lasers, and blowing up). This story is not about Manuel but about Bumi, Jake's four-year-old neighbor and a frequent visitor at the school (her mother helped Margaret manage the school library). Jake drew the picture shown in Figure 6.8 to go with the first part of the story, and the one in Figure 6.9 to go with the last part. His text, reproduced here, took four pages in his journal:

the story of the bubble Car

once there was a bubble car. a bubble car that can shoot darts out of the tires and shoot lasers out of the cannons. and the bad

Figure 6.8.   Jake's dart- and laser-shooting bubble car.

Figure 6.9. Jake's army base.

guys Are going to shoot at us and the bubble car is going to blow up the evil forces of Bumi and Bumi is ok but I will get Bumi. when I get Bumi I will shoot Bumi's ship But she has not seen the last of me. She is in the twenty-fifth-century and Bumi is being shot at By Buck Rogers. and Buck rogers is getting the whole force and I am going to take the bubble car back to the base but I see a dune buggy the End [April, Second Grade]

Jake's story anticipates and then moves through present time in a movielike script, although the last clause about the dune buggy is rather an awkward one. This clause was indeed tacked on. Margaret had come by as Jake was drawing his final picture. He was pleased with his drawn dune buggy and called Margaret's attention to it.

> JAKE: Margaret, this buggy, see? He's digging in the dirt.
> It's brown, it's going ( ) earth, then it will get out
> of there and the ( ) will blow up the whole thing.
> MARGARET: Oh wow! I wish I had read that in the story.
> JAKE: Yeah. I could put it in.
> MARGARET: You could. Good idea.

It *was* a good idea, but, since the dune buggy had evolved after the text for the Bumi adventure, it had no role in the written drama, although it was an appropriate part of the illustrated base.

Despite its concluding awkwardness, the Bumi text illustrates that, by the end of his second-grade year, Jake appeared to have developed a "script" or a global plan for an adventure story (not just for a bubble-car story), a repertoire of elements for fleshing out that plan, and a sense of moving through narrative time. Indeed, as the following journal entry will illustrate, he was able to move through fictional time without including himself or a peer and without ongoing dramatization. His written imaginary worlds included many elements (actors, actions, objects) and dialogues of his earlier dramatic play and drawing—but his text worlds were no longer dominated by those media. Listen to Jake's talk to himself during his last observed composing event. First he wrote,

> Once there was a men there from planet X and they are control-
> ling the world

He then remarked to himself, "Uh, I got to think of a counter [counter-force]. I got to think of something that's from, that's in the world. Uh, let's see." So, on his own, Jake reflected on his text, reaching out to the "real" world for help in forming his imaginary one. Having thought of a "counter," he continued writing:

> But the Russians had a bubble car and the bubble car is going
> to America.

Jake had gained distance from the many dramatic elements he had evolved, and he manipulated them to form a dynamic text world "on his own." He did not engage in social play with Manuel as he constructed this piece, nor did he argue about the experienced world with Hawkeye, but echoes of those earlier conversations were there as Jake interacted with and critiqued his own text in search of action and sense.

SUMMARY

Throughout his first- and second-grade years, Jake remained a talkative, sociable child, with an interest in words and a flair for the dramatic. During both years, his stories involved adventurous males and fast-paced vehicles. What changed was the dominant medium through which those stories unfolded.

During his first-grade year, Jake narrated and dramatized his imaginary adventures during drawing. His adventures served Jake well in his social world, as his spoken and drawn stories attracted the interest of his peers. Writing, however, was a struggle. He did indeed talk with others while writing, but task-involved talk was about spelling, not about the content of the story itself. Jake depended heavily on his pictures to help him compose his story content, and thus the majority of his written texts were at least partially art notes (see Table 6.3).

Jake's peers raised objections to his texts, pushing him to attend both to his written text as a distinct object and to the relationship between his imaginary world and the real world as experienced by himself and his peers. But Jake did not seem to use the content of his written worlds deliberately to socially engage his peers or to reflect on his experienced world.

During his second-grade year, Jake renegotiated the relationship between his symbolic, social, and experienced worlds. His bubble-car script, though developed through talk during drawing, gained him his independence from that drawing. Its length forced him to begin to draw additional pictures to illustrate its actual and anticipated events; moreover, its repetitiveness soon eliminated the need to draw before writing. Jake's entries contained primarily implied movement; they pushed but did not actually break through a single defined space.

When pressed to abandon his bubble-car topic, Jake turned to his peer Manuel for inspiration. In so doing he acquired a fictional character with whom he could interact while writing, both in his ongoing social world and within the imaginary world itself. Talk during writing became his most information-rich medium. Further, his texts, like his previous talk during drawing, became movielike, as they anticipated events and then moved through present time. Like Regina, Jake's assuming the role of an *interactive* participant within his imaginative world (even one who vacillated between observing and acting) enabled him to begin to move through time more easily and more extensively, and, just as importantly, to begin to convey the inner world of his characters. Jake's talk with others during writing demonstrated a sophisticated negotiation among

TABLE 6.3.   Movement and Stance in Jake's Written Products

	First Grade*		Second Grade**	
	% of products	No. of products	% of products	No. of products
Movement				
No movement	64	9	10	2
Implied movement	29	4	65	13
Movement	7	1	25	5
Stance				
Art notes	43	6	0	0
Art notes/observer	21	3	15	3
Art notes/actor	7	1	0	0
Observer/actor	0	0	20	4
Observer	0	0	60	12
Actor	29	4	5	1

* n = 14.

** n = 20.

imaginary, ongoing, and wider experienced worlds. For example, the well-known character Buck Rogers, a part of his experienced world, was also an actor in his imaginary world and a tool for engaging the interest of his friend Manuel in the ongoing social world. Thus, for Jake, writing was becoming both a more dramatically satisfying medium and a useful social tool.

As a first grader, then, Jake had worked from inside a complex, dynamic world of words and pictures, self and others. Through his own actions and the reactions of his peers, he confronted the tensions among differing symbolic media and perspectives of self and others. He seemed to separate drawing from writing and self from others, at the same time that he began more deliberately to manipulate differing symbolic media and differing perspectives (e.g., his own and Manuel's).

By the end of his second-grade year, Jake appeared to have developed, through his talk during both writing and drawing, a number of possible settings, actors, and actions, as well as interesting ways of capturing those elements in words. Encoding had become much less of a struggle, so, in that sense, he was freer to reflect on meaning during writing. He was beginning to be able to reflect upon his global plan and on the means for elaborating it. He could use dramatic elements to control a dynamic, written imaginary world, a world that might seem sensible to himself and to his peers.

CONCLUSION

Sadly, there is no epilogue for Jake's case. He reported at the end of his second-grade year that his parents wanted to move; by the opening of the next school year, Jake lived in a neighborhood far from the school. I missed his enthusiasm and his energy, his "kidness." I even missed the bubble cars. Luckily, though, I retain a beautiful memento.

During the spring of his second-grade year, the city sponsored a school-district art contest as part of its annual art fair. All of the children entered at least one picture. Jake decided to paint a picture of a bubble car. No one—not even Jake—thought a bubble car had a chance of winning. "It won't win," Jesse had said. "I know," Jake had replied.

To everyone's surprise—especially Margaret's—Jake did indeed win! As it happened, the judges had turned the boldly colored bubble car upside down, so that the wheels looked like eyes and the vehicle's body like that of an owl. Jake was quite indignant when he arrived at the fair and saw the "owl." He told the officials to turn it the right way—it was a bubble car!

Since Jake did not return to the school for the third grade, he was not there to claim the picture when the city sent it back in the fall. My assistant Carol Heller was there, however, and she asked Margaret if I could have the painting. It is hanging in my office, a fitting reminder of an imaginative young adventurer, a social leader, and a playful composer of pictures and words. His friends were the source of his artistic energy, first as a visual artist and then as an author of written worlds. The most important of those friends was a child with a distinctly different personality, the gentle, reasonable Manuel, to whom we turn in the next chapter.

Manuel

One upon atime
there was a maD
Scientist that maDe
a monster.The monster
killed two people
that won a race.

[March, First Grade]

174

Manuel's written world, a world where larger-than-life figures engaged in violent acts, contrasted sharply with his everyday external world, where a quiet, polite little boy searched for that tenuous, multifaceted quality called truth. Yet, Manuel's picture (Figure 7.1, seen above and in the color insert) does reflect his apparent sensitivity to the complex and dramatic nature of his experienced world. His "Castle Frankenstein" stands in front of huge mountains and behind the lights of a town and the torches of tiny townspeople. In his scene, lightness exists next to darkness, open curves next to closed ones, flowing lines next to stark ones.

Manuel clearly separated writing and drawing, as discussed in Chapter 4. Unlike Regina and Jake, Manuel neither drew stories nor wrote pictures. He attended carefully to each form of symbolizing, seemingly sensitive to their differences. But drawing was for him by far the more comfortable medium; its lines and shapes were more easily controlled than the letters and punctuation of written text.

Within the peer social world, where quantity, speed, and spelling expertise were valued, Manuel was sometimes singled out for his slowness as a writer and, on at least one occasion, his struggles with spelling.

> Manuel is sitting at a table with a group of his classmates. He is having difficulty spelling *in*, and so he asks for help. Naji, a second grader, raises his eyebrows.
>
> NAJI: Do you want to spell *on*?
> MANUEL: No, *in*.
> NAJI: *In*! That's the EASIEST word.
> SHAMARI: That's the EASIEST word.
> MANUEL: You guys. Don't you think you're overreacting?
> NAJI: It's the easiest word, when you're going on the third grade.
> MANUEL: I'm only a first grader.

Manuel seemed both realistic about and accepting of his struggles, despite others' comments. Moreover, he, like Jake, dreamed of public acclaim.

> Manuel is sitting next to Yamyha. He seems to think that Yamyha, who is black, wants to be a singer.
>
> MANUEL: You know what? When you grow up to be a rock star, Michael Jackson is gonna look like marshmallows.
> YAMYHA: I'm not gonna be no rock star.
> MANUEL: You aren't?

YAMYHA: No. I have to be a policeman like my daddy.

MANUEL: I wanna be an actor when I grow up. Maybe even a movie star.

YAMYHA: You wanna know what my daddy said? He said, "Hey you gonna be a policeman when you grow up." I said, "Why do I have to?" He said, "Because I'm one."

MANUEL: (laughs) That doesn't quite make sense, but—

YAMYHA: That's OK. That's a good enough reason for me.

Over the course of the next two years, Manuel did indeed become a star—at least, a classroom star. He found ways to connect drawing and writing to an overriding artistic goal and, through that connection, to use both forms of symbolizing to achieve individual expression and social recognition.

FIRST GRADE: TINKERING WITH DRAWN AND WRITTEN WORLDS

Keeping Boundaries; Making Sense

One day in class Mitzi had been trying to ease Sonia's concerns about where she would sleep at Mitzi's slumber party. Mitzi told Sonia that she might sleep with her baby brother, adding, "He is cute." Manuel intervened: "But all babies are cute. Is yours especially cute?" Manuel's remark exemplifies, as have other excerpts throughout this book, his sense of reason and order. While he was respectful and supportive of his classmates, he questioned them if he felt their comments were not sensible: "How do you know . . . ?" "But you just said. . . ." "What does that mean . . . ?" He could, of course, playfully enter into the dramas of his friends, especially Jake's, but he was more serious and more logical in his own responses to people and experiences.

Although he was a good conversationalist, Manuel, by his own admission, was relatively less knowledgeable about certain popular peer topics, most notably football and baseball. For example, in the midst of a football discussion among the first- and second-grade boys, Manuel voiced his preference for the Miami Dolphins, rather than the local favorite, the Forty-niners, but then noted, "Since I don't know that much about football I choose who I want to win by the name. That's why I chose the Dolphins."

Manuel was indeed a member of the gang, but his reflectiveness, concern for truth, and slightly bemused, comfortable stance toward himself—toward what he knew and what he did not know—made him a most distinctive member of that group. He was not a social leader like Jake, but he also was not someone who was easily led.

As illustrated in the "Mighty Mouse" event detailed in Chapter 4, Manuel's careful craftsmanship—his concern with pattern and sense—was clearly evident in his work during journal time. His artistic style was very different from both Jake's and Regina's. Manuel did not orally dramatize or narrate a story while drawing; rather, he was often silent, seemingly focused on the visual image he was creating. His resulting pictures were carefully detailed and often beautiful. Most typically, superheroes were boldly placed in the foreground of his pictures, while quieter landscapes filled the background.

When Manuel began to write, he had no story planned, just a desire for a story about his drawn figure, usually a superhero. As also illustrated in Chapter 4, however, Manuel did indeed desire *stories*—he wanted narrative action. In fact, even in the first grade, 63% of his collected stories (five of the eight), contained narrative movement. Moreover, since Manuel did not depend on his pictures to help him compose his texts, his writing did not typically reflect the tensions between the time frames of pictures and narratives that were so prevalent in Regina's and Jake's cases.

Manuel's efforts to plan his story slowed his writing process. He worked to make reasonable, sensible choices. For example, after silently drawing the castle piece depicted in Figure 7.1, Manuel knew that he would write a "Frankenstein" story, but he did not know exactly how that story would unfold. He began by copying "Once upon a time" from a previous entry. Next he sat and thought for awhile, then said—"That's an idea!" He continued:

[Once upon a time] there was a mad scientist that made a
monster. The monster killed two people that won

Here he stopped. He was concerned about the logic of his story. As in the Mighty Mouse event, Manuel grappled with the sense of the text; in the following comments, directed to me, he uses representational talk to reason about the event to be depicted: "How about "won the race"? Maybe they [the victims] could have been famous because they won lots of races." So Manuel added "a race" to his text (note the switch from the more definite spoken *the* to the written *a*), satisfied that there was some narrative sense in his tale: The two people that the monster killed were very famous, and, thus, the monster apparently had reason to attend to them.

While Manuel's peers also reasoned about the sense of their pictures, he was unusual in the careful reflection he engaged in during writing.

Moreover, during both drawing and writing, his representational, task-involved talk about his depictions was consistently focused on *planned* rather than actual depictions and was typically directed to an observer (adult or peer). Unlike Regina and Jake, Manuel did not use such talk to help convey the meaning elements of his story; that is, as an author and artist, Manuel was more director than actor.

Manuel found encoding stories, like planning them, a slow struggle, as noted in Chapter 4. In fact, of all the first-grade case study children, Manuel had the most trouble with the encoding system, a fact that greatly concerned Margaret. She worried about his progress and considered whether or not he should be referred for special help.

Manuel's difficulty with spelling may have resulted at least in part from his own attention to a larger unit of order—the drama. He appeared to keep his mind as much as possible on his story, relying at first on others to help him spell words, gradually leaning more on visual recall of frequently written words and at times on phonological analysis.

Despite this dependence on others, however, Manuel worked hard to manage his written text. He used directive language to access and monitor his unfolding message. Like Jake, though, he found it difficult to reread his text to accomplish these ends. Most often, Manuel tried to remember rather than actually reread his writing. He had particular problems with articles, often failing to encode them and thus facing a gap when trying to "reread" them. Indeed, the alphabetic nature of the writing system itself was problematic for Manuel. In one event, he stated his expectation that a word that orthographically differed from another only in its ending would in fact be spelled in an entirely different manner: that is, that *Spiderman's* should have a completely different set of letters than *Spiderman*. Perhaps to the ever-questioning, wondering Manuel, a writing system that equated a person and the quality of an object was odd.

Manuel, then, kept clear boundaries between his drawing and his writing, reasoning his way through both processes. He could easily spend two weeks working on one journal entry. His slowness was noted by his teacher, his peers, and Manuel himself. When his peers commented that he was "still" working on the same picture, Manuel calmly remarked, "Haven't you ever seen a slowpoke before?"

Negotiating Social Compromises

Despite Manuel's sensitivity to the sense of each symbolic process and product, he made no explicit reference to an audience's ability to understand his journal. But, like Jake and Regina, he both received and participated in critiques of drawings. These led Manuel, as they led all case study children, to engage in task-related talk with peers in the ongoing social world, talk about the relationship between his drawn world and the experienced world.

> Manuel is drawing the picture for his Mighty Mouse event (refer to Figure 4.6). Jake objects to Manuel's bold superhero flying upright against the blackness of the night and his barely visible feet.

JAKE: That's [Manuel's picture] a Halloween.
MANUEL: Halloween?
JAKE: Black is Halloween.
MANUEL: What you talking about, man? [Manuel here seems to˙ be talking in the black vernacular style Jake sometimes adopted when he was in his most energized, most "onstage" state.]
JAKE: I'm talking about that doesn't have any foot, man.
MANUEL: (thinks Jake said "fruit," not "foot.") Fruit? There's fruit in space?
JAKE: NO! Like this [points to his foot]. You need a foot foot.
MANUEL: I have a foot foot.
JAKE: Foot. Foot on that [picture].
    . . .
Foot on the superhero, Mighty Mouse.
    . . .
MANUEL: These are feet. I didn't have enough room to make them big enough. [Manuel responds to Jake's critiques by referring to his own drawing process.]
JAKE: Golly. Why didn't you make it [Mighty Mouse] upside down?
    . . .
MANUEL: You gotta be nuts. (smiles)
JAKE: Then he looks more like he's flying.
MANUEL: Nobody flies upside down.

As in Jake's case, Manuel's texts, as well as his drawings, were eventually subject to his peers' criticism. Manuel's texts were not as accessible as Jake's, primarily because his process was much slower, his talk much quieter; but he did not escape the comments of others. In another event, Manuel had drawn a picture of Superman, also flying upright, the buildings of a distant city visible in the background (see

Figure 7.2). Manuel knew he was "gonna write something like Superman so on and so on," but he was unsure of the direction of his piece. His thinking was interrupted when Margaret walked by the table and told the children to finish the sentence they were on, as it was time to clean up for recess. Manuel hesitated and then began his piece with a variation of his typical "Once upon a time" opening:

> One day I saw Superman. He gave me a lollipop. The lollipop tasted good. [April, First Grade]

This written text was quite different from previous ones. To begin with, the superhero did not engage in an act of magnificent proportions—he just gave a little boy a lollipop. In addition, the text included Manuel himself as an actor sharing the imaginary world with Superman. When Manuel reread his text, his peer Molik objected: Manuel's story

Figure 7.2.   Manuel's Superman.

violated "real-world" expectations for Superman. Further, as the following exchanges show, Molik's objection, supported by my own comments,
led Manuel to grapple with the differences in meaning elements represented in his picture and his text, the first time such conscious reflection
on drawing/writing relationships was observed.

MOLIK: He [Superman] wouldn't really do that ( ).
MANUEL: I should've made him with a lollipop. [He again
         refers to his own drawing process.]

At this point, I intervened, asking Manuel if he had planned to write
about Superman and a lollipop.

MANUEL: No, I wasn't thinking about the story [when I was
         drawing]. I knew it was going to be about Superman.
         Don't worry; this [the figure with two long ears in the
         foreground of his picture] is a bunny rabbit, not me.
         [Manuel was on occasion teased about his "big ears."]
MOLIK: Where are you?
MANUEL: I'm somewhere over here. [Under pressure from Molik,
         Manuel is verbally elaborating on the sense of his vis-
         ual world, given his verbal one.]
MOLIK: You mean you're Superman?
MANUEL: No I'm not Superman. (irritated) Superman is Clark
         Kent. And Clark Kent is Christopher Reeves [the actor].

In this exchange, Manuel and Molik were considering Manuel's picture
and text in the light of the first graders' standard use of writing as an
accompaniment to a drawing. Manuel's next three written texts, the last
three of his first-grade observation period, were at least partially art
notes—present-tense comments on his pictures. For example, after the
Superman entry, Manuel composed another about Frankenstein to accompany a drawing of the monster and his resistant victim:

**The Frankeinmonster is killing a girl But the girl is squeezing the
franmaoster nose. [May, First Grade]**

As Manuel said, pointing to his picture, "I write that. See?"
    This new style of working—"copying offa the picture," as his friend
Jake put it—allowed Manuel to produce entries quite quickly; each of his
last three entries took only two days. Manuel was very pleased with the
speed the style change allowed: "OK. God. That was only 2 days too!"

Figure 7.3.   Manuel's Frankenstein and his resistant victim.

Writing a description of a picture with action in it was quicker and easier than painstakingly constructing a "nice little adventure story."

At the end of his first-grade journal, Manuel drew a picture that suggested an explanation for this sensitive, sensible little boy's fascination with the violent actions of superheroes. The picture, presented in Figure 7.4, was of a showman in a top hat and, in a large spotlight, the face of a cartoon mouse. Perhaps Spiderman, Superman, Mighty Mouse, and the other superheroes were a part of this aspiring actor's fascination with the dramatic, the performative: His drawing suggests that his imaginary characters were part of his real world of compelling media events ("Superman is Clark Kent. And Clark Kent is Christopher Reeves.").

In the second grade, the topic of Manuel's journal and his ways of negotiating among his imaginary, social, and experienced worlds would change notably. While Regina and Jake began to liberate their texts from

Figure 7.4.   Manuel's showman.

their pictures, Manuel would work to coordinate his pictures and his texts more closely, not by making art notes but by finding words for visual images without abandoning narrative action. Discovering a way to bring his own visual sense and his reflective style into his dramatic texts would contribute to Manuel's emergence as an acknowledged artist—a social star—in the second grade.

SECOND GRADE: DRAWING AND WRITING AS DRAMATIC PERFORMANCE

Manuel retained his polite, patient, but questioning interactional style in the second grade, as illustrated in the following vignette.

It's April 1st, April Fool's Day. In honor of the day, Jake has been "getting" people all morning long. In the middle of journal time, he turns to Manuel and says, with great urgency, "Look!" Manuel immediately looks. "Got him," says a very pleased Jake. Jake pursues his teasing a bit further:

JAKE: Hey, Manuel!
MANUEL: What?
JAKE: Your face is red. His cheeks are red, like a girl. LOOK! His cheeks are red! [By now, Manuel's cheeks are indeed quite red.] Lookit! His cheeks are red like a girl.
MANUEL: Men can't have red cheeks? (with dignity)
JAKE: How do you spell Manuel? (Jake is writing a Manuel adventure.)
MANUEL: M-A-N-U-E-L.
JAKE: Thank you.
MANUEL: You're welcome.

Despite Jake's loud, triumphant teasing—and his own embarrassment—Manuel was at least verbally unruffled. To further illustrate, Manuel quietly but persistently questioned a claim by Jesse that "Everybody was born in the USA." He mediated a dispute between Jesse and Sonia on the nature of dog/cat relationships, pointing out to the irritated Jesse that Sonia's dog might indeed be gentle with her cat "because he's used to the kitty." Manuel also retained his playfulness. As illustrated in Jake's case history, Manuel participated in imaginative play initiated by others; he joined in as well when children, often led by Jake or Jesse, began chanting a commercial (McDonald's hamburger chants were especially popular) or singing a pop song.

Despite his blushes and shy grins in response to public compliments or teasing, Manuel kept, too, his desire for fame, as revealed in the dialogue reproduced in Chapter 3, in which he said, "I want to be in a movie. . . . I also want to be a famous artist or singer." Sonia's reply to this was, "I think you would be better at the artist." In fact, in the second grade, Manuel's peers began more and more to recognize him as an artist. Although on occasion a child, notably Sonia, had acknowledged Manuel's artistic skill in the first grade, most peer comments about his work had been about his slowness. Manuel had taken these comments in stride, agreeing that he was slow and that he did not spell well, but, after all, said he, "I'm a first grader." In the second grade, however, all of the observed case study children in his classroom, and many other children as well, commented on the beauty of Manuel's pictures and on his "neat" journal story. Jake even wrote about his admiration of Manuel. In a brief period of artistic disorientation, after his bubble-car period and before the Manuel adventures, Jake composed this journal entry to accompany Figure 7.5:

> Flying around the world would be fun But I want to be a jet pilot when I grow up and my friend manuel wants' to be an artist when he grow up because he is a good artist. The end I like manuel!

The reason for Manuel's local fame was his story, which took up an entire journal entitled "The Snowman." As will be seen, not only did this effort gain him the admiration of his peers, it allowed him the narrative space to construct a well-reasoned story, the narrative guidance to lessen his struggle with such a story, and the opportunity to reflect upon and take advantage of the distinctive strengths of visual and verbal art.

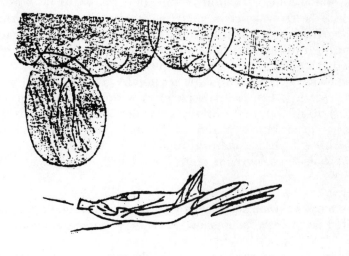

Figure 7.5.   Jake's picture of himself as a jet pilot and Manuel as an artist.

Negotiating Between Symbolic Media: Visual and Verbal Magic

Throughout his first-grade year, Manuel's meticulously drawn pictures had provided him with minimum support for developing his stories. Instead, his plans for his stories seemed drawn from his knowledge of superheroes. During the second grade, Manuel began to plan for his entire "book" (as he now referred to his journal). His scheme again seemed inspired by stories he had heard: He intended to write about a snowman who comes to life in a dream, a script common to children's stories but one which Manuel brought to life, to art, for himself.

The most notable characteristic of Manuel's early second-grade journal entries was a focus on the visual scene. Indeed, 7 of Manuel's 12 entries in his "snowman" journal made explicit reference to objects in the physical environment. He not only described the physical world but used it as a major agent of narrative change. Thus, like Jake, Manuel renegotiated the relationship between drawing and writing in the second grade. But, while Jake was struggling with the separation of talk from pictures and the incorporation of talk into his writing ("I'm really getting into 'keechew, keechew, peechew'"), Manuel worked to bring his drawn and written art closer together, capturing the physical beauty of his pictures in his texts. This new quality of Manuel's writing greatly impressed Margaret; she even commented to the class about Manuel's ability to evoke "word pictures" in her mind.

The very first two journal entries in Manuel's "snowman" book illustrate how the physical world was revealed through his texts. In the first, written to accompany Figure 7.6, Manuel verbally portrays physical beauty, while, in the second, illustrated by Figure 7.7, he conveys the power of that beauty over his central human character, a fictionalized self.

One day I was walking down a lonely road. The sun's light glimmered on the new fallen snow. [Entry 1, February, Second Grade]

I fell in to a deep trance because of the beauty. Soon I lost track of the time. [Entry 2, February, Second Grade]

Manuel was often silent while drawing, but his occasional task-involved talk reflected his concentration on the visual scene unfolding before him. Using directive language, he commented on his own process—his need for this color, that marker, or a particular sort of shape. Using personal language, he assessed his pleasure or frustration about the rightness of a color or line ("Oh, God." "Oh, no. This is wrong.").

Figure 7.6.   Manuel's walk in the snow.

However, in this search, Manuel also kept in mind the language of
the story he was developing. He was creating visual art, but he was
working within the tension between language, on the one hand, and line,
color, and shape on the other. This movement was particularly evident as
Manuel worked on the third drawing in his book (see Figure 7.8), because
he explained his process and his artistic vision to a greater extent than
usual, as his peers were exceedingly curious about his efforts. While he
clearly wanted to be polite with his attentive peers, he had an equally
strong desire not to compromise his artistic intentions and to remain in
control of his imaginary world.

Before beginning to draw, Manuel turned back to review his previous
texts and pictures, apparently to see exactly where he had been and where
he should go in his unfolding tale. He then began his "midnight snow"
drawing, in which his human character—the little boy—wanders in the

Figure 7.7. Manuel's trance-inducing scene.

"glimmering" snow. Sonia and Jake watched as Manuel painstakingly colored the falling snowflakes. He used unusual "snow" colors for a second grader, shades of blue and yellow. Sonia wondered why he didn't just use white and then decided to pick up a blue color and help him. Manuel objected. Table 7.1 presents an analysis of his interaction with the curious and persistent Sonia.

In his talk with Sonia, Manuel displayed his careful attention to visual detail and, at the same time, his movement between visual and verbal symbols: "Don't you know around here is supposed to be a magical area, in my story? Special snow falls down glimmering." Indeed, Manuel's verbal involvement in his imaginary world is reflected in his use of task-involved talk focused on his depictions, not on his *planned* depictions. While common in both Regina's and Jake's first-grade cases, such talk had been rare in Manuel's first-grade case; Manuel's focus had been on his own drawing and writing processes. In this event, the social pressure of explaining the sense of his depictions to Sonia led him to use

Figure 7.8.   Manuel's midnight snow scene.

verbal symbols to rationalize his visual ones, just as had happened (although in a much less extensive way) when Molik had questioned him about his "Superman-and-the-lollipop" story as a first grader.

Neither drawing nor writing seemed dominant in Manuel's work; they had different roles in the construction of the imaginary world. Manuel himself said, "I don't write about my pictures. I just write stories." This was exactly the inference drawn on the basis of my observations of him in first grade. But, in his first-grade year, the story was represented in the text and the text was typically related to the picture only in topic. In his second-grade year, both picture and text cooperated to represent a story world, whose qualities found expression more easily in different media.

For example, the completed picture for this event displays the detailed snowy night scene and the walking boy, both of which figured in

TABLE 7.1. Manuel's "Midnight Snow" Event: Functions of
            Drawing and Talking

Manuel's Interaction	Function/Strategy	Comment
Manuel: Don't you know around here is supposed to be a magical area, in my story?	Interactional-representational/ labeling, elaborating,	Manuel's talk here is task-involved and referring to the experience depicted in his previous text about glimmering snow; at the same time, his talk is socially involved, as he tries to justify his color choices to his curious peer.
Special snow falls down glimmering	reasoning, elaborating	
		Sonia persists, however, despite a directive from Jake to "leave him [Manuel] alone." Sonia tries green around a snowflake.
Sonia: Then there's one magical green piece of snow. Mmm-kay, one green.		
Manuel: Oh no. Oh God.	Personal/ evaluating others	
Don't wreck it anymore.	Directive	
D--don't! I said, Sonia, don't!		
Sonia: Oh no! It's too deep purple [to let the green show].		
Manuel: Good, that's what I want.	Personal/ evaluating others	
I want it to look like it's pretty misty.	Representational/ elaborating	

TABLE 7.1. (continued)
_____

Manuel's Interaction	Function/Strategy	Comment

_____

Sonia: It is?

Manuel: I think   Reasoning
this might give it
a misty effect.

Sonia: God, you
want misty effects?

Manuel: (sighs)
Well, I don't want
special effects. I
want misty effects.

Sonia: Misty effects.
God, you have a
weird sense of humor.   Finally, Manuel
                                         lets Sonia help
                                         him, but under his
                                         direction. Misty
                                         effects, he tells
                                         her, require a
                                         "certain touch."

_____

previous texts. The picture also foreshadows future text developments: The garbage can contains the snowman's clothes and the magical key to bringing the snowman to life. Also depicted are figures that are never mentioned directly in the story's text but that carry strong thematic threads: the animated figures of Nature, including the trees, the moon, and the sun; and the clock tower. All of these reappear often in the story's pictures. In addition, the man's face expresses surprise, an emotion not mentioned in the text, although its probable cause is.

Manuel's text further reveals the tension between verbal and visual art, when it is considered both with its accompanying picture and with the pictures and texts that preceded it. At the same time, his writing illustrates his ability to move between those art forms in order to achieve more extended, more elaborate, more involved narratives. Following is Manuel's text about this magical snow scene:

Soon it was midnight. I saw a plump of snow. It glittered in the
moon light. Since I was lost I built a snowman. [Entry 3, March,
Second Grade]

Like Regina and Jake, Manuel renegotiated the relationship between
drawing and writing and thus was better able to develop his stories. Like
Jake, he used a succession of pictures to capture narrative time. But, like
Regina, he used certain distinctive written language structures to establish temporal movement within his texts. Perhaps Manuel's decision to
write a book—and thus the necessity, for him, of using booklike language—accounted in part for the rather dramatic change in his writing.
Rather than brief action-centered stories, one tale was slowly unfolding
in his journal. Manuel's pictures gained momentum as they were juxtaposed, thus revealing the changes in color and objects as night changed to
day, as the moon gave way to the sun. His written texts more explicitly
established such movement through adverbials such as *one day*, *soon*,
and *since*. However, Manuel seemed to reveal more easily the apparent
underlying themes of his work—the power of nature and its ever-ticking
clock—through his pictures. Put into words, these themes seem beyond
the powers of a young child, but the pictures suggest their presence.

Manuel's text about the midnight scene also suggests that, like Jake
and Regina, Manuel could more easily reveal the inner world of his
characters when he himself moved into the text. In his written words, we
experience the outer world through the inner world of Manuel's major
character, a fictive "I." This experienced universe is remarkably visual, a
realm in which one falls into trances and loses track of time, as did
Manuel himself. Moreover, it is a place in which reasonable, thoughtful
decisions are made: "'Since I was lost I built a snowman.''

In producing his text about the midnight scene, Manuel began, as
with his drawing, by briefly looking over all the pictures and texts in his
book. He occasionally returned to his previous work during the actual
writing. He again worked quietly; however, his intermittent talk suggested that, as in the first grade, he maintained two foci during writing—
message forming and encoding. Although clearly engrossed, Manuel did
interrupt his work to join in ongoing discussions with his peers, particularly when someone's comment seemed not quite right, not quite sensible.

Manuel's task-involved talk, when not related to encoding, appeared
to occur primarily when he reasoned about his text for the observer or an
interested peer. He thus appeared to be struggling to ascertain what, in
the experience behind the words and the pictures, was not being made
clear. Such reasoning about his writing had occurred during the first

grade, but in the second grade he no longer worried about the plot's logical next action but rather about how to make his already planned ideas clear—how to flesh out his images through words.

For example, in writing his text about midnight, Manuel stopped to reread his previous entries, and, in the course of that rereading, spontaneously explained to Carol Heller, the observer, why the character had fallen into a trance. Manuel reread: "Soon I fell into a deep trance, because of, the beauty." He paused and commented: "Because of just looking around I started to . . ." But he still couldn't find quite the right words.

Although Manuel did reflect upon his story, he no longer struggled in the same way that he had in the first grade. The momentum of his planned story appeared to be solid support for his message forming. This easing of the writing task and, at the same time, his greater experience with written language in school may account for his increased and more successful attention to encoding in the second grade. As Manuel himself said, he "used to ask for every word," but now he did not. Like many of his peers, he spontaneously studied the spelling patterns of puzzling words, commented occasionally on words in his stories that reflected characteristics recently discussed by his teacher (e.g., homonyms), and began to engage regularly in phonologically based spelling. In the midnight event, Manuel requested the spellings of only 6 of the 25 words. The excerpt from the event analyzed in Table 7.2 illustrates his behaviors.

In addition to a clear concern with encoding, Manuel was as meticulous about the mechanics of his writing as he had been with his drawing. He continually got up from the table to sharpen his pencil, and he reformed letters that apparently struck him as not quite right. He was exceedingly careful about his periods and capital letters, and he clearly understood how they were to be used. A pleasing visual presentation of text seemed important.

Dramatizing in and out of Text: The Birth of the Snowman

As is evident from the preceding discussion of Manuel's midnight event, his peers admired his beautiful pictures, and they were increasingly impressed by the length of his snowman story as well. As reported in Chapter 6, it was his admiration of Manuel's story that led Jake to decide to "write the rest of [my] book about this story, 'Me and Manuel.'"

While Jake was producing his first "Manuel" story, Manuel was working on bringing his snowman to life. Manuel's pleasure at Jake's attention was suggested, not only by his ever-present grin, but also by his periodic interruptions of his own work to notice Jake's. The interactive

TABLE 7.2.　Manuel's "Midnight Snow" Event: Functions of Writing and Talking

Manuel's Text	Composing Code	Manuel's Talk	Function/ Strategy	Comment
I saw				
a	OV	a	Directive/ monitoring	
	OV	/pl/	Directive/ encoding	
p	OV	/p/ /p/		
lump	OV	a plump		
of	OV	of	Directive/ monitoring	
	P			Manuel attends momentarily to Jesse's talk.
	RR			Rereads silently.
	P			Turns to the snowman picture on his cover.
	OV	( )		Mumbles.
snow ...	S			
	OV	Since	Directive/ planning, encoding	
	IS-A	Does since start with a c or an s?	Heuristic/ seeking information	Asks for help in stages; apparently wants to try it first by himself. Carol tells him that it begins with an s; he tries unsuccessfully to locate it in his dictionary.

TABLE 7.2.   (continued)

Manuel's Text	Composing Code	Manuel's Talk	Function/ Strategy	Comment
		Will you write <u>since</u>?	Directive/ seeking information	
	OV	/si: n: s/ /si: n: s/		Seems to study the word before writing it.

KEY: IS-A--Interruption Solicited from Adult; OV--Overt Language; P--Pause; RR-Reread; S-Silence (adapted from Graves, 1973).

play between the two boys figured significantly in Jake's case, but here, in the midst of Manuel's world, it bears repeating.

> Manuel seems completely involved in his drawing process, as Jake begins writing. While Jake starts to unfold his adventure, Manuel works on his own developing scene. He seems to be constructing a picture already in his mind's eye, but sometimes the picture in his mind and the one on his page are frustratingly dissimilar ("Um, that is the bad part." "I want— Damn it!"). Manuel interrupts this intense working, however, when he hears Jake say, "Manuel."

MANUEL: What are you writing about?

JAKE: You. I'm gonna make it bad.

MANUEL: What do you know about me? [His initial expectation is of a realistic, rather than imaginative, piece.]

JAKE: I'm going to talk about you. I'm, I'm just gonna make sure you get blown to pieces.

MANUEL: (retaliating playfully) In my story you're going to meet a magician who's going to turn YOU into a snowman.

JAKE: Well, actually, guess wha—

MANUEL: And melt you flat.

JAKE: (backing down) Actually, um, I, I'm, I— We're gonna, I'm writing about um us flying the fastest jet in the world.

Both of us isn't gonna get blown to pieces because it's
the fastest jet. It can outrun any bullet.

Later, however, Jake repeats his original threat.

JAKE: Manuel, you're still gonna get blown to pieces.

MANUEL: And a magician is still looking at you, and you're
gonna turn into a snowman, and be melted in the sun.

JAKE: That's fine with me, but I still can be water and
splash you.

MANUEL: Yeah, but that won't be half as bad as being blown up.

In this exchange, the dynamic force of Jake's imaginative style contrasted with the gentler magic of Manuel's. Both boys were using their
fictional creations—Jake's explosions and Manuel's snowman—to play
with and enjoy each other. However, their differences in ways of creating
graphic worlds were clear, too. Although they were both using representational (narrating) language, Jake was actually writing his adventure; that
is, the interactive narrative that unfolded during his talk with Manuel
appeared in his written text. Manuel's world was set; he could adopt and
play with Jake's style, but for him it was purely verbal imaginative play.
Nonetheless, as will be illustrated, Manuel himself did begin to incorporate
dialogue into his texts. For him, as for Regina and Jake, dialogue became
an important means for movement both into the mind of his character and
through the time sequence of his plot. Unlike Jake, however, Manuel did
not begin using written talk by putting cartoonlike bubbles in his pictures;
his early dialogue appeared in his texts, a development consistent with his
apparent sensitivity to distinct qualities of visual and verbal art.

Despite his intermittent play with Jake, Manuel almost managed on
this day to complete his drawing ("I need to put green in there [hills in
background], and that should be all."). The next day, he added that
green, and the picture of the magical snowman was completed (see color
insert, Figure 7.9). In the accompanying text entries, he elaborated on
how his human character built the snowman:

I found a garbage can. In the garbage can there was a coat.
There was also a carrot. There was a box of raisins. [Entry 4,
March, Second Grade]

deep in the garbage can I found a note. It sed Illdenanay. I sed
the magic word. [Entry 5, March, Second Grade]

Slowly I started to see a blue light arounder the snowman. Then
over the blue light I saw a orange light. Slowly over the orange I
saw a red light. [Entry 6, March, Second Grade]

In the picture for entry 6 (refer to Figure 7.9), the boy looks aston-
ished, as glowing lights encircle the still inanimate snowman; in the
distance, the hot sun begins its daily ascent. In the next drawing (see
Figure 7.10), the snowman and the boy are seen close up. The faces of
both figures are vivid against the dark sky. The snowman's face is similar
in construction to that on the previous page, but it is clearly animated.
The eyes are no longer dark, round circles, but have pupils that move,
eyebrows that tilt. The boy is smiling and turned toward the snowman,
arm uplifted in apparent greeting.

Both pictures capture particular scenes in the unfolding drama, yet,
by themselves, they do not smoothly convey the passage of time. As in
previous events, Manuel began writing his text for Figure 7.10, a text that
would explicitly connect the scenes, although it would not capture the
orange light of the dawning sun or the joy of the characters whose eyes
are fixed upon each other's.

Before beginning that text, Manuel looked over his previous work,
rereading the texts and looking at the pictures. When he began writing,
he again worked relatively quietly, using directive talk to access, monitor,
and encode his words. Manuel's increased interest in and confidence with
encoding were evident as he made at least partially phonologically based
attempts at spelling words (e.g., *wat, sede*). He also reread and apparently
studied words he had already written. He gave no verbal indication of
planning. His pauses and glances at his previous work suggested that, as
he had said, "I always have the idea," and that coming up with the exact
words for this section of the story was not as much of a struggle—quite a
striking contrast to the obvious search for words during the first grade.
Manuel's completed entry 7 was as follows:

> Boom Bang zap zoom zep. After the explosion I saw that my
> snowman was alive. He sede happy birthday. I didn't know wat to
> say. [Entry 7, March/April, Second Grade]

This entry marks a turning point in Manuel's book. In his first six
entries, Manuel's central character had observed his surroundings and
reacted to them. In the seventh entry, another character was born, a
snowman, and thus Manuel's boy had someone to talk to. The snowman
says, "Happy Birthday," and the boy is speechless. For the next four
entries, dialogue, both actual and described, moved the text through time,
until Nature, ever present in the book's pictures, finally reasserted itself
and brought the story—and the dream itself—to a close.

Manuel seemed very pleased with the birth of his snowman. He
spontaneously reread his piece, attending carefully to needed periods and

to spellings that did not look quite right. He explained the reasoning behind the "Happy Birthday" remark to Carol: "Because it's his . . . I mean he just was pouring out of the magic words, so that's why he says, "Happy Birthday." The snowman had been born through the power of words, although the image of that birth was a remarkably visual one.

Social Support and Social Tension

Throughout this chapter, illustrations of Manuel's writing events have suggested his peers' increasing attentiveness to his efforts. Their interest gave him opportunities both to reveal and to reflect on his own artistic intentions, to use "spaces of dialogue"[1] to help him think about the relationship between his visual and verbal efforts and to assess the sensibleness of those efforts. At times, adult observers also provided similar opportunities, but, as observers, we initiated few interactions with the children, although we were interested and, as illustrated throughout the book, the children did spontaneously comment to us on their work. Manuel's peers, however, deliberately acted on their interest in his efforts. They both critiqued and imitated his products. For example, Jake and Sonia both attempted long stories, like Manuel's; Sonia and Jesse attempted to create similar visual effects; and, as seen in Chapter 3, Jesse reproduced as closely as he could details of Manuel's pictures and texts, in hopes of pleasing his admired friend ("Like it, Manuel?").

While Manuel resisted his peers' attempts to influence his creations directly, as seen in his response to Sonia's "magical green piece of snow," he clearly valued their interest and worked to make his visual and verbal work clear for them. Indeed, from the beginning of the first grade, Manuel demonstrated concern that his pictures and texts be sensible; an awareness of audience seems implicit in such a concern. In the second grade, though, Manuel's concern became explicit. As will be recalled from the previous chapter, even his narrative play with Jake revealed his audience sensitivity. When Jake told Manuel that indeed he was going to be blown up in his story, Manuel responded,

MANUEL: Just at the very end when they're just so happy, it's almost—they're just so happy and they read the entire story and they loved it, I get blown up.

JAKE: Yeah.

MANUEL: And they cry and cry and cry and cry— It's so dramatic.

---

[1]The concept of creating "spaces of dialogue" in classrooms is eloquently discussed in Maxine Greene's *The Dialectic of Freedom* (1988, p. 13).

And so Manuel envisioned his ongoing play with Jake as a social drama that would be replayed for others through Jake's text.

Manuel's concern with his own audience was made quite explicit in his talk about the transition between his next two journal entries—8 and 9. It was indeed a subtle one; readers needed to make inferences based on both pictures and texts. In entry 8, to accompany Figure 7.11, Manuel's boy and snowman have begun a conversation:

> The snow man and me wanted to tock. we were right in the
> middle of a conversation win we came to a house. [Entry 8,
> April, Second Grade]

In Figure 7.12, for entry 9, the scene has changed to the back of the house. The snowman is looking at a thermometer, and he seems panicked—his mouth open, his head flung back, his hat tumbling off:

> The snow man said I must go into this hous. I did'nt know wat to
> thik. The snow man wint in back of the hous. [Entry 9, April, Second Grade]

Manuel's text did not explicitly mention the action behind the house, perhaps because the story was being told from the boy's point of view. From his perspective, the snowman leaves and then, in entry 10, returns. Further, although the snowman tells the boy that he (the snowman) must go *into* this house, he actually goes *in back of* the house—"because he's a snowman," as Manuel explained. These subtleties seemed to pose problems for Josh, an admiring peer who was sitting next to Manuel as he drew his picture for entry 9.

JOSH: Oooh. That's [your picture's] nice.
MANUEL: Thanks. (Manuel's face flushes, as it tends to when
          he receives a compliment.)
JOSH: What's this?
MANUEL: This?
JOSH: Yeah.
MANUEL: It's a house.

Josh continues to attend to Manuel's efforts. After Manuel begins to write, Josh leans over to read his entry. He stumbles over the words *went in back*:

JOSH: Went inside, went inside?
MANUEL: No, he didn't go inside. He went right by, there on the
          other side of the house. See, they're on this side of the

> house. (turns to previous picture showing front of
> house) Then they went in the back. (turns to current
> picture) This is the back of the house.

The next day, Manuel worried aloud about this page to the adult observer: "I think this page is a little bit hard, how he went into the house." Manuel seemed to think it was "hard" for his readers: "Went into the house, I mean, went *by* the house. . . . I think people can tell just by the picture that um (laughs)—but I hope they can cause I don't know how I'm gonna write it so that this is . . ." and he pointed to the pictured back of the house.

Manuel thus displayed his understanding of the multiple worlds within which he had to act and within which his text had to exist. His imaginary world and that of his readers were mediated by his symbols, his pictures, and his texts; and those depicted symbolic worlds had to be both true to his imagined experience and sensible to his readers. For, in the social world, readers not only judged his imaginary world against their experienced world, but they in fact could find insensible texts "hard" to read.

Manuel's comments also revealed his awareness of the multiple perspectives involved in a literary experience, in this case, his own perspective as the all-knowing creator, that of the major human character (the "I," whom Manuel sometimes referred to in conversation as "he"), that of the snowman, and that of the prospective readers, who included at least the child readers who daily demonstrated their interest in his work.

After reflecting on his previous entries, Manuel began his next picture (see Figure 7.13). He seemed to have a clear image of what this picture should look like. He proceeded quietly and intently, ignoring the conversations around him and occasionally mumbling to himself about the adequacy of his efforts. First, he made the outline of the boy and the snowman and then worked on the section of the picture containing the snowman's hat, filling it in with blue. He did the very top of the hat in turquoise. Next he moved to the top of the snowman's nose, which he did in orange. He then colored first the left and then the right side of the snowman's vest blue. At this point, Manuel paused and looked over his work, adjusted his sweatshirt, and then began on the inside of the snowman's torso with yellow, moving from there to the bottom of the snowman and finally to the face. Manuel used meticulous strokes, doing first the sides of each round shape and then the bottom and top.

The only interruption in this intense focus on the unfolding drawing came when Manuel first formed the outlines of the snowman and the
boy (refer to Figure 7.12). The snowman is visibly smaller relative to the
boy, the result, we can infer, of the hot sun now high in the sky. Manuel
used representational, task-involved talk to report on the internal condi-
tions of the characters in this scene—perhaps to explain their calm
smiles, despite the need for the boy to readjust the snowman's arms: "As
far as going away, he [the snowman] doesn't notice it. It's going away. It
seemed to melt. This guy [the boy] doesn't notice it, either."

With the picture completed, Manuel examined it, turned back and
reread the previous text (for entry 9), glanced again at his new picture,
and began writing. In his text, Manuel resumed the perspective of the boy
and connected temporally with the previous text, in which the boy had
seen the snowman go off:

Whin the snowman came out of the house he said it is getting
hot for me. I must go. [Entry 10, May, Second Grade]

Notice that Manuel did not directly express the boy's ignorance of the
melting snowman in this text; since the story was told from the point of
view of the boy, such an expression was not possible.

In writing this text, Manuel engaged in no verbal planning. His talk
was directive and focused on encoding, as he monitored the word he was
writing, reread to access the next, and worked to encode that one through
phonological analysis. Manuel requested the spelling for only 2 of the 19
words. Moreover, although he requested the words *getting* and *came*, he
never actually looked at the provided words. Perhaps he simply wanted the
comfort of knowing they were there if needed. Manuel finished his text in
record time—five minutes. This was quite a change from the first-grade
days when 40 minutes of intense work might yield four or five words.

Manuel's increased confidence as a speller was at this point very
evident in the group activities that preceded writing time. When Margaret
orally quizzed the children about the spellings of words, Manuel regularly responded by eagerly raising his hand. Most often, Margaret's questions were about words the children were studying for their weekly
spelling quiz, and Manuel did learn these words. His oral errors indicated, though, that Manuel was not memorizing the words by rote but
figuring out their orthographic sense (e.g., his spelling of *cleaned* was
C-L-E-E-N-N-E-S). Marcos, his first-grade brother, often grinned and
gave a victory fist when Manuel got the words right, and Manuel gave
Marcos the same support.

**Social and Artistic Satisfaction: The Completion
of the Snowman Book**

As Manuel began the last few pages of his snowman book, he seemed
to have mixed feelings about nearing the end. He reread his book with
great pride (and great fluency), smiling throughout. He seemed especially
pleased with his magic word; upon reading it, he paused and laughed,
and then commented, "Oh great. I love this. God, I don't know how I
made up those words. Never heard of them before." He enjoyed as well
his verbal depiction of the fantastic explosion—"Boom bang zap zoom
zep!"—which he read with a great grin on his face. He regretted that he
only had two picture pages left and thus did not have room for a picture
of the snowman melting or the boy crying by the abandoned hat. Still, he
conceded, "It's starting to get a little boring." A new story would be nice.

Manuel began his picture for entry #11 by drawing the church and
the outlines of the boy and three other people shown in Figure 7.14. He
wanted to make the time of day depicted appear to be similar to that
depicted "way back to the beginning of the second page." Thus, by entry
11, it is late in the day, and the snowman is "totally gone." So Manuel
drew the snowman's hat on the ground, which his classmate Arrison
found puzzling.

ARRISON: So, what is it?
MANUEL: Oh, just um.
ARRISON: A snowman?
MANUEL: Well, yeah. Well, it's no longer a snowman. It's
melted. Here it is. That's just a hat.

Manuel quietly sketched in the sun and then began meticulously to color
first his figures and then the smiling sun. In the picture, the boy is
talking to another fellow, seemingly oblivious to his departed companion. In the accompanying text, the boy discovers his loss:

I started to tock again. All of the sudden I saw that there was no
snowman he had melted. [Entry 11, May, Second Grade]

The very next day, Manuel began his final picture, commenting on it
to the adult observer.

MANUEL: You know, I like this picture better than any of my
pictures.
HELLER: You do?

MANUEL: This is— I've been thinking about this picture for a
				long time. Since I started the book—how I'd make the
				end.

Manuel's comments suggest the importance of pictures to his writing process. His drawing before writing did not seem to be simply a ritual left over from his kindergarten days, when Margaret encouraged all the children to draw first. Rather, for him, drawing pictures seemed to be a productive and personal way of working. The pictures provided the anchoring scenes; the text provided the temporal connections and, at times, more explicit—or, at least, more verbal—renditions of the narrator's internal reasonings.

As Manuel begins his final picture, Jesse, who is sitting several chairs away, is very attentive to Manuel's efforts. When Manuel pauses to look for a marker, Jesse immediately offers his own.

JESSE: You need this color?
MANUEL: No. Right now I need black.
RUBEN: Black doesn't work.
JESSE: Any black is purple or blue.
MANUEL: (picking up a black marker) This black is purple or
				blue. You're right. (tries another) It's worse.
JESSE: That's brown.
MANUEL: That's brown—oh my God. That was black. [The
				outside of the marker looked black.]
JESSE: You want my black? Use my black (watches Manuel
				take a brown crayon) Use my black, Manuel. Manuel.

Manuel begins coloring with brown but is almost immediately interrupted again, this time by Sonia, who wants to look at an old picture of his.

MANUEL: Are you still looking at it? Are you finished looking at it?
SONIA: Yeah.

Manuel begins again, and this time Regina stops him.

REGINA: Is that—is that a girl?
MANUEL: (stands up) Not a she.

At last Manuel was able to work. Soon he completed his final picture (see Figure 7.15), a boy sitting up in bed, tears running down his face, a cartoonlike bubble (Manuel's first) rising up and containing the boy's remembered snowman. The ever-present sun is peeking in the bedroom window. "It might be," Manuel remarked, "the nicest picture I ever made."

Figure 7.15. Manuel's boy awaking from a dream.

Like all his texts, Manuel's last one was within the boy's point of view, and, as before, it established the temporal flow:

All of the sudden there was dark. Then I felt my pillow. Nexed I felt tears. I was in my bedroom. My snowman had only bin a dream. [Entry 12, May, Second Grade]

When Manuel finished his story, he decided to reread the whole book yet again; he chuckled as he turned way back to the beginning. Margaret announced to the class that Manuel had finished his whole journal, and so, tomorrow, it would be shared with the class. Manuel blushed, giggled, and turned to me. "I'm proud of this story," he said. (Unfortunately, the next day Manuel had chicken pox.)

In the first grade, Manuel seemed to be a child who persisted in his work despite the criticism of others ("Haven't you ever seen a slowpoke before?"). By the end of the second grade, he was not just persisting but glowing in his recognized accomplishments as an artist. During the first grade, he worked very hard and seldom commented positively on his work to others. During the second, Manuel worked just as intensively and sometimes with evident frustration ("Damn!"), but he also found great pleasure and pride in his work. In the end, even his snowman smiled at him, as shown in Figure 7.16 (see color insert) which Manuel drew on the back cover of his book.

SUMMARY

Throughout the initial two years of the project, Manuel remained a sensitive, searching child, one with a strong sense of order and of pattern in both the imaginative and real worlds. In the first grade, he kept firm boundaries between his pictures and his stories. While drawing, he talked only occasionally, primarily to monitor and report on his own procedures and, at times, to reason about the logicalness of his drawings. When writing, those drawings provided minimum support for developing his story, as he did not tell a story during drawing. Manuel deliberately planned his written story, choosing words with the care with which he had chosen colors and strokes for his drawing. As he did during drawing, he also occasionally revealed through his talk his struggle to come up with a reasonable "little adventure story"—his sparse stories only hinted at the thought behind them. Manuel wrestled, too, with encoding those stories and with rereading what he had in fact encoded.

Despite Manuel's slowness and his apparent difficulty with "language arts," his pictures were often beautiful and his texts, while not fully developed stories, displayed more narrative movement than did most first graders' (see Table 7.3). Moreover, Manuel himself did not seem discouraged. He struggled, but any frustration he felt seemed to come from some discrepancy between the image he wished to convey and the one he realized on his paper, not from others' judgments.

During the second grade, Manuel renegotiated the relationships between his visual and verbal worlds, and among his imaginary, ongoing social, and experienced worlds as well. His search for aesthetic and logical order began to appear within his texts, not only in his talk about his texts. Moreover, his blank and lined pages combined to form a stage upon which this thoughtful, aspiring actor could perform a dramatic but sensible story for his friends.

TABLE 7.3.   Movement and Stance in Manuel's Written Products

	First Grade*		Second Grade**	
	% of products	No. of products	% of products	No. of products
Movement				
No movement	25	2	17	2
Implied movement	13	1	0	0
Movement	63	5	83	10
Stance				
Art notes	25	2	0	0
Art notes/observer	13	1	0	0
Art notes/actor	0	0	0	0
Observer/actor	0	0	0	0
Observer	50	4	0	0
Actor	13	1	100	12

*$\underline{n}$ = 8.

**$\underline{n}$ = 12; Manuel's entire second-grade journal comprised one story; he however, divided the story into "parts" that could be "finished" (as in, "I finished that part."). Therefore, "parts" rather than entries are counted for the second grade.

Certainly both Manuel's teacher and his peers—his audience—expected that pictures would be "illustrations" for texts, and thus they provided some social pressure for bringing his verbal and visual worlds into closer collaboration. Manuel, however, had not done that during most of his first-grade year. During the second grade, he was aided by his intention to represent an event (a snowman coming to life) rather than a figure (a superhero). As in the previous year, his initial plans for his story seemed more visual than verbal, and he also still maintained his sensitivity to the time and space differences between pictures and stories. But his planned event yielded a series of visual images, each of which could then be joined through linguistic symbols of time ("then," "next," "sud-

Figure 7.1. Manuel's castle of the mad scientist.

Figure 7.9. Manuel's magical snowman.

Figure 7.10. Manuel's meeting between the boy and the snowman.

Figure 7.11 Manuel's conversing boy and snowman.

Figure 7.12. Manuel's snowman and the thermometer.

Figure 7.13. Manuel's hot snowman.

Figure 7.14.   Manuel's oblivious boy engaged in talk.

Figure 7.16.   Manuel's winking snowman.

denly"). Thus Manuel was able to describe his pictures—to take advantage of his visual images—without violating his sense of narrative time and space.

Manuel's planned event may have aided his encoding as well, just as Jake's planned bubble-car event seemed to aid his. But Jake's story was continually replayed, thus allowing him to spell the same words repeatedly and to attend relatively less to encoding than he had in the first grade. In contrast, Manuel's overriding plan may have given him a sense of narrative direction, which in turn permitted him to attend relatively less to planning his story and more to encoding.

Like Jake and Regina, Manuel as author was also supported by his own entry into his stories (refer to Table 7.3). For Regina and Jake, the fictional, talkative "I" had seemed to aid narrative movement, but Manuel's texts had always contained this. In the first grade, however, that movement had been limited (e.g., "The doom roller shot spiderman. Spiderman fell down."). Manuel's fictionalized self helped him to coordinate his movement through a more extended narrative time and space; in particular, he relied on his central human character's (his *I's*) reactions to move the story along. The use of this first-person stance also allowed the internal world of Manuel's human character to become more visible, just as it had aided Regina and, more notably, Jake. In the first grade, Manuel's reasoning about his character's actions had existed in his occasional mutterings about his texts; in second grade, it began to appear inside the text in the form of his character's inner motivations and confusions ("I didn't know wat to thik.").

Most important, Manuel, like Jake, seemed to be increasingly aware of his texts' embeddedness in—and their capacity for influencing—his ongoing social world. Manuel was increasingly talkative about his work, thereby both responding to and encouraging the interest and admiration of others. For him, as for Jake, writing no longer seemed to be simply a representation of a logical story, but also an occasion for interaction. Manuel, however, did not collaborate with others within his text in the literal way that Jake did (e.g., he did not actually put Jake inside his text world). Rather, Manuel sought to anticipate and guide others' responses to (interactions with) his words and pictures. He wanted others not only to understand his story, but to come to understand it in a certain way. For example, he did not want his readers to know until the end of his book that the snowman's birth had only been a dream ("I don't reveal that 'til the end."), but he did want them to understand that the snowman was fading because of the passage of time, the rising of the hot sun. Clearly Manuel viewed his work as being for others, others who, like Manuel himself, expected, reacted, judged, and admired.

Thus, over the two years of the project, both Jake and Manuel became socially and critically sensitive manipulators of symbolic worlds. Jake, the dramatic actor, found his way out of his imaginary worlds and thereby gained a director's control over them, as he began to reflect about his dramatic actions in a literary way (e.g., "I got to think of a [counter-force]."). Manuel gained control by finding his way inside his literary worlds, so that his actions made dramatic sense; that is, the distant director (e.g., "Gotta get some action in here.") gained the dramatic involvement of an actor (e.g., "As far as going away, he doesn't notice it. It's going away. . . . This guy doesn't notice it either."). Both children were becoming artistic weavers of words, who could be inspired, but not dominated, by other symbolic forms and other people.

EPILOGUE

Manuel returned to the school for his third-grade year. It seemed strange to see him without Jake. The interplay between these two young artists had been critical in highlighting the dynamics of writing development. They had pushed each other across symbolic and social boundaries, pointing out the permeable boundaries between the imaginary and the real, the individual and the group. And that interplay had also provided much of the human drama of the project.

Nonetheless, Manuel was very much a part of the action unfolding in his new second/third-grade class. During the seven formal observations made in the spring semester, Manuel chatted with his friends about their stories (pictures and texts) and about a range of other topics as well, including many familiar ones—Mitzi's baby brother, the existence of Santa Claus, the pleasures and tribulations of pet owners, space travel in the twenty-first century, and Manuel's tendency to blush. (In the epilogue to Regina's case history in Chapter 5, Regina was seen collaborating with her friends to write a playful description of the blushing Manuel.)

Moreover, Manuel seemed a confident author and artist, his past accomplishments providing a rich social and intellectual context for his present efforts.

HELLER: So, is this a long story, Manuel?
MANUEL: Yeah.
HELLER: Like your first journal kind of? Like your snowman journal?
MANUEL: Uh-huh.
SONIA: Manuel?

MANUEL: Yeah?

SONIA: Are you doing—are you doing a story like you did
um and you you know um in your other um journal?

MANUEL: Last year?

SONIA: I mean— ⌈ Yeah.

MANUEL: ⌊ Yeah.

SONIA: With the snow. The whole journal was about snow.

MANUEL: ⌈ The whole   is about snow.

SONIA: ⌊ someting like that

MANUEL: Yeah, well it's maybe not the whole journal this time.
It might be a little short.

SONIA: So you start from the beginning about this?

MANUEL: Yeah. I'm just now—yeah.

SONIA: OK. 'Cause I just wanted to know 'cause I thought
that was sorta neat.

Many characteristics of Manuel's earlier "neat" work were still in evidence. Throughout the second half of his third-grade year, Manuel wrote a story about a "magic fish." This story, like Manuel's snowman story, seemed inspired by others he had heard, particularly fairy tales. Moreover, this new story contained many familiar elements from his earlier ones, including a central human character who became lost, who dreamt, and who doubted his dreams; a magical nonhuman character who was brought into the story by human effort; talk between these central characters; and Nature, particularly in the form of the sun, who was an empathic companion for the human.

There were new developments in Manuel's work as well. Most notably, the drama within Manuel's story became less visual, more verbal. Many subtle emotional interplays between his characters, which were suggested primarily by gazes and facial expressions in his snowman book, became evident in the dialogue of his fisherman piece.

To tell Manuel's "magic fish" story briefly, a good and kind fisherman had two mean, lazy brothers. These horrid brothers depended upon the good and kind third brother to catch and sell fish for their livelihood (see Figure 7.17). One day the fisherman caught a "huge fish" (see Figure 7.18), whose beautiful colors suggested its magic, just as had the colors of the magical snow. (Note how Manuel's pictures displayed the sun's concern and then pleasure for the struggling fisherman.) Manuel wrote,

The fish was a golden color. In its middle the fish had sum red skalles. It was butiful. If you looked at it you would see something magecal. [February, Third Grade]

Figure 7.17.   Manuel's struggling fisherman.

Manuel's fisherman began to walk home, lugging the heavy fish:

> He noticed that the fish was much heavier than other fishes that the man had had. There was no light, the stars were hidden, and the moon was behind a cloud.

As Manuel later explained to Christopher, the fisherman became lost, although Manuel never explicitly wrote this. Rather, he had the fisherman going to sleep in the woods, without reaching home:

> The man sat under a big tree and he made camp there. Meanwhile at the three fisherman's house the other two were having a huge party. they were hoping that the third fisherman would die. [February, Third Grade]

Figure 7.18. Manuel's successful fisherman.

This dual scene was depicted in the drawing in Figure 7.19.

As these excerpts suggest, in the first part of his book, Manuel still depended upon his pictures to establish the key scenes of his story, and then on his text to connect those scenes temporally. The preceding passage was unusual for Manuel, in that it described characters' actions in two different scenes, yet it was supported by a picture that also had two different scenes. Also as in previous texts, Manuel shared his characters' insights in both pictures and texts. Unlike the snowman text, however, in the magical fish text Manuel revealed the thinking of several fictional actors—the pair of evil brothers and the good brother, who was his major character. This character, like the boy of his snowman book, was a thoughtful, reasonable human who nonetheless found that things are not always as they seem. Also as in his snowman book, Manuel depended upon Nature's rhythm to guide his narrative. His sleeping fisherman woke up with memories of an awful dream.

Figure 7.19.   Manuel's three fishermen in two scenes.

It was early morning when the third fisherman woke up. He sat up
straight. the sun was just coming up. He had an oful dream. Or
was it. He looked around. It had not bin a dream. he was in a
forest. [March, Third Grade]

Manuel began writing the very next entry without first drawing. His
upset fisherman wished that he could be back home, and found—"all at
ones"—that he was home. "He looked at the fish. It smiled." In response
to a curious Christopher, Manuel suggested both the power of the fish—
and its ultimate demise.

MANUEL: (rereading) The fisherman wished that he—
CHRISTOPHER: Would catch a fish?

> MANUEL: No.
>
> CHRISTOPHER: What did he wish then? That he caught a magi-
> cal fish?
>
> MANUEL: He's lost. He caught a magical fish and he's lost.
> He doesn't know he caught a magical fish. It's a
> beautiful fish, but he doesn't know it's magical.
> He got lost in the forest—and he ( ) back home
> because the fish heard him. But the problem is
> the fish is dying.

Yet Manuel's fish did not die. The text was taken over by a dialogue
between the fish and the fisherman. As the following entry—corrected for
spelling and punctuation—shows, this was a dialogue much like those
between Manuel and his peers—both playful and demanding of reason:

> He could not take his eyes off the fish. "It's not polite to stare,"
> said a voice. "Who, who, who said that?" "Don't be scared," said
> the voice. "Did you say something?" said the fisherman. "Who,
> me? Na." All at once the voice grew loud. "Of course I said that.
> Who else?—Superfish or the fishermen from the black lagoon?"
> Sorry, said the bewildered fisherman. [March, Third Grade]

"Be reasonable," the fish seems to say, in the midst of this fanciful scene,
just as Manuel himself would exhort his friends in the midst of their own
imaginative stories. Manuel had abandoned the limited superheroes—
"superfish"—and their noisy, violent actions. In their stead, he turned to
the more literary magic of folktales and fairy tales, where impossible
occurrences occur in the lives of reasonable, wondering people. The
following was the end of Manuel's story:

> The fisherman and the fish became best friends. He was never
> heard of again. Some say he turned greedy and just as uncaring
> as his brothers. Some say the people of the town made him king
> and he ruled a peaceful land. And by far the best idea of all was
> that he lived a simple life in the country. But these are just as I
> said ideas. [May, Third Grade]

This conclusion, focused as it was on what people "say," was comfortable for Manuel, who was given to thoughtful questions and reasonable speculations during dialogue. In the next chapter, we turn to Mitzi,
another child whose social and literary life involved much talk. Unlike

hers, though, Manuel's written dialogue evolved against the landscape of
Nature; in fact, the physical world provided the source of his most
powerful literary characters (the snowman, the fish) and, indeed, of his
first extended narratives. In contrast, Mitzi's dialogue evolved against an
emotional landscape of relationships, not between Nature and human-
kind, but among humans themselves.

Mitzi

Once there was a cowboy.
I hated the cowboy a Lot.
Do You Like cowboy's?
But I like You alot.
Sometimes I Like The cowboy.
TueSdaYs I Like The cowboy.
The End
        [February, First Grade]

Figure 8.1.   Mitzi's cowboy.

Of all the case study children's texts, Mitzi's first-grade entries most straightforwardly displayed the multiple worlds within which authors work. In her writing, the imaginary world of the indefinite past coexisted with the current experienced world of feelings and relationships; the imagined distanced world, cast in the third person, was placed next to an ongoing social world as realized by the first and second persons; the visual image provided the topic for a written rendition of a talklike commentary.

Mitzi's cowboy piece, for example, reflected the influence of her pictorial world (the drawn cowboy) and her memories of the daily experienced world she shared with her baby brother (whom she loved, "but not always"). Her text began in the imaginary past, with her as observer ("Once there was a cowboy"), and then moved to a socially inviting present, where she seemed to ask How about you? How do you feel about cowboys? While her texts thus implied social dialogue, this was only a simulated effect, not yet anchored to her ongoing social world. (see Bissex, 1980, for a report of simulated socializing in a study of a five-year-old's writing.) Over time, Mitzi's vague "you" gave way to specific characters, and, while her written worlds became much more unified, Mitzi herself as artist and author became a more skillful manipulator of multiple worlds. Like Manuel, she coordinated more carefully her pictures and texts, and she entered into her imaginary worlds in order to take action within them and within her ongoing social world as well. For Mitzi, however, literary action was not a dramatic performance, as it was for Manuel; rather, it was an intimate revealing of confidences. This chapter, then, presents Mitzi's efforts to bring together her imaginary, ongoing social, and wider experienced worlds in new ways and thereby to create within her texts an integrated but complex "personality—a role complex" (Halliday, 1978, p. 15).

FIRST GRADE: JUXTAPOSING MULTIPLE WORLDS

Written Formulas for Visual Displays

Mitzi was a child concerned with relationships. Her talk during journal time was about her experiences with and feelings about family and friends as the following exchange illustrates.

Mitzi is drawing a picture of a rainbow and a house. As she works, she engages in a nontask-involved discussion of the "best" and "worst" children in her class.

SONIA: Rebecca [the first/second-grade homeroom teacher]
         thinks I'm the best one in the class.
MITZI: Uh-uh. You just want her to think that.
SONIA: Then who is? Who does she— Maggie [a substitute
         teacher] always thinks Reba's the best one in the class,
         huh?
MITZI: Nyema's the baddest.
SONIA: I'll—I'll—I'll tell you who's the baddest.
MANUEL: Reba.
MITZI: NYEMA. NYEMA. 'Cause she always follows Bessie
         around in group conferences [the afternoon activity
         period] and sits next to her and all this mean stuff!
         And pinches her and Bessie doesn't want her to. And
         she tells her and she keeps following her and following
         her. (Mitzi's voice is quivering at this point. She is al-
         most in tears.)
SONIA: Are you just telling a story?
MITZI: Uh-uh. Even ask her yourself!
SONIA: (turns to me) Is she telling a story?
MITZI: No. Ask Bessie.
MANUEL: She (referring to me) wouldn't know.

Mitzi's social talk, such as the foregoing, was not directly involved in her
ongoing drawing and writing; indeed, her fast-paced, formulaic approach to the journal activity did not allow others easy entry into her
efforts.

As discussed in Chapter 4, during drawing Mitzi concentrated on her
design. She preferred figures formed with clean, bold lines and dark
colors. Little girls, rainbows, clouds, and hearts were all favorite figures,
although elaborate houses drawn in three-dimensional perspective sometimes appeared. While writing, Mitzi typically began by introducing her
central figure ("Once there was a . . .") and then commenting that she—
or "you"—likes, hates, might like, or might be liked by that figure. Of
her 22 first-grade texts, 17 contained the words *love* or *like*.

Because Mitzi's texts were affective comments on figures, 86% contained no movement through time, yet they were not art notes. Mitzi
marked her written worlds as independent of her accompanying visual
art; for example, the drawn cowboy was a present-time representation of a
figure who in text was cast in the indefinite past ("Once there was a
cowboy."). Even so, she did not maintain the third-person stance inherent in that traditional introduction to a make-believe world. In over half
(59%) her texts, she shifted her stance as author from an observer of an

imaginary world set in the past to a sociable actor in the present, just as she did in the cowboy piece. Following is another example, this one of a girl and her less likable brother, written to accompany Figure 8.2:

Once there was a girl. I like the girl. I Hate the Girls Brother a Lot. The End [February, First Grade]

Early in her first-grade observation period, Mitzi produced two texts that did indeed move through time. This narrative movement was accomplished through fictional dialogue, as the following text for Figure 8.3 shows:

Figure 8.2.   Mitzi's frowning girl and crying brother.

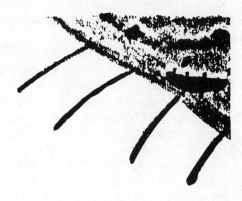

Figure 8.3.   Mitzi's girl saying "Hi."

I like You. Are You a girl? Yes' I am. The End [February, First Grade]

Like other case study children, then, Mitzi used a talkative first person—indeed, two talkative first persons—to accomplish movement through time, without moving beyond the time frame of her picture. But this dialogue seemed based on pure affect, not grounded in any particular interaction with others inside or outside the text's boundaries. It was simply an extension of her formulaic "I like you."

The repetitive use of "I like" no doubt eased Mitzi's encoding task: As discussed in Chapter 4, she produced her texts quite quickly and wrote about twice as many entries as did either Jake or Manuel. Any task-

involved talk during writing thus focused on encoding, as there was little
planning required.

Nonetheless, Mitzi's texts were not merely texts of convenience. They
reflected, as did her talk, her concern with relationships. Her "once-
upon-a-time" openings were sometimes followed by affective statements
about real others ("I love my mom."). Her written texts thus suggested
the tension that can exist between the real and the imaginary, a tension
that sometimes surfaced explicitly in peer talk about her *oral* stories.
Sonia, especially, raised this issue, as she did in the conversation about
Nyema's treatment of Bessie and in the following one, about earning
money by typing (a conversation in which the "truth value" of Mitzi's
account seems more problematic).

> During a conversation about people's weight—and whether or
> not being a little bit chubby is essential to the body's functioning
> —Mitzi remarks that her mother's girlfriend is quite heavy, and
> then she changes the topic.
>
> MITZI: I hate her [the girlfriend]. Once I had to go to her
>   work. I had to work for her.
> SONIA: What did you have to do?
> MITZI: I had to type papers.
> SONIA: What did they have to say?
> MITZI: And then people came to me and said, "Can I have one
>   of those pieces of paper?"
> SONIA: Mitzi, are you telling a story?
> MITZI: Nope. And I got some money because I gave her the
>   papers which I typed.
> SONIA: How much did you get?
> JAKE: Three hundred and fifty-five cents?
> MITZI: No.
> SONIA: How much? I mean in dollars.
> MITZI: A hundred. But I already spent them.
> SONIA: A hundred dollars. (laughs)
> MITZI: I spent them on a um, on a couch!
> MANUEL: On a couch? A couch is that expensive?
> MITZI: Yeah. But we gave it away because we needed room for
>   my brother's crib.
> SONIA: I thought so.
> MANUEL: That makes sense.

Over the course of the next year and a half, Mitzi would make great
progress in making sense within her written stories. To do so, she would

begin to enter into her stories and thus to confront more deliberately her movement between real and imaginary relationships—real and imaginary "I like you's." One helpful support in this process was the very real response her affective statements could elicit in her ongoing social world.

The Social Consequences of Written Formulas

> This is a story about AbcdefGhiJklMnoPQRstuvwXYz. One day there was a A. And One DaY There was a B. And One Day there was a c. I Like aBcdefGhiJKlmnoPQrstuvwxY And Z The End [February, First Grade]

A quick story about ABC would not be likely to engender an intense response from one's peers; however, if, instead of ABC, one substitutes the names of those peers, then the quick story has the capacity to elicit involvement—and so it happened with Mitzi.

> Mitzi is completing her journal entry about the girl who lived under a rainbow (see Chapter 4). As she writes, she talks with Sonia about her upcoming birthday/slumber party.
>
> SONIA: Where am I going to sleep?
>
> MITZI: Me and Bessie are gonna sleep up on the top [of Mitzi's bunk bed]. Me and Bessie and Sally.
>
> SONIA: Oh. Who's gonna sleep on the bottom? Your brother. Where am I gonna sleep, Mitz?
>
> MITZI: You're gonna sleep in my sleeping bag.
>
> JAKE: I knew that was going to come up. (laughs) Sleeping bag.
>
> MITZI: Or maybe sleep with my brother [who is 2]. He is cute.
>
> SONIA: He's cute, and I like to squeeze babies too.
>
> JAKE: Yeah. Squeeze him so hard, the baby's gonna have a dent. (Jake and Mitzi laugh very hard; Sonia seems upset.)
>
> MITZI: And then you'll be in trouble, and he'll die—from my mother. [Sonia will be in trouble "from" Mitzi's mother.] She'll [Sonia] kill him. (Jake and Mitzi continue to laugh hard.)
>
> . . .
>
> SONIA: I'm not gonna squeeze him *that* hard. (very sincerely)
>
> . . .
>
> MITZI: My baby *is* cute.
>
> MANUEL: But all babies are cute. Is yours especially cute?

When Mitzi finishes her piece, she begins writing a new journal entry *without* first drawing. She composes it very quickly; it includes the names of all the children invited to her party:

I like Sally. And I like Sonia too. And I like Bessie. And I like Elizabeth P. And I like Sarah. The End (March, First Grade]

Sonia hears Mitzi reread her text and is immediately attentive.
SONIA: Mitzi, you love me. (very pleased)
MITZI: I said *like*, not *I love*. (firmly)

. . .

SONIA: Who else do you like besides me, Mitzi?
MITZI: Sally.
SONIA: Why can't I sleep with you and Sally and Bess?
MITZI: Because that's all. That's enough.

. . .

SONIA: Mitz, mine's gonna be an overnight one, and I'll ask my
         dad if he can make a bunk bed with both of our [my
         little sister's and my] beds. And you'll sleep on the bot-
         tom with my sister.
MITZI: I'm not gonna come then.
SONIA: OK. You can sleep on the top with me.
Mitzi next draws an accompanying picture of three little
girls—Elizabeth P, Sonia, and Bessie—each bearing a present.
The pictured Elizabeth is calling, "Happy Birthday."

In the preceding event, Mitzi abandoned her typical "once-upon-a-time" imaginary frame and commented directly on her feelings about real people. These remarks figured into her ongoing social life: Sonia was heartened by their presence and attempted once again—although unsuccessfully—to gain a place in Mitzi's top bunk.

Despite Sonia's interest in her written personal commentary, Mitzi returned in subsequent events to her "collage" texts, those juxtaposing varied space and time worlds. But these texts, too, sometimes became the focus of peer interest, for, as has been seen in all previous case histories, the children as a group were increasingly attentive to each other's efforts. Mitzi herself both commented upon others' texts and received commentary about her own, the latter forcing her to begin to justify the tensions among her different worlds.

A particularly revealing peer response occurred during Mitzi's "mean-looking-witch" event (see Figure 8.4). Mitzi labored intensely as she drew this witch and was quite pleased with her result, remarking that

Figure 8.4.   Mitzi's mean-looking witch.

this was her all-time "favorite story." She then began to write. As was typical for her, she used self-directive talk to monitor her encoding of the text. She seemed to rely primarily on visual recall, requesting help on only one word: *witch*. Her completed story began with the familiar opening:

> Once there was a witch. She is my mom. I love my mom. [April, First Grade]

Table 8.1 analyzes her talk while writing this passage.

In the mean-looking-witch event, the varied worlds Mitzi moved among as a writer were quite visible. There was the present-time, two-dimensional "story" of the carefully drawn witch, with the overlapping "once-there-was" realm she shaped with written words; these symbolic

(*text continued on p. 226*)

TABLE 8.1. Mitzi's "Mean-Looking-Witch" Event: Writing and
            Talking

Mitzi's Text	Composing Code	Talk During Writing/Comment
		As Mitzi begins writing, her talk is task-involved and self-directed, assisting her in directing the encoding of her story:
Once there	OV	Mitzi: Once there
	P	
	RR	Mitzi: Once there
was a	OV	Mitzi: was a
	OV	Mitzi: witch
	IS-A	Mitzi: How do you spell witch? . . . Mitzi continues to write, soon completing another sentence:
witch. She is my mom.		
	RR	"She is my mom." (The principal walks in and Mitzi is momentarily distracted; she then restates her text.) "He was my mom."
		Jenni intervenes. Mitzi's talk with Jenni is at first task-involved and metasymbolic, as she and Jenni focus on Mitzi's pronoun choice; then the talk becomes task-related, as she and Jenni focus on Jenni's personal experiences.
	IU-P	Jenni: He?
		Mitzi: She.
		Jenni: You said, "He."
	RR	Mitzi: She is my mom.
		Jenni: I have a witch mother.
		Mitzi: What?
		Jenni: I have a real witch mother. My mother's a friend of a witch.

224

TABLE 8.1.   (continued)

Mitzi's Text	Composing Code	Talk During Writing/Comment
		Mitzi: A bad one?
		Jenni: No, a good one/bad one.
		...
		Mitzi may be feeling uneasy about referring to the witch as her mother, for she now writes:
I love my mom	OV	"I love my mom"
		Bessi and Jenni overhear Mitzi's self-directed talk. They, too, seem to be feeling uneasy about her text. In response to their concerns, Mitzi engages in talk that is at once task-involved (focused on her written and at least partially imaginary rendition of her mother) and task-related (focused on her real-world feelings about her mother).
	IU-P	Bessie: You shouldn't share it.
		Mitzi: She's a bad witch.
		Jenni: Then you're a bad girl.
		Perhaps a little girl who writes that her own mother is a witch is a bad child indeed, from Jenni's point of view. Mitzi appears to interpret Jenni's statement similarly:
		Mitzi: No, I'm not. I might not even like my mom, or I love my mom.
		At this point, Mitzi draws a conversation bubble next to her witch and writes:
I am Bad	OV	Mitzi: I am bad.

KEY: Dialogue: IS-A--Interruption Solicited from Adult; IU-P--Interruption Unsolicited from Peer. Monologue: OV--Overt Language; P--Pause; RR--Reread (form adapted from Graves, 1973).

realms were embedded within the ongoing peer social world and within her wider experienced world, as her feelings about her mom pulled in the world beyond the classroom walls.

In this example, Mitzi's text was related to her ongoing social life in less direct ways than in the previous "slumber party" example. Mitzi's social relationships with her friends were mediated by the written world she created (and they re-created), which was separate from and yet embedded in their shared world. This created world affected others' behaviors toward her, just as did the more direct "I like Sonia." Thus, in both events, the reactions of Mitzi's friends seemed to have highlighted for her both the text world itself (e.g., *like*, not *love*) and the social world within which it existed. Mitzi, like Jake and Manuel, was learning that authors do not simply represent or comment on their feelings in their texts; written texts are sites of social interaction, not just individuals' representations.

Social Judgments About Written Truths

Late in her first-grade year, Mitzi's texts, which had implicitly raised the issue of truth value, evoked explicit peer talk about that issue. For example, one month after her witch event, Mitzi wrote another piece about her mom that also inspired much task-related talk:

> Once there was a teenager. She was my mommy. when she was a teenager, And she loves me. [May, First Grade]

This entry led to a lively debate about the age at which it was possible to have a baby.

In a later event, Mitzi discussed the truth value of her work during the course of her drawing and writing, rather than after it had been completed and thus the consequences of that conversation were evident in her work. Mitzi had brought in some stickers of the cartoon dog Snoopy and a small bear. She announced to the children at her table that she was going to make a beach scene; she even wrote the title at the top of her paper: "At the Beach." (She was working on a single, blank piece of paper, rather than in her journal.) Sonia was very interested in Mitzi's activity, and most especially in her stickers. Table 8.2 presents an analysis of the functions of Mitzi's talk during this event, as she carried on a conversation with Sonia.

As can be seen from the table, Sonia's questions about Mitzi's drawing helped Mitzi to think more clearly about what she was producing and

TABLE 8.2. Mitzi's "Snoopy-and-the-Bear" Event: Functions of Talk

Mitzi's Talk	Function Strategy	Comment
Sonia: Are they friends, Mitzi?		Sonia is referring to Mitzi's Snoopy and bear stickers.
Mitzi: Yeah.	Interactional-representational/labeling	Mitzi's talk here is task-involved and refers to the figures in her drawing; at the same time, it is socially involved, as she responds to the inquisitive Sonia. Indeed, Mitz engages in much more task-involved talk than in any previously observed event.
Sonia: Mitzi, what's this? Is this gonna be the water?		Sonia is referring to a blank spot on Mitzi's paper.
Mitzi: No, this is the story. Sonia: Oh. Where's the water?	Interactional-representational/labeling	
Mitzi: Maybe--I know how to do it.	Personal	Sonia's questioning to support Mitzi's planning.
That will be the water. ... Sonia: Mitzi, why did you do that? Oh, you're gonna put the story up?	Directive/planning	Mitzi is drawing sand where she had earlier said the story would be.
Mitzi: No. I'm drawing a picture of Yosemite's beach.	Interactional-representational/reporting	Mitzi's talk is task-involved but focused on her own actions, as she explains her efforts in her ongoing social world.
Sonia: I went to Yosemite and Lake Tahoe, and I'm gonna go--		Sonia initiates task-related talk about personal experiences, but she abandons her topic, perhaps because Mitzi is intent on her drawing.

to make it understandable to her audience. The conversation trailed off when Sonia saw how engrossed in drawing Mitzi had become.

Sonia then began to concentrate on her own journal activity. Mitzi worked quietly, although she intermittently responded to Sonia's requests for spelling help. Soon Mitzi herself began to write. The following was her completed text:

At the Beach

Once there was a bear. And there was Snoopy too. They were sister and brother. And they were at the beach. Snoopy is a boy and the bear was the girl. The End. [May, First Grade]

Mitzi's text seemed disjointed. She began from an observational perch set in the indefinite past but abandoned it to make a "real-world" observation about Snoopy being a boy. And that observation, as Table 8.3 illustrates, was motivated by the concerns of her friend, Sonia.

Despite Mitzi's consistent combining of the "once-there-was" opening with references to apparently real and present-time others, she herself sometimes objected to such mixtures in other children's journal entries. Indeed, the day before the Snoopy event, she had accused Jake of "lying" in his story when he wrote about seeing a jet shoot the sun (see Chapter 6).

In the second grade, Mitzi would begin to manipulate more deliberately her combining of social, experienced, and imaginary worlds. Her affection for others, her worries about their affection for her, and her concerns about—and liberties taken with—the "truth" would become increasingly evident in her talk about her texts, just as they would also become less starkly evident within those texts.

SECOND GRADE: MELDING MULTIPLE WORLDS

For her second-grade year, Mitzi was placed in Bill's second/third-grade classroom. Margaret did not feel that Mitzi had done her best in the first grade; for example, Mitzi's repetitive texts had not seemed to reflect much thought. Nonetheless, Margaret did feel that Mitzi was progressing satisfactorily and would be able to manage in the older children's classroom. Sonia, Jake, and Manuel thus were no longer her classmates; Jenni, however, also went into Bill's classroom, making that relationship more intense.

Friendship itself continued to be a consistent theme of Mitzi's journal-time behavior. Moreover, the content of her drawing and writing

TABLE 8.3. Mitzi's "Snoopy and the Bear" Event:
           Writing and Talking

Mitzi's Text	Composing Code	Talk During Writing/Comment
Once there was a bear. And there was Snoopy too.		
	They were	
		Mitzi stops and makes a planning comment about her writing, the first such comment I have heard from her:
	OV	Mitzi: OK, they'll be a little tiny sister. (referring to the bear sticker)
sister	S	
		Sonia overhears Mitzi's comment. She again engages Mitzi in talk, first focusing on Mitzi's imaginary world and then on their shared experienced world:
	IU-P	Sonia: They were sisters?
		Mitzi: Yeah
		Sonia: Snoopy isn't a girl.
		Mitzi: I know. Sister
and	OV	AND
brother.	OV	brother.
	IS-P	(to Sonia) Why are you copying?
		Sonia: Mitzi, I'm not. It's something about my sister.
	RR	Mitzi: Once there was a bear and they [text: there] was Snoopy too. They were sister and brother.
	IU-P	Sonia: Why don't you put-- because, you know, Snoopy is not a girl.
		Mitzi: I know. That's the boy.

KEY: Dialogue: IS-P--Interruption Solicited from Peer; IU-P--
Interruption Unsolicited from Peer. Monologue: OV--Overt
Language; RR--Reread; S--Silence (adapted from Graves,1973).

229

became more integral to these classroom friendships. For example, in the following interactions, Mitzi was attentive and supportive as she talked with her friend Jenni about the latter's decision not to finish the story she has been working on in her current journal.

> MITZI: You need to write "to be continued in the next journal."
> JENNI: In my next journal I'm gonna finish this story.
> MITZI: Then write "in the next journal"! This is how you spell *journal*. Just copy offa mine's. I'll write it—I'll write it right here.

Despite Mitzi's straightforward, confident manner, she sought her classmates' support for her own efforts; she called others' attention to her drawing and writing sometimes by offering self-evaluative comments like, "Ugly, huh?" and, "Like it?" She seemed to need connections with and approval from her friends. Further, her relationships with others seemed increasingly complex, and Mitzi displayed greater reflectiveness about this complexity, especially about her own motives and feelings and those of others. In the following excerpt, Mitzi reacted to Jenni's statement that she was using Mitzi's pencil. The conversation demonstrated Mitzi's—and Jenni's—ability to consider the perspectives of others.

> MITZI: I already know about that. That's about the 15, 15 thousandth time you told me. I know you're using my pencil, and it doesn't bother me a bit.
> JENNI: What do you mean, "I know I'm using your pencil"?
> MITZI: I know. And it doesn't bother me a bit.
> JENNI: Well, what do you mean by that?
> MITZI: It doesn't bother me a bit that you're using my pencil.
> JENNI: I don't know what you mean. 'Cause I know that you knew that I was using your pencil. What do you mean?
> MITZI: I didn't know that. I didn't know that YOU knew that I knew that I—I knew, I didn't know that you knew that I knew that you were using my pencil.

In Mitzi's writing, her straightforward but sensitive style was clearly evident. Her concerns about the truth value of texts continued, and she continued as well to write about feelings. But, like Regina, Manuel, and Jake, she developed more sophisticated ways of moving among multiple worlds—among multiple space and time structures—and, as a result, her texts changed.

Acting in the Ongoing Social and Imaginary Worlds

Before beginning her second-grade journal, Mitzi organized a table of contents. Mitzi, like her friend Jenni, seemed to use the table as a planning device—a way of figuring out beforehand what to write about—rather than as an aid for anticipated readers. Her planned second-grade stories were

1. Me and my friend
2. Me and my dream
3. Me and My
4. Me and My

While I had inferred Mitzi's concern about human relationships in the first grade, no such inference was necessary in the second. As Mitzi said of her journal, "It's going to be me me me me me and and and." When Bessie and Jenni described their stories as being about bunnies and cats, respectively, Mitzi commented, "Mine are about people."

Although Mitzi's concerns remained the same, her composing behaviors changed. Her imaginary worlds were increasingly meshed with her social world. She began to share her texts spontaneously with her peers, as entertaining them with her stories became socially more important. Further, rather than straightforward "I like you" statements, she more often incorporated peers and family members into her texts as characters: 53% of her second-grade texts contained the names of peers and/or family members, compared with 23% in the first grade. She frequently included herself as the character "I" and then used the narrative form to play out her relationships dynamically with others. So, in the second grade, Mitzi's texts, like Jake's, more often moved through time: 53% of her second-grade texts were narratives, compared with 14% in the first grade.

Further, fictionalizing herself and those close to her seemed to help Mitzi, as it helped all case study children, to create texts that conveyed the internal world of her characters. It no longer was only she (the "I") who liked and hated, but her characters as well.

Finally, Mitzi's use of drawing changed. In the first grade, she had most often begun her journal entries by drawing; in the second grade, she more often reversed this procedure, using the drawing to illustrate her ideas. This shift may have been related to her abandonment of her repetitive text routine. Rather than building affective statements around her drawn figures, she tended to construct her texts by relying upon real or fictionalized personal experiences. And in those experiences, affective comments were part of the unfolding drama.

To illustrate, early in her second-grade observation period, Mitzi again wrote a piece about a witch. She put both herself and her friend Jenni into this story; indeed, Jenni was the witch. The feelings of this fictionalized Jenni toward Mitzi provided the emotional energy of the story. Mitzi's decision to place Jenni in this fictional role seemed to be made quite suddenly. She began by writing a more familiar text, one about what promised to be a bothersome boy:

Me and My Dream

I had a dream and My dream was a BiG NiGhtMare and This is My NightMare. Once there was a boy.

Mitzi then turned to Jenni, who was sitting beside her.

MITZI: Now this is going to be a true dream.
. . .
This is a nightmare I once had and the girl was you.
JENNI: Yeah?
MITZI: And you really hated me.
JENNI: No wonder it's a nightmare.

In her opening exchange with Jenni, Mitzi engaged in self-initiated, representational talk about the event to be depicted in writing; she labeled the event ("This is a nightmare I once had") and elaborated about its details ("and the girl was you"). Moreover, this talk was focused both on the anticipated text world and on her peer in the ongoing social world.

In producing this text, Mitzi concentrated more notably on text planning than in any previously observed event. Letting go of her "I-like-you" variations necessitated such planning. In addition to her comments to Jenni, Mitzi's pauses and occasional self-evaluative remarks further suggested her concern about what to write. Her behaviors while writing are illustrated in Table 8.4.

Mitzi's completed text contained the ideas she had discussed with Jenni. It vacillated between the past and the present, reflecting Mitzi's own movement between her apparently imagined past and the present world she shared with Jenni:

Me and My Dream

I had a dream and My dream was a BiG NiGhtMare, and This is My NiGhtMare. Once there was a Girl and her name was jenni and she hated Me. but I do not know why. and she had a magic bulb.

TABLE 8.4. Mitzi's "Nightmare" Event: Writing and Talking

Mitzi's Text	Composing Code	Talk During Writing/Comment
Me and My Dream I had a dream and my dream was a BiG NiGhtMer*	RR	Mitzi begins by rereading the text she wrote the previous day, then continues on:
and this	S	
	IU-P	Jenni shows Mitzi her text page, which is full of references to cats. Mitzi leaves her own task and becomes involved with Jenni's. Together the two girls read: "Cat cat cat cat the the the the." Mitzi finally returns to her own task.
Once	S	
there	S	
	P (10 sec.)	She listens to a conversation between Jenni and Sally.
was	S	
a	S	
boy	S	
	///	Mitzi erases boy.
	IU-P	Jenni: My daddy and mommy got married 6 days after--I mean 6 days before I was born. Mitzi: That's cute too. (pointing to Jenni's picture) Mitzi's talk is focused on Jenni's drawing.
boy	OV	Mitzi: boy. Mitzi's talk is now involved in her own task, as she uses directive talk to monitor her own encoding processes.
	P	
	IU-P	Jenni starts a pencil duel with Mitzi.

TABLE 8.4. (continued)

Mitzi's Text	Composing Code	Talk During Writing/Comment
	IS-P	Mitzi tells Jenni about her planned "true dream"; her talk is focused both on her own task and on her peer in the ongoing social world.
	/////	She again erases boy.
Girl	S	She writes the following text, using primarily directive talk to monitor her encoding; her fluent writing is interrupted once, as she seeks help with bulb:
Her name was jenni and she hated Me. but I do not know why. and she had a magic bulb her bulb had		
		At this point, Mitzi seems to reconsider her direction:
	OV	Mitzi: No
	///	She erases had.
was	S	
a very	S	
	IS-A	She seeks help with powerful.
	IU-P	Jenni: Is that the nightmare with me in it?
	RR	Mitzi reads this part of her text to Jenni.

* Spelling of this word later corrected in response to adult help.

KEY: Dialogue: IS-P--Interruption Solicited from Peer; IS-A-- Interruption Solicited from Adult; IU-P--Interruption Unsolicited from Peer. Monologue: OV--Overt Language; RR--Reread. Other: P--Pause; S--Silence;///--Erasing (form adapted from Graves, 1973).

her bulb was a very powerful bulb. it was so powerful it turned Me
into a Powerful bulb and now she has Two Powerfull Bulbs. The
one that is Me is even Powerfuller than the other one. The End.
[February, Second Grade]

As soon as she finished her text, Mitzi turned to Jenni and asked, "OK,
want me to read this to you? It's very funny."

As shown in Table 8.4, Mitzi produced her text with ease, correctly
using periods and spelling most words without any obvious attempt at
figuring them out. She requested spelling help for only 4 of her 85 words.
While her writing fluency suggested that she was visually recalling most
words, her reaction to the spelling of *bulb* suggested an attentiveness to
the orthographic sense of words. First Mitzi copied the word *bulb*: "B; B,
bulb." She paused and then studied the word, just as Manuel studied
requested words whose spellings puzzled him. Mitzi talked softly to
herself: "Bulb? Oh, I don't know. Bulb. Bulb." Mitzi often studied her
written words, adjusting spellings; rethinking her decisions about
whether one word was in fact two (e.g., she erased *NightMer* several times,
trying it both as a single word and as two separate words); and eliminating unnecessary apostrophes, which she sometimes inserted before plural
s, a very common tactic in her class.

After completing her nightmare story, Mitzi drew an accompanying
picture that fleshed out the fanciful quality of her dream. (see Figure 8.5).
In the first grade, Mitzi, like Manuel, had kept firm boundaries between
visual and verbal art; that is, she did not use talk extensively during the

Figure 8.5.   Mitzi's nightmare.

drawing process to create the depicted world, nor did she use her text to summarize or re-create her drawing/talking experience. Her pictures were of figures, and she commented on those figures in her text. In second grade, Mitzi, like Manuel, was able to bring drawing and writing into closer harmony, thus forcing a negotiation between visual and verbal art.

As in Manuel's written texts, the action in Mitzi's story was detailed in her text, while the picture portrayed a scene. But while Manuel drew a series of scenes to reflect time's passage, Mitzi drew only the concluding scene—the result of the action of Jenni's magical bulb. Like Manuel, however, Mitzi included elements of meaning in her drawing that were not conveyed by the text itself. In the text, Jenni is simply Jenni with a magical bulb; in the picture, Jenni has witchlike nose and hands and the bulbs look like crystal balls.

Finally, as in 12 of her 17 second-grade entries, Mitzi incorporated words into her picture to convey nonvisual information. Like Jake, she made frequent use of cartoonlike, conversational bubbles. The simulated dialogue of her earlier pieces was gone; in this and her next nine pieces, any direct quotations were anchored to her drawings. Thus, in this piece, Jenni, in appropriate witchlike fashion, is saying, "He, He, He."

Abandoning the Imaginary World and Reconstructing the Real World

Fictionalizing real people and real experiences highlighted the relationships between the experienced, the ongoing social, and the symbolic worlds, and more particularly, the issue of truth in fiction. In Mitzi's nightmare piece, she resolved this issue, as Manuel did, with the realistic notions of "magic" and "dreaming"—realistic, that is, from a child's point of view. She could thus incorporate the real-world Jenni into an imaginary realm ("This is a true dream.") and, by so doing, engage her in the ongoing social world as well.

In order to meld the imaginary and the real worlds in comfortable ways *without* the use of dreams and magic, authors contextualize the essence of a real experience in an imaginary one. And, as just suggested, Mitzi was beginning to do this; ambivalent emotions were part of an imaginary drama. And yet, she seemed increasingly uncomfortable with the tension between the imaginary and the real, a discomfort evidenced in her struggles with beginning her pieces.

Shortly after her nightmare piece, Mitzi produced Figure 8.6 and the following text. In this piece, her emotions were again contextualized; but, despite the once-upon-a-time opening, they were embedded within her *experienced* world:

Figure 8.6.   Mitzi's little brother.

Me and My BaBy Brother

Once upon a time there was a girl Which is Me. I had a little
brother. My brother is very bad some times. Some times I love him
but not always. The End. [March, Second Grade]

This text was very similar to the piece she had written over a year earlier
to accompany Figure 8.2 (see p. 218).

Once There was a girl. I like the girl. I Hate the Girls Brother a
Lot. The End. [February, First Grade]

But in her second-grade piece, it was not just any girl whom she liked and
whose brother she hated. She herself was the girl, and her own brother
was the object of her wavering affections.

During the months of March and April, Mitzi abandoned the imaginary and instead produced real-world texts, which, like her text for
Figure 8.6, often began with "Once upon a time." As with her first-grade
texts, she would introduce a person or a pet and then include an affective
or evaluative comment about that figure. The latest pieces, however, were

more detailed, perhaps because she was writing about known figures in her experienced world.

Of the eight texts Mitzi wrote during this period, her first four were not narratives. In order to capture movement within her realistic texts, Mitzi would need to play out, at least schematically, a recalled event, just as she had played out her dream adventure with Jenni. Further, if she went on with her "once-there-was" openings (however unconventional they were for personal narratives), she would need to use them—and their setting of time, place, and character—to frame the recollected or, more accurately, the re-created event.

Mitzi's first new tactic, however, was to begin, not with "Once there was," but with "One day," an opening that framed a particular recalled event, rather than a recalled figure. In the following text she erased "dad" in two places because she remembered he had not gone:

Me and My Mom and [Dad erased]

One day me and mom and [dad erased] went for a walk. It was fun because my brother Was not with us. We went to San francisco Zoo. [March, Second Grade]

In her very next text, Mitzi included both the indefinite "there was" and a more definite "once".

Cat's by Mitzi

Onec there Was a gang of cat's that was Mean. I hate those cat's. Onec one of them almost killed Me. It was so scary I almost fainted. My MoM came runing out side, and she almost fainted too. The end [March, Second Grade]

Mitzi's accompanying picture was an illustration of the narrative's conclusion (see Figure 8.7). In it, Mitzi and her mom were smiling at three quite small and innocent-looking cats. In the background was her house. And, as was Mitzi's usual procedure, she labeled her figures ("Mom" and "Me") and included a conversation bubble: Her mother was saying, "That was a clos whon." While this event probably came from her memory of a real-world event, notice that Mitzi's picture is not entirely realistic as her mother and she are dressed in "once-upon-a-time" costumes.

Mitzi was certain that her friend Jenni would like this entry. Indeed, she remarked, "Jenni, you're gonna like this one." Given Jenni's attraction to cats—and Mitzi's attraction to Jenni—this belief was understand-

Figure 8.7. Mitzi's gang of cats.

able. Throughout the observation period, Mitzi had listened to Jenni reading her cat stories, which Jenni sometimes referred to as re-creations of true events, like Mitzi's "gang-of-cats" piece. For example, once, after reading her story about putting a cat into her purse and having another cat hiss at her, Jenni commented, "It really did [i.e., this story is really true] because it [the cat in the purse] doesn't like the other cat—the neighbor's cat." However, Jenni also sometimes talked about her stories as fanciful, like her "once-upon-a-time" story about a cat named Winfield who "has a crush on a big black cat." (Mitzi told Jenni that she liked the affective part of this latter story—the fact that Winfield "has a crush.")

Mitzi was very knowledgeable about Jenni's family life and about the tenuous role of cats in that life. For, although Jenni wrote about *cats*, those cats were very much a part of her relationships with other people, including family members and friends. In fact, her parents wouldn't allow Jenni to have a cat! Mitzi's attentiveness to Jenni and her relationships with and about cats were illustrated in the following conversation initiated by Aimee, another second grader.

AIMEE: Jenni, do you think your brother likes cats? [Jenni's brother Ian—her twin—was also in the second/third-grade group.]

JENNI: No, he doesn't.

MITZI: Yes, he does. You told me that he does. He does.

JENNI: I don't think he— I think he's beginning to hate them 'cause he— Yesterday he took his dart gun and shot another cat.

MITZI: And what happened?

JENNI: He got hissed at.

. . .

MITZI: You shouldn't have one 'cause your dad is allergic to them.

JENNI: I know. So what— Ian said we can keep the cat in the closet all day.

Mitzi herself wrote more directly about the quality of her relationships with family members and with Jenni herself. As has been illustrated throughout this section, Mitzi's challenges seemed to center on how qualities are particularized in time and space: What, she seemed to ask, is the relationship between the "once upon a time" and the "once"? Between the "liking"—or the "hating"—and the particular events that energized that emotion? Indeed the particulars had sometimes been in her pictures, even while qualities alone had existed in her texts. Recall the little girls going to the birthday party, drawn after Mitzi's "I like Sonia" and other statements of affection, or the pictured little brother crying "Mommy" that accompanied the statement "Some times I love him . . . ." Further, Mitzi seemed to have been in temporary retreat from her grappling with the connection between these real relationships and the imaginary ones they inspired. However, this theme of truth and fiction—so dominant in both the first/second- and second/third-grade classes—could not be long avoided.

Negotiating among the Experienced, Imaginary, and Ongoing Social Worlds

Just as Mitzi seemed to use "once upon a time" and "once" as structures for exploring the relationship between qualities of existence and particularities of events, she began to manipulate the openings of her stories to explore the dynamics between real and imaginary pieces. Her first imaginary text, after the lengthy period of reports of personal experiences, seemed connected to an upsetting classroom event.

During the month of April, the children in all classes were making a surprise book for Rebecca, the retiring reading teacher. They had been faithfully working for weeks on their individual pictures and essays for the book when its existence was revealed to Rebecca. In the opinion of Mitzi and her friends, this revelation was a serious breach of trust.

> The children sitting by Mitzi are complaining that Alexander and Rachel have told Rebecca about the book. Alexander was apparently the first to reveal the children's secret.
>
> IAN: Rachel knew that Alexander told, so she told her, Rebecca, and she already knew that Rebecca knew.
> MITZI: Mm mmm. But she knew that they were gonna get Rebecca to not know that—she knew that they were gonna get her to not know that, the real surprise.
>
> . . .
>
> IAN: I hate Alexander for what he did.
> MITZI: I hate Rachel for doing it, 'cause she did it too.

Secrets and potential betrayal were the themes of a piece Mitzi entitled, "How My Life Was." The story featured Mitzi and a twin sister. And this sister seemed to be intent on repeating Alexander's and Rachel's misdeed:

> I said to my sister one day that I was going to run away. My sister screamed, "Oh no." My mother and father ran down the stairs. "What happened" they said. My sister was beginning to say that I was going to run away When I ran across the room and covered her Mouth. The End. [April, Second Grade]

While this piece marked Mitzi's return to imaginative texts, this narrative did not begin with a variation of "once upon a time." Instead, in small letters, above the piece, she had written "not true." Perhaps she anticipated some objection from her peers about the truthfulness of the reported "one day." It was, after all, Mitzi's first imaginative text in almost two months, and such a glaring untruth as having a twin—revealed only in the picture, not in the text—would certainly be noticed, especially by Jenni, who was herself a twin.

Mitzi's story was fleshed out in a more elaborate way than in any of her previous texts. Like Regina, Jake, and Manuel, Mitzi accomplished this in part through dialogue, dialogue now contained within the text itself, rather than in the picture. She was an actor in a particular event, unfolding the details from her knowing vantage point. Further, she did not need to proclaim "I hate her for that [for almost telling my secret]"; her negative evaluation of the event was in the very grammar of her text: She slowed down the narrative's pace with a progressive verb (My sister was beginning to say . . .) and then added an adverbial clause to depict her own quick action in this frozen moment.[1] Indeed, Mitzi's text portrays the event, including its affective quality, much more vividly than her accompanying picture, which is of quite a peaceful scene (refer to Figure 8.8).

Mitzi continued for the next month to mark her imaginative stories "not true." Nonetheless, she was both more flexible and more conventional about openings and about her texts in general. She began her imaginative texts in varied ways and also consistently wrote them in past tense. Further, she no longer began true written texts about friends or family with "once there was." For example, following is Mitzi's recollection of an outing with her neighbors.

The new car

About 4 days ago my upstairs neighbors were going to buy a car. The kids wanted me to come with them. Their parents said, "o.k." Then I went downstairs and asked. My Pop said, "ok." So we went to Berkeley. Me and my neighbors played circus. (emphasis added.) [April, Second Grade]

In another text, Mitzi used literary constructions (other than "once upon a time") to convey a true experience, in this case, her move to a new home:

Next door to Me there lived a kind lady that had a cute cat. I still love that cat.

These literary features of children's narratives have been studied by Purcell-Gates (1988), who builds especially on the work of Chafe (1982). Literary constructions evident in Mitzi's text include literary phrasing ("there lived") and literary word order (the preposed adverbial "next door to me").

---

[1]Labov's (1972) analysis of personal narratives informed my view of how Mitzi and her peers expressed evaluations of experience in their texts.

The little Attic

Figure 8.8.   Mitzi's family scene.

Mitzi clearly had become more comfortable with the relationship between real and imaginary worlds. She seemed to understand that imaginary worlds conveyed some essence of the real world—a person with secrets could be vulnerable in both sorts of worlds. Further, she seemed to grasp that the real world, when replayed in written narrative, assumed an imaginative quality—it, too, was a verbal construction, a product of human symbolizing.

In the final observed event of her second-grade year, Mitzi wrote a deceptively simple text about cats. This piece, unlike the cowboy piece that began this chapter, presented a unified world, but Mitzi, as author, moved among worlds. And she did so in an impressively sophisticated fashion, for her imaginary text was firmly embedded within her ongoing social and experienced worlds. She had decided to write about cats, a topic that, as noted already, provided a social link to Jenni. Days earlier, Mitzi had written the title for this entry in her table of contents. So she knew that the story had to have something to do with "The Surprise Party."

MITZI: Jenni, what can I write about? Um, I'm thinking about cats. It's gonna be a surprise party about cats. What should I write about? You're good, you're good at that. You're good at this [i.e., writing about cats], Jenni. Jenni you're good at that! (pause) I know! A bird that'll go and kill a cat!

YAHMYA: A vulture?

MITZI: NO! They're my made-up cats. Once I made up some cats. Once I made up some cats. And there were some birds. BIRDS! And they eat 'em, too.

YAHMYA: They eat CATS?

MITZI: Mm mmm. [Yes]

Mitzi seemed to be trying to justify her story to Yahmya by clearly separating her imaginary world from the real one ("They're my made-up cats."). When Mitzi finally began writing, however, she wrote about cats that eat birds. Perhaps Yahmya's critique of the reverse situation had made her reconsider. After writing her piece, Mitzi began drawing a tree and soon realized that she needed "dead birds down here" underneath it.

JENNI: Cats?

MITZI: Yeah—listen:

Once there was a bunch of cats. Then all of a sudden there came a flock of birds. This was a BIG surprise to the cats. At once the cats started to kill them.

DARIUS: Meow, meow, meow. [Darius is another classmate.]

Mitzi read, "the cats started to kill them," although she had actually written, "they started to kill them." The confusion in her ongoing social world, with Yahmya and then with Jenni, over who was killing whom— and her own change of plans—may have led to this adjustment. (Later, Mitzi erased *they* and substituted *the cats*.)

After listening to Mitzi's story, Jenni suggested a strategy for avoiding a picture full of dead birds: "You could put some flying away up here." Mitzi paused and then had yet another thought: "No, I know what I'm going to do." She then added "and eat them" to the last line of her text, thereby eliminating the need for dead birds. As shown in Figure 8.9, she drew one bird; it was crying as it hovered near the tree.

In this event, Mitzi produced an imaginative narrative in which she herself was not a visible actor. She constructed it using literary language ("Once there was . . ." "Then all of a sudden there came . . ." "At once . . ."), yet it contained familiar elements from her real world, such as the familiar cats with their capacity to kill. And the theme was a familiar one as well, that of sudden, unanticipated misfortune (at least for the birds).

Mitzi, then, had carefully coordinated her picture and her text, which combined to tell a sensible, imaginary tale to her interested, inquisitive friends. As the event illustrates, she had progressed from "I like you"

Figure 8.9. Mitzi's sole surviving bird.

journal entries surrounded by social talk to written worlds in which characters themselves liked and hated, were surprised and saddened, betrayed and befriended. Her journey to dynamic literary worlds was mediated, as was that of all the case study children, by her interactions with her supportive, if critical, peers.

SUMMARY

Throughout the years of the study, Mitzi remained a child for whom friendship mattered. She paid attention to the details of her friends' lives and revealed the details of her own. She gave and expected loyalty and support from these special others, qualities realized in the small efforts that solidify relationships—sharing secrets and pencils, sitting together and exchanging phone numbers, publicly denying a friend's chubbiness or complaining of another's ill-treatment.

From the beginning of the project, Mitzi's concerns about relationships were reflected in her texts, but those products seemed unconnected with her ongoing talk during journal time. Rather, her texts were formulaic and thus produced with ease and efficiency. They were generally nonnarrative pieces through which Mitzi proclaimed the existence of a drawn figure and then commented on her—or another's—feelings about that figure. Mitzi's writing thus seemed to be based upon her general concerns about relationships rather than any *specific* story suggested by her picture or by her ongoing interactions with others. Moreover, her stories were collages of space and time structures: Past imaginary worlds coexisted with her current experienced world; her statements as an observer were juxtaposed with her rhetorical actions as a social participant.

Mitzi's friends, especially Sonia, Jenni, and Bessie, were increasingly attentive to her efforts. Her quick "I like somebody's" could elicit strong social reactions, like Sonia's pleasure at being "loved"; similarly, her juxtapositions of the imaginary and the real could also evoke a response, like Bessie's admonition not to share the story about the witch who happened to be Mitzi's mom. Mitzi's texts, then, mattered in her social world; they could elicit social commentary, which in turn encouraged Mitzi's reflections on her text and on her intentions as well ("I love my mom.")

During her second-grade year, Mitzi's multiple worlds began to mesh more comfortably. To begin with, Mitzi, like Manuel, brought her drawing and writing into closer harmony, thus forcing a negotiation between visual and verbal art. Rather than commenting on a pictured imaginary figure in her texts, she drew upon personal experience for inspiration for both picture and text. For a period, she tended to draw and write about known people or pets. While she would still describe and make affective comments about these significant others in her stories ("Some times I love him [my baby brother] but not always."), in her pictures she would contextualize them into a time and place. Indeed, she would provide space for these characters' own voices, such as where her pictured baby brother is screaming for their mother.

In time, however, Mitzi leaned upon particular events for inspiration for her written texts as well. The language routines of other authors and storytellers appeared to help her negotiate between states of being and the particular actions that energized those states: *"Once upon a time there was* a gang of cats," she wrote; not only were these cats mean and thus deserving of intense negative feelings ("I hate those cats"), *"once* one of them" brought its meanness to bear on poor Mitzi.

Mitzi's re-creation of personal events contributed to the greater frequency of narrative texts in the second grade (see Table 8.5). Moreover, in time, the details of the event moved from the picture to the text. Like Jake, she moved from incorporating dialogue into her pictures to incorporating dialogue into her texts and thus beginning to talk herself through her written world.

In addition to her negotiation between visual and verbal media, Mitzi struggled with the relationship between her experienced and imaginary worlds. "Once-upon-a-time" framed her recalled ("real") as well as her imagined worlds, although their presence reflected Mitzi's awareness of the permeable boundary between these worlds. Like the other case study children, she seemed to resolve, at least partially, the tension between them by fictionalizing herself and others, while still retaining within her text the quality of her relationships with those others. Retaining that quality—that essential "psychic reality" (Bruner, 1986, p. 14)—allowed her to reveal confidences through her writing, not literally by sharing secrets, but by revealing more subtly the intimacies of her life.

Through this fictionalizing, Mitzi could also deliberately use her written worlds to help her take action in her ongoing social world. She learned to make connections with others in more complex ways than, for instance, by writing, "I like you." Incorporating another as a character in her story, revealing the thoughts and feelings of that character, and choosing a special topic for a story (e.g., "cats") were all ways of reaching out to others.

In time, Mitzi no longer consistently used her "once-upon-a-time" openings. She stepped more definitively into both her imaginary and real worlds ("About 4 days ago . . ."; "I said to my sister one day . . ."; "One day I came home from school . . ."). Still, even a recollection of a real

TABLE 8.5.   Movement, Stance, and Inclusion of Others in
             Mitzi's Written Products

	First Grade*		Second Grade**	
	% of products	No. of products	% of products	No. of products
Movement				
No movement	86	19	41	7
Implied movement	0	0	6	1
Movement	14	3	53	9
Stance				
Art notes/actor	0	0	6	1
Observer/actor	59	13	29	5
Observer	18	4	18	3
Actor	23	5	47	8
Inclusion of others				
"You"	36	8	6	1
Names of peers and family members	23	5	53	9

* n = 22.

** n = 17.

event could be fashioned into, in Britton's (1984) words "a celebratory plaque, a monument to experience" (p. 326). These monuments were fashioned with literary language ("Next door to me there lived . . ."; "One day . . . my mother greeted me in the nicest way . . . because she knew that it had been the most hardest day in my life.").

Mitzi, then, like all the case study children, became a more deliberate manipulator of multiple worlds. And, like her peers Regina, Jake, and Manuel, her growth as a writer was sensible, given her intentions and style as artist and as friend. The socially sensitive Mitzi abandoned, within her texts, the formulaic movement between the past and present. Rather, she began to construct socially involving experiences for her future readers by drawing upon her own past and present experiences. "Want me to read this to you?" she had asked Jenni, confident that her story would be well received by her close friend. The affective world that had surrounded Mitzi's journal entries began to permeate it and thus to support both artistic unity and social satisfaction.

EPILOGUE

Mitzi returned to the magnet school for her third-grade year. She renewed her friendships with Manuel, Regina, Maggie, and, especially, Sonia, all of whom were in the second/third-grade room. As in previous years, Mitzi continued to capture her friends' attention with talk about her family and friends.

During the seven formal observations in her classroom, the themes of Mitzi's talk were familiar—special trips with her mother, the bothersome baby brother, and lovable and loathsome animals—such as attacking dogs.

In the following conversation, Mitzi is telling the children at her table about her old dog's best friend—a dog named Ralph. Just as in other exchanges noted throughout this book, Mitzi is holding the attention of an inquisitive Manuel and a doubting Sonia.

MITZI: Ralph bit this old man because this man—old man was trying— They thought that this old man was try—was trying—to break in. He was just walking by and um and then they and then Ralph um happily killed him.

MANUEL: What?!

MITZI: Ralph happily ⌈ killed him.

SONIA: ⌊ For real?

MITZI: So um, he killed um—he killed, um—sued my mother but um my mother— He *tried* to sue my mother, but he didn't get away with it. So, uh—

MANUEL: Happy ending?

MITZI: No, but um— (whole group giggles)

MANUEL: Not being sued.

MITZI: But, um, but um—the—Ralph, but Ralph did get um—Ralph did have to be given away to, I think, the police.

Also as in previous years, these themes became incorporated into Mitzi's journal entries. In the following excerpted event, Mitzi's talk about pets was related to a specific journal entry she had just completed. In this entry, she had commented on the "liking" and "loving" of cats, a theme that continued to fill her journals:

> MITZI: I'm done.
>
> NICOLE: Can I read it? (Begins to read Mitzi's story.) I feel that animals are very special and I have much feeling /a/, bout—
>
> MITZI: about
>
> NICOLE: them, about them, about them. But I'm not a vegetar—
>
> MITZI: But I'm not a vegetarian.
>
> NICOLE: I'm not a vegetarian.
>
> NICOLE: ⌈ I love cats the most.
> MITZI: ⌊ I love cats the most.
>
> NICOLE: Cats are cute. (Nicole has finished reading.) You didn't say that you don't eat cats, but that you like them.

And Mitzi added the suggested lines.

Mitzi's entries clearly varied in style. They included personal commentaries, like the text just cited, and chatty reports of personal experiences, such as the following:

> On mother's day I gave my mother six presents, or was it Five, well any way, we went to Robert's park. . . . [May, Third Grade]

Most impressive of all was a lengthy story about the adventures of two best friends. This text revealed Mitzi's further artistic growth. It was unified and coherent, but Mitzi herself seemed freer to move within her imagined world, elaborating, explaining, and, perhaps, playing. Her opening lines skillfully set the stage for the initiating event:

A Piece of Gold

Once there were some best friends. Ann was the oldest one, Molly was the youngest one. **One day** they were walking home from school and they saw a fair so they went home to ask their mothers if they could go. but their mothers said, "No, you can't because we have to go to Santa Rosa." Molly and Ann lived in Napa Valley. "but you can go tomorrow." "O.K." said Molly and Ann. The next day they headed on down the street. (emphasis added) [April, Third Grade]

Mitzi's text world was an imaginary "Once-there-was" one. Yet its links to the real world were there, for example, in the use of realistic city names. Moreover, Mitzi seemed to be interacting with her readers, interrupting the progress of her story to explain about the current residence of Molly and Ann.

As she had begun to do in the second grade, Mitzi continued to reveal the "feelings" of her characters, by both labeling them and externalizing them in characters' actions. For instance, in the next passage from the story of Ann and Molly, Ann got "so excited" when she saw the fair, "she couldn't look." Characters' feelings were evident not only in their own words but also in how they spoke those words, a new development. She wrote, *Ann exclaimed, "GOLD!"* As apparent in Mitzi's emboldened *gold*, the graphic nature of print could be exploited to convey affect. (The use of such graphic stylistics is termed the "WOW phenomenon" by Cook-Gumperz and Gumperz, 1981, p. 102).

Mitzi highlighted the critical moments in her unfolding story through the manipulation of time. In the following text section, she explicitly labeled time's passage as "sudden" and "quick," from Molly's and Ann's point of view; but she slowed down time's passage for herself and her readers, so that they could carefully observe the girls' "quick" actions and reactions—each sentence added successive detail.[2] As the story continued, then, the journey to the fair was apparently uneventful, as Mitzi did not dwell on it. But then the action began:

> When they got there, Ann was so excited she couldn't look.
> Suddenly "look," said Molly, "everything is gone." Quickly Ann
> looked. All they could see was a tiny little piece of gold. Ann
> exclaimed, "GOLD!" Molly picked up the piece of gold and said,
> "this is not an ordinary piece of gold." Ann looked at it too and
> said, "It has a kidnapping signal on it." Ann and Molly were so
> scared, They started to run home.

But the girls were kidnapped! "Meanwhile," just as the girls were being "plopped into a big bag, . . . their moms were screaming because their children were gone." The police were called, and they rescued the children, who finally "went to the fair."

Amidst the textual renditions of alternatingly excited and scared little girls and their worrying mothers were illustrations of essential

---

[2]Dixon and Stratta's (1986) analysis of 12-to-18-year-olds' portrayal of fictional time informed my own analysis of the focal children's depiction of time.

objects. For example, one page contained only a large bag (the bag supposedly containing the little girls) on which was written "Help" in large print. Another page contained only a telephone receiver (the one used to call the police), while another had an archway on which was written "Fair." The story was thus particularized in time and space within the text itself, and the pictures each highlighted one aspect that symbolized an important subepisode of the story.

Mitzi's social style during journal time, then, remained essentially the same across her primary-grade years. She was a child with much feeling for people and animals. And she told stories of the things done to and by those beings, stories that emphasized the emotional life: Children brought each other comfort and hassles, giggles and tears, as did adults and children. Yet, as an artist, Mitzi's feelings were not initially embodied in written renditions of characters' actions and reactions. Any reported feelings belonged primarily to herself—Mitzi, the "I," was the one who liked, loved, and hated.

By third grade, she had become an accomplished eight-year-old author, who could still foreground those feelings in her written commentaries ("I love cats.") but could also infuse them into her imaginary stories, energizing her characters and coloring their experience of time and space. The emotional landscape particularized through the social talk and actions surrounding Mitzi's productions was clearly evident in the talk and actions contained within it.

Perhaps, too, this process of detailing an imaginary world reverberated in the talk and actions within her experienced and ongoing social world. "Ralph happily killed him," Mitzi had said to her friends, sounding very literate with her -ly adverb. "Happy ending?" Manuel had inquired, sounding as if he were discussing an imagined world. The real and the imagined, the individual memories and group constructions, the word pictures and pictures of words—all are the essential instruments orchestrated by authors, artists, and friends.

9

Reflections:
The Multiple Worlds
of Child Writers

In the prologue's opening anecdote, Maggie and Manuel reflected on the beginnings and ends of a long "thinking cap." The beginning, Manuel explained, is a matter of the observer's perspective. Through this book, I have offered a new perspective on young children's writing development, particularly their story writing, within the context of a special kind of community—a classroom. This view evolved from long looks at individual children participating in the artistic, social, and intellectual life of their school. In this chapter I no longer foreground the case studies but, rather, the perspective on writing that they engendered.

I first clarify that perspective by comparing its angle with those of other possible theoretical approaches to writing growth. I discuss the developmental tensions children confront as they discover how and what written language "means" as a symbolic medium and a social tool (Halliday, 1977). The next section highlights another sort of tension, that between the particulars of *a child's* life and the interpretive power of generalizations about *children*. I aim in this section to illustrate the necessity—the theoretical appropriateness—of this tension, which is inherent in qualitative, observational research (Genishi, 1982). In the third chapter section, I consider both these sorts of tensions from the points of view of those whose daily lives are filled with the stories of children and with children as stories—the teachers of young children. I conclude with some thoughts about children as friends and writers.

PERSPECTIVES ON BEGINNINGS

Visions of literacy's beginnings have changed dramatically over the last decade. When significant professional concern with young children's literacy began in the 1930s, a five-to-seven-year-old child stood in a picture frame, alone and "preliterate" (Johnston, 1984). Over time, researchers and educators developed varied sorts of tests as lenses through which to view that child, as they searched for the essential prerequisites that signaled the child's "readiness"—visual and auditory perception skills, letter-name knowledge, and vocabulary breadth.

Beginning most notably in the 1970s, educators observed that indeed young children do read and write, even before they have received formal instruction, although in their own "emergent" ways (Clay, 1966; Hall, 1987). Thus, the literacy behaviors of preschool and early elementary school children have been allowed into the frame, as the "picture" has given way to a number of films—documentaries focused on varied aspects of literacy development. Research questions have centered on children's reading and writing behaviors or on children's interactions with adults during literacy activities (McNamee, 1987; Teale, 1987). Questions that researchers have asked include, How do children's early scribbles evolve into conventional print (Clay, 1975)? Into conventional spelling and punctuation (Cazden, Cordeiro, & Giacobbe, 1985; Edelsky, 1983; Read, 1975)? And into conventional genres (King & Rentel, 1981; Newkirk, 1987)? How do children develop "expert" planning and revision processes and, particularly, what instructional circumstances seem to foster these processes (Calkins, 1983; Graves, 1983; Sowers, 1985)?

In this book, the observed children departed in some ways from the genre of developmental films about literacy. They brought each other into focus, so that the documentary on literacy seemed at times a drama about children's social lives. The children were companions and co-workers in an environment filled with both adult demands and their own desires to be competent and special in each other's eyes.

Further, Margaret and the children suggested a different theme for the developmental film. As discussed in Chapter 4, using a symbol system involves both mapping skills (being able to use culturally agreed-upon conventions for representing meanings, such as the spelling and punctuation conventions of written English) and being able to capture and communicate personal experiences. Most studies of young writers have focused on the development of conventions, but the focus of this observed school and of Margaret herself was relatively less on the children's mastery of conventions and relatively more on children's "self-expression." I, too, then, as camera person and editor, found myself examining the children's selves as expressed in their drawings, talk, and texts—their often imaginary worlds.

Thus, in studying the efforts of Regina, Jake, Manuel, Mitzi, and the other young writers who shared this classroom, the focus was not on their writing alone, because writing does not evolve only from writing. Rather, the focus was on the meanings each child intended to communicate, that is, on the symbolic worlds being deliberately formed. And those worlds were revealed in the children's drawing, talking, and playing, as well as in their writing. Moreover, each child's symbolizing was seen as an expression of that child and shaped by the child's ongoing experiences in school and by her or his reflections on the wider world.

In brief, from the perspective of this book, writing development is viewed as evolving within and shaped by children's interactions with other symbolic media and other people, including their peers. Both the developmental challenges children face as writers and the resources they lean upon are found in the varied symbolic and social worlds within which they, and all authors, work.

This way of viewing writing development leads to a re-viewing, a rethinking, of two basic developmental concepts or, more particularly, developmental relationships—that between embedded and disembedded language and that between an understanding of print's function and an understanding of its inner workings.

Rethinking the "Embeddedness" of Young Children's Story Writing

For young children, print is meaningful within the context of the activity—the talk and action—of which it is a part. A letter is meaningful because of the interactional activities surrounding its sending and its receiving; a list is sensible because of the talk and action accompanying its writing and its reading. And, more relevant to this book, the meaning of a young child's written story, which may consist of squiggly lines and circles, may be found in the talk and drawings that accompany its production and eventual reading.

It is tempting, then, to describe children's writing development as a process of separation, in which children "disembed" or "decontextual-ize" their written work from other symbolic media, so that it will be sensible to anyone in any situation (Donaldson, 1978; Olson, 1977).

There is, though, another way of thinking about children's development as writers. From the children's point of view, writing is not embedded in their lives as it may be in the lives of adults steeped in a literary tradition. That is, for young children, texts do not have the functional power implicit in adults' perceptions of written language. As suggested in Chapter 1 and illustrated throughout the book, within the context of story writing in school, children may gradually realize print's social and evaluative functions, and this understanding supports their efforts to find new ways to capture their experiences and engage in social interactions within the texts themselves. The expansion ("disembeddedness") of children's written texts thus comes from the expansion of the social worlds within which those texts figure (are "embedded").

Rethinking the Developmental Role of "Function"

This vision of children discovering the functional power of writing leads to questions, not only about notions of embedded and disembedded language, but also about the relationship between function and form. Children are often viewed as attaining "functional knowledge" about written language *before* they attain knowledge of exactly how that written system works (i.e., function comes before form) (Mason, 1980; Taylor, 1983). By functional knowledge, educators and researchers most often mean an understanding of print's representational function—that "particular and meaningful words and messages have printed counterparts" (McCormick & Mason, 1986, p. 91). Sometimes, however, this knowledge is more broadly defined as an awareness of the purposes for which people use that print, for example, to provide information or pleasure for others (Holdaway, 1979; Taylor, 1983).

This conception of the developmental process—that of function driving form—is sensible. As noted, children can write stories composed of pictures, talk, and scribbled writing well before they can write a convention such as "once upon a time." And yet, the young authors examined herein suggested a more dynamic relationship—a dialectic— between children's understanding of written language's functional possibilities and their understanding of its systemic workings. Within the context of their daily journal time, the observed children went beyond a grasp of print's representational function to discover its multifunctional power.

To make sensible this changed perspective, I return to the Vygotskian concepts introduced in Chapter 1. A child's developing knowledge of a system, such as written language, acquires new characteristics because of "changes in interfunctional connections and relationships" (Vygotsky, 1987, p. 299). In other words, children's ways of writing change as children begin to sense new functional possibilities in their activity, ends that were previously fulfilled through other means. Children's sense of what can be accomplished through writing evolves as others respond, both playfully and critically, to their efforts. New ways of writing engender new responses, which in turn engender the discovery of new functional possibilities.

In Margaret's classroom, children initially used writing primarily either to represent a nonnarrative, imaginary world—one existing through their deliberate symbolic efforts—or to comment on the world represented in their pictures. The majority of the kindergarteners' written texts (67%) were "art notes"—comments on their drawn pictures (see Appendix D). On the other hand, the children used drawing and its accompanying talk to serve an interactional as well as a representational function; children might, for example, engage in dramatic play with their friends *during* drawing. In addition, drawing and talk could also serve to evaluate the real world, as the children argued about the sensibleness of each other's drawings.

Children's story writing gradually came to fulfill these same functions. Their simple texts of existence, affection, or description ("This is the flower princess.") were indeed the seedlings of written worlds to come. More powerful literary action came about at least in part because of the children's involvement with other symbolic media—imaginative play, narrative and dramatic talk, and drawing—and with other people.

To elaborate, both the classroom structure, organized by Margaret, and the children's spontaneous interest in each other's work helped their written worlds, like their drawn ones, to become legitimate objects of attention for their teacher, their friends, and themselves. Teacher and peers focused their attention on the compatibility of their drawn and sometimes spoken worlds, on the one hand, and their text worlds on the other and thus supported their differentiation of these diverse symbolic media. "It [the text] can't say that," worried Regina, as she compared the pictured little girl holding up her dress with the written-about child who was unaware of the mud on her legs.

In addition, the children's reading of their own and each other's texts led to joint reflections on real-world rationalizations for those texts, including in that reality both the objective world of things and events and the more subjective world of feelings and relationships. ("I have a witch mother," said Jenni, in response to Mitzi's story about "a witch" who was "my mom.")

Further, from the beginning of their schooling experience, social interaction about the content of their written worlds *followed* writing, as Margaret guided the children's sharing of their work with the larger group. Gradually, however, the children's responses to each other *during* writing helped the texts themselves to become places where not only were meanings represented, but social interactions occurred. The children began to discover that not only could they elicit others' attention and approval through their texts, they could also manipulate the response or, more accurately, that interaction with their texts. "Just at the very end when they're [the readers] just so happy . . . they read the entire story and they loved it, I get blown up," said Manuel after he had played through Jake's story writing with him. The children were thus learning how authors themselves guide readers' interactions with their stories via the maps—the textual hints—they create (Bruner, 1986).

In the children's growth, however, there were struggles. The focal children's unexpected oral and written excursions into varied space and time structures (unexpected shifts of tense and author stance, movement realized in talk but only implied in text) suggested that young authors wrestle with, and at times get caught on the borders between, differing symbolic and social space and time structures, differing worlds. Worlds first discovered through talk and pictures do not so easily fit on a page. Current feelings and past experiences must be transformed if they are to find expression within imaginary worlds. And, to add to the challenge, those imaginary worlds, often set in the distant past, are the author's means for interacting with future (and, for the observed young authors, with their present, sitting-right-beside-them) readers. Writing thus presents very confusing challenges of time and space.

To meet these challenges, the observed children depended upon familiar activities—drawing, talking, and playing with their friends—but they did these things in new ways. They began to use talk with others—dialogue—not only outside but inside their text worlds, allowing them to move more easily through time and to reveal the inner worlds of their characters. They began to sequence their pictures to capture movement, and they began as well to write before they drew, using drawing to cooperate with and extend the written rendition of their story. Most strikingly, they themselves entered into their imaginary worlds, and they brought their friends and their experiences with them. They thus found firmer ground upon which to act, feel, and move forward within the imaginative realm, while maintaining connections with their social and experienced realms. Their lively social, intellectual, and artistic lives did not simply surround their written texts but began to be mediated by them.

For Jake, Mitzi, and Manuel especially, story writing became a way of representing meaning, of interacting with others, and of reflecting on personal experiences. Moreover, these multiple functions began to mesh with one another. The most vivid and engaging written representations of story worlds were those that rendered characters talkative, scenes imaginable (picturable), plots sensible. Further, the *imaginary* realms that engaged their friends were often those that captured for the author some *real* quality of their shared world—such as Jake's dynamic and playful adventures, Mitzi's worries about acts of friendship and loyalty, and Manuel's reflections on nature. The broad power of written language—its capacity for action in multiple worlds—thus supported and was supported by the children's differentiation of the symbolic tools of talk, text, and pictures and by their efforts to render sound and images in socially engaging and sensible written worlds.

THEORETICAL PERSPECTIVES ON VARIATION

In the preceding section, I presented a view of writing development emphasizing the sorts of transitions and challenges children confront, not the particular behaviors they exhibit. As first discussed in Chapter 4, children's behaviors vary even when they are engaged in a seemingly identical activity. And yet, it was the close study of individual children's particular behaviors that led to the broad theoretical frame suggested here. In effect, the research method involved alternating observational perspectives, moving close to one child and then moving back, to reflect comparatively on all of the case study children.

The differences among the observed children seemed rooted in their very individuality—in their styles as symbolizers and socializers. Indeed, a central idea of this book has been that an individual's ways of interacting with people and symbolic materials is an organizing force in writing development (Dyson, 1987a). These children had different styles—their journal activity was supported by different symbolic and social processes—and thus their ways of carrying out this activity differed as well.

The children's initial approaches to journal composing reflected their preferred ways of responding to a new activity. And, as in studies of children's stylistic variations in other areas of symbol development, these children's symbolizing activity gradually became more complex (Bussis et al., 1985; Nelson, 1985; Wolf & Gardner, 1979). That is, over time, individual children began to incorporate into their own approach to the composing activity various stances first made visible by others. It was, in fact, such changes that suggested the guiding metaphor of this book—that learning to compose written stories is learning to negotiate the boundaries among multiple worlds.

To illustrate, I summarize here the progress of the two most strikingly different children—Jake and Manuel. In the first grade, Jake

crossed symbolic boundaries to compose his imaginary worlds, interweaving talking and drawing. He himself adopted the role of actor in
those imaginary worlds, playing his part with visual swirls and dramatized words. Jake's completed drawings shaped his writing—he "copied
offa" his pictures. Jake crossed social boundaries, too, incorporating
peers into his spoken and drawn worlds as fellow actors.

Manuel kept firm boundaries between drawing and other symbolic
media, and he adopted the role of careful director of those media. His
written stories were not copied from his pictures but were deliberately
structured narrative worlds. Manuel kept social boundaries as well; his
peers were his audience, not his collaborators.

In time, Jake became more aware of the boundaries between drawing, talking, and writing; he attempted to coordinate and negotiate those
boundaries, intending to capture sound effects and visual action in
printed texts. Indeed, Jake's first extended texts incorporated his dramatic and spoken dialogues into his written stories. In time, he also began
to differentiate and more deliberately negotiate social boundaries; his
peers were becoming not only collaborators but audience, an audience
whose reactions could be anticipated and manipulated. At times he
sounded like Manuel, a director wondering if his story would seem
complete, logical.

Manuel also began to coordinate his symbolic media; his text worlds
were elaborated as he rendered his visual world in written words, and his
written stories were enriched by his visual portrayals of hard-to-verbalize
feelings and themes. His talk, too, suggested that he was beginning to use
his text not only to please his audience but also to guide their interaction
with—their construction of—his imaginary world. Manuel's talk suggested that he also was entering his text worlds; at times he sounded like
Jake, orally conveying his characters' feelings and actions.

Focusing on children with such different ways of using symbolic and
social resources illuminated the nature of learning to compose imaginary
worlds. Whether a child melds together or firmly separates symbolic
worlds, eventually the boundaries between symbol systems must be deliberately negotiated; similarly, whether peers are invited into a child's
imaginary world or kept at the borders, social boundaries, too, must be
differentiated and negotiated. And, whether given to performing the role
of director or actor, in order to develop as a writer the child must both
direct the unfolding action in the created realm and—at least internally—
enact that drama, feeling the human responses that energize it.

Indeed, this dynamic vision of development is sensible, given our
understanding of literary discourse (Bruner, 1986) and of symbol develop-

ment (Nelson & Nelson, 1978; Werner & Kaplan, 1963; Wolf & Gardner, 1979; Wolf et al., 1988). There is no reason to isolate children's literary development from that of symbol development in general (a process of differentiating the features of each medium and integrating those features into a system) or from the sort of discourse they are learning to produce, a discourse of truthful lies that, despite the aloneness that often accompanies its reading and writing, is an antidote to loneliness and isolation.

Even acknowledging, however, that the nature of children's literacy tasks—and thus particular child behaviors—will vary, the essential developmental challenges seem generalizable. For example, young children may write stories on blank paper, which does not physically separate drawing from writing. In such a task, they may mix media (Dyson, 1982; Gundlach, 1982; Harste et al., 1984), as in Sara's picture (Figure 1.2) in Chapter 1, where the written words and pictures are all enveloped in one told story. Nonetheless, the children's developmental questions remain the same: What of the story is actually recorded? In what symbolic media? How can the interaction with others that surrounds the writing be incorporated within the written words themselves? How can imaginary worlds be made sensible to others? Such questions would seem to arise both from the children's own actions as drawers, talkers, and writers, and from the social responses their work engenders. The questions activate the tensions inherent in the children's multimedia efforts, and those tensions, those productive conflicts, set learning and exploration on its way (Piaget & Inhelder, 1969).

And what if a child is in a classroom where writing is expected, but without any other accompanying media? Again, the basic developmental challenges would seem the same, although the symbolic and social resources would certainly differ. With fewer alternatives, the children may experience fewer conflicts. For example, Cazden (1971) commented on the composing of young British children using the Breakthrough to Literacy program, in which children select and arrange word cards to compose sentences. Since these children did not create sentences to accompany their drawings, they did not use "This is a _____" sentences. Yet, whether the text is "My cousin is skinny" (Cazden, 1979, p. 138) or "This is my cousin. He is skinny," the composing child must still discover the precise nature of the meaning rendered in written text and thus communicated to others.

Ultimately, to become composers, children must learn how to bring their ways of experiencing their symbolic and social worlds into their texts, so that each child's "cast of mind" is more fully evident in written words (Geertz, 1983). In Margaret's classroom, therefore, it made developmental as well as literary sense—it made the case history satisfying—that Jake's first elaborate stories were energized by oral adventures and Manuel's by sensitive visual images. It seemed sensible, too, that Manuel's texts achieved narrative *depth* through their *connections* with his pictures and that Regina's texts achieved narrative *space* through their *differentiation* from her pictures. And how fitting that Mitzi's written stories became gradually more sophisticated renderings of critical moments in relationships—moments of loving, hating, befriending. Each child's development was not predictable, but it was sensible, given a theoretical frame that places writing development within the context of each child's symbolic and social processes.

Indeed, researchers and educators observing children in different sorts of literacy environments describe selected children as achieving a written "voice"—a literary personality (Bissex, 1980; Calkins, 1987, Edelsky, 1986; Genishi & Dyson, 1984). For many children, this voice emerges toward the end of the primary-grade years, when their texts are longer, more fluid, more filled with visual images and talkative characters structured with written language.

This emphasis on individuality contributes to an understanding of certain key issues in writing development that focus on variation both within and across children: What is the function of repetition and variation within one child's work? Across children, are there fixed or variable patterns to children's development of writing conventions? In the remainder of this section, I briefly consider these issues.

Learning As Repetition and Variation

Theories of child development tend to view the process of growth either from the inside out or from the outside in; that is, they tend to emphasize how children's internal processes influence their external actions or how their external interactions structure their internal processes.

It is the former approach that stresses the developmental meaning of repetition and variation in children's behavior (Piaget & Inhelder, 1969). From this perspective, which emphasizes children's internal worlds, repetition allows children to consolidate their actions, to experience control over them, and thus to form a firm basis for further development, for reorganization of those actions to meet newly perceived external demands. In many different areas of child development, including children's acquisition of drawing schemata (Goodnow, 1977; Smith, 1983), grammatical structures (Slobin, 1979), and conceptions of the written encoding system (Clay, 1975; Ferreiro & Teberosky, 1982), children are described as repeating and gradually transforming forms already controlled. In the area of graphic symbolism especially, children seem to study their own handiwork. "Flower," a child might say, sensing a new possibility in his or her drawn circles and lines.

In the case histories of Margaret's children, repetition was clearly evident. To begin with, most children had recurrent topics that dominated their journals. Repetition of writing topics was interrelated with repetition of drawing topics. For example, Regina's tendency to draw little girls contributed to her tendency to write about them. Similarly, Jake enjoyed drawing vehicles, especially jets and bubble cars and, not surprisingly, this is what he tended to draw and write about in his journal as well.

For children who relied on drawing as a resource for writing content (e.g., Regina and Jake), increasingly eiaborate pictures seemed to contribute to increasingly elaborate texts (Graves, 1983; Zalusky, 1983). But it was not simply that the drawing was becoming more elaborate, but also that the talk surrounding the drawing was becoming more elaborate. These meanings, spilling over the picture frame, became not only a resource but also a source of tension: Of all that was said and drawn, what should or could be written? How might certain kinds of meanings—like sound effects or swirling lines—be written?

Not only topics were repeated and varied. Children also could repeat, with variations, the very content and structure of their texts. There were, for example, Mitzi's "I like" stories and Jake's bubble-car adventures. Such repetition allowed children a ready plan for action and thus seemed to contribute both to greater writing fluency and to greater ease in spelling frequently written words. Children like Sonia and Manuel, who had more variation in their story content and structure, tended to be slower writers.

Repetition also allowed a basis for elaboration. Jake's descriptive stories about vehicles or adventurous men began to push against his pictures' frames; hence, his figures' progressive actions (what was being done) became predicted or implied actions (what was going to be done) and, eventually, successive actions being accomplished. Mitzi's personal likes became her characters' likes (and hates) and, eventually, particular moments of liking or hating.

The explanation for these changes in the children's work could not be found only in the children's interactions with their texts. As argued throughout this book, changes in children's story writing were interrelated with shifts in their conceptions of the functions fulfilled by those stories, and these modifications were supported by their interaction with

264 MULTIPLE WORLDS OF CHILD WRITERS

other people and with other media. Written symbols were differentiated from drawn and spoken ones and, at the same time, those written symbols began to serve functions previously fulfilled by other media. Children could deliberately use imaginative stories as avenues for social interaction and for reflection on the real world. For example, dialogue began to appear more frequently in their stories, and it resembled the talk that the children acted out with friends. Fictionalized selves and others also began to appear, as the children adopted literary roles, just as they had done in their play. More detailed word pictures also occurred, as the children worked to make sensible texts, just as they had worked to make sensible if imaginary pictures, sometimes in response to inquisitive or critical peers.

With such a view of development, I return to a Vygotskian frame, but one that differs from those emphasizing children's independent enactment of activities originally performed in collaboration with others (e.g., Brown & Ferrara, 1985). Rather, my view stresses the internal reconstruction of those activities.

Consider, for example, how it is that children come to understand the discourse features of stories. Clearly, as many point out, children initially "learn" these features because they have read books with adults and been read to (Holdaway, 1979; Teale, 1982; Wells, 1985). Yet, ultimately, these features must be analyzed and incorporated into each child's evolving understanding of what it means to compose a "story," just as children gradually analyze and reconstruct most features of their language into an increasingly more useful, powerful system (Lindfors, 1987; Pappas & Brown, 1987; Villaume, 1988).

In Margaret's classroom, the discourse features most in evidence were the language routines of story writers (and tellers)—conventions such as "once upon a time" and "one day." These discourse features could be catalysts for thought and for productive confusion, as Mitzi so vividly illustrated. She originally used "once upon a time" as an opening for her texts, whether or not they were imaginative stories. Her routine opening, however, came to be a textual marker for her apparent deliberation, both in interaction with peers and then on her own, about what in fact was "imaginary" and what was "real."

Similarly, Regina's written-language-like dialogue (i.e., "she said" rather than "she is" or "she was saying") was an external marker for her differentiation of the space and time dimensions of stories from those of pictures. Manuel's adverbials similarly marked his own deliberate attempts to negotiate between pictured and told stories.

Thus, "book language" or "written language registers"—including written dialogue, formulaic openings, adverbs, and past tenses—are not just ways of using language that are learned from being read to. These features help individual authors mark the permeable boundaries of an imaginary and textual world. The boundaries between imagined and experienced, monologues and dialogues, and multisensory images and written renditions are wrestled with by all authors.

In sum, writing development indeed involves repetition and variation of forms the child already controls, as today's actions contain the possibilities for tomorrow's. But this gradual evolution of the child's work is shaped by social processes learned in interaction with others; moreover, even particular discourse features learned in interaction with others are not simply imitated. They, too, are subject to—and the catalysts of—children's deliberations about the nature of text worlds and their own role in those worlds.

In fact, this would seem to be so not only for specific discourse features of a certain genre—such as stories—but for whole genres themselves. From the observed children's point of view, the essential writing issue did not seem to be how to compose a conventional "story"—a narrative about an imaginary world—but what sort of stance or role to adopt vis-à-vis their social, experienced, and symbolic worlds. Imaginary worlds are not necessarily in a narrative form, nor are they in any way "opposites" of the "real" worlds of expository texts. Indeed, the picture-dependent art notes that I have viewed as early stories are very similar to those Newkirk (1987) describes as early expository texts. Undoubtedly both views can be correct.

For example, imagine that a child has drawn a picture of a cowboy and then writes "cowboy" or "This is a cowboy." It is difficult from the product alone to judge whether or not the child's intention is to represent a "real" or a "pretend" world. The child's talk might suggest that the cowboy is an imagined one, with particular characteristics and/or engaged in specific actions ("This guy is going to the rodeo."). The child's talk might instead suggest that the cowboy is primarily a representative of real-world cowboys ("Cowboys have big boots."). Moreover, the boundary between the imagined and the real is permeable, especially for young children. The key to writing development thus is not what is written on the page but what the child is trying to accomplish in the world beyond the page.

Pattern and Variation in Writing Development

Rather than examining variation in one child's behavior over time, in this section I highlight variation across children in how they develop as writers. The literature on beginning writing presents contradictory messages about this variation, that is, about whether or not there is a fixed sequence of emerging writing behaviors (at least, among children learning an alphabetic written system). This issue of developmental order has centered on children's control of writing conventions, in other words, on what is on the paper. Some argue that there is no such fixed order (e.g., Clay, 1975; Dyson, 1985; Harste et al., 1984); others provide carefully documented descriptions of evolving behavior (Ferreiro & Teberosky, 1982; King & Rentel, 1981; Read, 1986).

There is sense, however, to the apparent contradiction. As previously discussed, most documentaries of writing development have presented a single aspect of that development. Indeed, most researchers who argue for a relatively invariant order focus on children's understanding of the encoding system—their ways of spelling messages or, more broadly, their understanding of the relationship between a read or spoken message, on the one hand, and written graphics, on the other. For example, Read (1986) analyzed the phonological basis of young children's alphabetic spelling, while Ferreiro and Teberosky (1982) investigated the nature of children's prealphabetic encoding. Within any one strand of written language knowledge, patterns in how children perform particular sorts of writing tasks can be identified.

On the other hand, researchers who do not find a fixed order of development are also not focusing on a "fixed" phenomenon; that is, they have not focused on one aspect of children's development of writing conventions. Rather, they have tended to study children's literacy behaviors more holistically, examining children's engagement in a variety of activities in home or classroom. There is a difference between studying children's displays of a particular strand of writing knowledge (as revealed by a particular task) and studying children engaged in the actual activity of orchestrating that knowledge to compose a message, encoded in letter graphics, for a particular purpose (Bussis et al., 1985; Dyson, 1987a).

As illustrated by Regina, Jake, Manuel, and Mitzi, writing is an enormously complex activity, involving the orchestration of message-creating and message-encoding processes. Children may simplify this process within any one writing activity by focusing upon certain aspects of the system rather than others (Jacob, 1985; Weaver, 1982). Children's ways of managing literacy tasks depend upon their work style, the support system within which the tasks take place, and individual children's overriding intentions (Dyson, 1985, 1987a). Thus, the ways in which children display and make use of any one aspect of their written language knowledge will vary.

To illustrate, primary-grade children's major spelling strategy is often described as phonetic: Children sound out their messages phoneme by phoneme. (For a thorough discussion of the literature on spelling, see Read, 1986.) In Margaret's classroom, the children's use of phonologically based encoding varied, and this was not attributable in any simple way to individual children's developmental level. Indeed, when asked to spell unknown words, with no social support, as they were in my encoding assessment tasks, the children could invent phonologically based or prealphabetic spellings using strategies described in the literature (see Appendix C). The children's variation in actual use of phonological spelling can be explained at least in part both by individual children's styles and by the nature of the classroom literacy activity.

First, as already discussed, the children's differing ways of interacting with symbolic materials and with other people influenced their ways of composing imaginary worlds, including their ways of planning and encoding messages. For example, since Jake and Regina initially leaned on their drawn pictures for help in formulating written stories, they were relatively free to concentrate on encoding while writing. Mitzi did not formulate verbal stories while drawing, but she initially wrote repetitive sentence patterns; thus, encoding posed few problems for her. On the other hand, Manuel at first had great difficulty encoding; relative to the other children, he rarely engaged in phonological analysis, relying instead on requested and recalled spellings. But Manuel also devoted relatively greater attention to planning his written messages, and he attempted the most ambitious stories, as he neither "copied offa the picture" nor used repetitive sentence patterns.

Second, in Margaret's classroom, the children participated in the same task from kindergarten through third grade. During the kindergarten, the children built up expectations for "journal" language. Further, in the first/second-grade classroom, when independent writing during journal time was more generally expected, the first graders sat amidst the more experienced second graders, who not only could provide needed words but who also were producing relatively extended texts. No first grader began independent journal writing by producing labels, an initial writing form reported by other classroom observers (Newkirk, 1987; Newkirk & Atwell, 1982).[1] The children's longer messages may have made them more apt initially to request spellings; in fact, visually recalled and

---

[1]Despite the dearth of label writing during journal time, labels do indeed seem to be critical in young children's discovery of the nature of the written-language encoding system. Certainly, in Margaret's kindergarten, children were interested in and often wrote a special kind of label—people's names. For further discussion of the importance of labels, see (in addition to Newkirk, 1987) Dyson (1982) and Ferreiro & Teberosky (1982).

requested spellings tended to dominate in the children's initial independent encoding efforts within the journal activity.[2] And too, for Margaret,
the guiding objective of journal time was to encourage children's self-
expression; she did not define writing as dependent upon independent
spelling (cf. Graves, 1983, p. 184). Spelling help was given when requested, although Margaret often encouraged children to figure out
spellings for themselves.

Despite their initial reliance on visual encoding, all children began
to analyze the spelling system, and phonologically based spellings increased over the course of the project. This increase was due in part to the
children's growing experience with written language, and perhaps their
greater involvement with their writing made them less likely to interrupt
that process to seek spelling help. And, as noted in Chapter 3, the ability
to spell independently became a matter of competence within the peer
group as well. As with comprehending the nature of story language,
ready-made information such as recalled or copied spellings must eventually be made sensible within an evolving internal understanding, in this
case, of how the alphabetic encoding system works. (For a discussion of
the critical importance of children's independent analysis of the written-
language system, see Dyson, 1984). Jake's *and*, for example, was one day
spelled *"an* (with the quotation mark taking the place of the *d*, he
reasoned)—a mark of Jake's analysis and integration of information into
a systemic understanding of spelling.

In brief, as in learning any system, young writers search for order—
the interrelated structure of parts (e.g., letters, words, sentences) and the
rules governing the arrangement of those parts in varied contexts. The
developmental literature, whether dealing with children's invention of

---

[2]In another project, focusing on kindergarteners' spontaneous writing at a classroom
writing center, I observed a variety of encoding strategies (Dyson, 1983, 1985). When
attempting to encode long messages, the observed children were most apt to use the least
analytical encoding procedures; for example, they would use "cursive" or wavy line writing
or request spellings from others. (For similar findings, see Sulzby, 1985.) In Margaret's
classroom, the observed writing task was not so open-ended. The children were not asked
"just to write" but to produce an illustrated story to be read by teacher and peers. To
produce their long messages, they did not choose to use encoding procedures they themselves regarded as unintelligible by others. As they concentrated on their long messages, they
focused initially on analyzing the sentence into words, rather than breaking words into
sounds. Individual children's experience with and interpretation of the task, then, contributed to their initial use of requested or recalled words, a writing strategy observed in other
studies of young schoolchildren (e.g., Amarel, 1980; McCaig, 1981). In a more open-ended
activity, like free writing at a classroom writing center, Margaret's children may have made
different choices.

words or worlds, illuminates the general nature of the challenges children face as composers. But within any one task, children will orchestrate—draw upon—their developing knowledge in diverse ways. Thus, the extent to which children's writing displays any written language convention in expected ways depends upon the extent to which children choose or are able to attend to that convention. Across differing literacy tasks, children might manage a specific writing task differently, and thus attend in different ways to its varied aspects.

Such variation suggests that there can be no definition of how young children write, nor any simple prescription for how teachers should help. There seems to be little reason to support, and much reason to refrain from, expecting all children to carry out literacy tasks in similar ways; nor would there seem to be any one sort of literacy task that will help all children learn all aspects of literacy.

To elaborate, I am not sure what would have happened in Margaret's classroom if Manuel had been required rather than encouraged to "sound 'em out," or if Mitzi had been told to incorporate the parts of a "good" story into her entries. If we as educators are too rigid in what we expect from children of varied age and grade levels or in what we conceive of as "good," we risk cutting children off from "the seat of their best judgement" (Bussis et al., 1985, p. 196).

With these last comments, I have turned to the teacher's response to the variation of child writers and thus to my final topic.

SUPPORTING CHILDREN'S DEVELOPMENT AS AUTHORS, ARTISTS, AND FRIENDS

In the preceding sections of this chapter, I have reviewed the developmental challenges children face as composers of imaginary worlds, as well as the challenges researchers and educators face as they seek to understand children's overall development by studying the rich and varied behavior of individual child writers. In the following pages, I consider the pedagogical implications of these challenges, beginning with a familiar image for early childhood teachers, one of children at play.

It's early morning in the dramatic play center, and kindergartener Regina, the "mom," is trying to get her "boys" to eat their breakfast.

REGINA: Eat your eggs. (to Jason, the "father") Even if we take them out to dinner they don't behave.

. . .

See? These kids don't know how to act.

JASON: I know. They don't know how to eat.

REGINA: That's why I don't know what to do. (dials the phone)
         Could you please take the kids to jail? They didn't eat
         their food.

Helping Children Play Inside Written Words

The overriding metaphor in this book has been that of multiple
worlds—of children learning to join together to construct an imagined
world by transforming their real one. And yet, as Regina and her peers
demonstrated, this is what children do early on in their play (Garvey,
1977; Genishi & Di Paolo, 1982). We might imagine Regina dashing off a
note to "her children's" teacher or adding the need for more eggs to a
grocery list; that is, we can imagine her playing *with* written language in
her story of the bad children and the eggs. But it is more difficult to
imagine Regina, as a kindergartener, playing with others *inside* deliberately composed written words.

Educator and author Vivian Paley (1988) argues that young children's composed stories are only empty shells until those stories are
brought to life through the children's dramatic play: "The unacted story
is the unlived-in story" (see also Paley, 1981, 1986). In her classroom,
Paley forms a stage area with masking tape on the rug and then, inside
that stage, the children literally play out—and in—their dictated stories.

My question, then, has been, How do children learn to play with
others inside the words themselves? That is, how does this living outside
the texts become transformed within and by them, so that children can
have play partners who are not physically standing on the stage with
them, and so that the nuances of their actions and talk can be rendered
into black-and-white squiggles?

To answer that question, I have portrayed, throughout this book,
children confronting and resolving the challenges inherent in this question. Through their actions and their talk with others about those actions, children set in motion the conflicts that lead to their own questions
and resolutions. Children thus learn to differentiate the potential stage
within the words, to bring others inside those words, and to make the
action on that stage sensible to their play partners. They have to, for, in
this new kind of play, their partners must cooperate without the lively
role negotiation and action justification that are found in the three-
dimensional variety. (e.g., "Let's pretend that . . ." and "No, don't laugh,
because doctors do not laugh." See Genishi & Di Paolo, 1982, p. 62. For
related work on older children's play during writing, see Daiute, 1988.)

The experiences of Regina, Jake, Manuel, Mitzi, and their peers suggest that, just as in other developmental areas, children benefit from learning situations that allow them to explore and to experience in their own ways the symbolic and social medium they are learning, and they benefit as well from "authentic" experiences that highlight, rather than obscure, the nature of that medium (Edelsky, 1986; Goodman & Goodman, 1979). Regina and her peers seemed to orchestrate their artistic experiences spontaneously during journal time, in a classroom and in a school that provided them with opportunities for drama, painting, song, and literature. Many teachers provide children with deliberately structured experiences with the arts that may well augment and nurture children's own orchestrations.

Since young children are growing, not only as writers but as users of varied media, they need such opportunities to discover the interrelated purposes and powers of all these forms of expression. Children can use their written texts as scripts to be acted out (Paley, 1981), or they can talk and write after enacting a drama, thus shaping their lived experiences into words (Wagner, 1985). In either case, children can begin literally to experience the time and space dimensions of their linear, printed words. Too, children might visualize the settings of both their own and professional authors' texts through drawing; capture those texts' moods through movement and rhythm; and feel characters' emotions through their own dramatized facial expressions, bodily movements, and raised voices. As Margaret's children illustrated, in attempting to convey meanings in several media, children are given opportunities to see what is lost and what is gained when multidimensional worlds are shaped with linear strings of words. (Among the pedagogical discussions of such child experiences are Glazer, 1981; Hennings, 1986; and Hough, Nurss, & Wood, 1987.)

Experiences with the arts seem more in the spirit of Margaret's children's composing challenges and triumphs than teacher-directed discussions of "complete stories" and "clear language." In our concern that children become literate—and as literacy programs and pedagogical publications for early childhood teachers multiply—it is easy to pull written language out of the constellation of symbol systems of which it is a part and within which children experience it. Moreover, it is easy to treat that written language as a subject for the child to learn in school, rather than as a tool for the child's playful and thoughtful expression. In Vygotsky's (1978) apt words, written language must be "cultivated," rather than "imposed," or the child's "activity will not be manifest in his writing and his budding personality will not grow" (p. 117).

In addition to opportunities for drawing, talking, acting, and singing, young writers also need each other. As illustrated throughout this book, Margaret's classroom was one in which children were appreciated, not only as budding writers, but, more importantly, as interesting people with experiences, opinions, and ideas to share, not only with Margaret, but with each other. In such a classroom, children's interest in each other and in the work they do can provide a nurturing context for writing as social participation and intellectual discovery. In time, the peer talk interwoven with the children's activity may invest writing with powerful meanings, as written messages begin to figure into children's reactions to and relationships with each other.

Indeed, in Margaret's classroom, the children became a kind of literary collective; their knowledge of each other—their memories of their own past—included the stories they had shared. A year after Manuel had written his snowman story, Sonia remembered it with appreciation. And as a third grader, Regina, the child who had been so concerned with peer approval, recalled with her friend Marissa their intertwined literary history.

The case histories of Margaret's children thus highlight the sources of support teachers may offer young authors, including opportunities to interact with other symbolic media and with other people. But teachers do more than offer resources; they observe how children respond to and make use of those resources (Almy & Genishi, 1979; Genishi & Dyson, 1984).

Observing the Faces in the Classroom Crowd

The professional language arts literature has emphasized the teacher's role as responder to children's work.[3] Teachers are encouraged to provide children with opportunities to share their work formally, which Margaret did. And teachers are encouraged to respond appreciatively and with genuine curiosity to children's efforts, which Margaret did. But, in the context of activities where products matter (and, for the observed children, products mattered), teachers cannot rely *only* on their own responses to children's written stories, nor on those response opportunities they formally organize. Not only are there limits to the time available, there are also limits to the teacher's role. Teachers are authoritative "experts"—the ones who set down the rules, who tell parents how children are doing. And, as vividly illustrated in Chapter 3, children are intelligent and cannot be fooled on this point. Indeed, Margaret evalu-

---

[3]Perhaps the most influential book on elementary school children's writing has been Graves's *Writing: Teachers and Children at Work* (1983).

ated the children's journal writing regularly. She pointed out to individuals what she thought they were doing well, and she had them erase and do over things she thought were not up to an individual's standard.

Margaret's children, then, could not so easily learn from her one of their most critical lessons—that, from the point of view of the writer, social interaction does not come *after* but *during* the writing, even when that writing is taking the form of a story, not a letter. Margaret's success in language arts teaching, therefore, was not found only in the formal group activities she orchestrated but, moreover, in the talk her activities so influenced—the talk among the children themselves. Her teaching triumphs were found in Jake's yelled warnings to Manuel before the impending but written blowing up ("Watch out, Manuel"), in Mitzi's deliberations with Jenni about cats and dead birds ("I know what I'm going to do" to avoid all those pictured dead birds), in Manuel's worries about Josh's ability to figure out where his snowman went ("I think this page is a little bit hard" for my readers).

The importance of the peer group to writing development suggests that, as teachers, we can enrich our understanding of each child as an author by attending not only to the individual child's writing but to how that writing figures into the child's relationships with other people. In any classroom, children may be found who have potentially problematic relationships with their peers, relationships that may influence their use of written language. To illustrate briefly, I bring to the foreground two of Margaret's children who have been in the background in other children's cases—Jesse and Ruben.

Throughout this book, Jesse's admiration of his older schoolmates Jake and Manuel has periodically surfaced. It would be an understatement to say that Jesse's social ambitions infused his writing; indeed they seemed to overpower it. As a kindergartener, Jesse had a very dynamic artistic style, much like Jake's. In the pages of his journal, motorcycles raced, good guys fought bad guys, bombs exploded. In his real-world classroom interactions, Jesse sometimes became embroiled in tension; he could become quite angry, filling the room with his loud crying.

In the first/second grade, Jesse worked hard to become one of the boys. He attended carefully to the actions of Jake and Manuel, both of them self-assured, slow-to-anger second graders. Jesse visibly worked to maintain his composure when upset, and he made progress in this area. Yet, so great was his admiration of Jake and Manuel that he copied pictures and key words from their stories. While all of the children copied ideas from others, Jesse did not seem to incorporate those ideas into his own evolving style. The implied narratives composed during the latter half of his kindergarten year gave way, not to adventures, but to brief descriptions of his pictures. He used the forms of drawing and writing but not their potentially interactive processes or substance to connect with others. ("Like [my picture], Manuel?" "I can spell *king* without looking.")

Jesse did not return to the magnet school for the second grade, so his story is incomplete for me. I do not know if he would have found new ways to connect with Jake and Manuel through story writing. Certainly it was the more experienced second graders who most exploited the interactional possibilities of the journal activity. Perhaps, too, in the light of Jesse's tremendous effort to compose himself, thoughts about his composing of stories pale in importance. Further, insight into Jesse's social and literary challenges does not lead to any simple prescriptions for how a teacher might support him, but just to reflections on the possible consequences of possible teacher moves (for example, manipulating Jesse's table companions during writing time, or structuring certain kinds of interactions between Jesse and other children, such as a conference in which a child talked with him about his own work).

Such consideration of ways of influencing children's interactions during writing are prompted by Ruben as well. Relative to Margaret's other students, Ruben had an unusually private way of composing. As a kindergartener and a first grader, he would cover his pictures and texts with his arms and head whenever peers showed an interest in them. While Ruben would talk with his friends about spellings and letter names, the content of his journal entries was private business. Some of Ruben's topics were potentially of interest to his peers; for example, like other children, he drew good guys, bad guys, and blown-up spaceships. But Ruben did not share his pieces with them, outside of Margaret's formal sharing time. His texts were most often descriptions of his pictured objects, rather than recalled or imagined experiences involving those objects.

Margaret was very respectful of Ruben's work and appreciative of his journal during sharing time. She would sometimes sit beside him, talking about his picture and story. But Ruben was not talkative about his efforts; he gave her, as he gave his peers, no ready access to any meaning beyond that on his pages.

Given the luxury of hindsight, we can again only consider some possible moves. If Margaret and I could go "back in time" (to use one of Jake's favorite story devices) perhaps we could find a way for Ruben's writing to be linked to other sorts of symbolic activities. For instance, Ruben did interact to create dramas with his friends in the home center; with adult help, these might have been recorded. Playing in—dramatizing—published stories by other authors is another way Ruben might have built bridges between actions and words. As with Jesse, perhaps manipulating Ruben's table partners during writing time could have helped. Indeed, in the second grade, Ruben did talk about his journal-writing efforts with Mark, an inquisitive but very accepting first grader. Even though Ruben's text on that occasion was still a description of his picture, his talk was filled with ideas about his pictures. Certainly generated ideas would give both Ruben and his teacher a matrix of potential things to talk about and upon which to build written language.

With Ruben, then, as with any child, we might consider the interaction between child and activity in the light of our own goals as teachers (Dyson, 1986b). I have examined children's story writing as experienced in a specific classroom and within a particular activity frame (i.e., the journal). And that activity was the window through which I learned about children, stories, and development. But manipulating the window can allow children and ourselves other viewpoints on writing and on themselves. As earlier argued, across differing literacy tasks, children might manage the writing system differently and thus experience and display different sorts of skills. Playing word games, acting out a drama and collaboratively writing it down, and responding in a dialogue journal to teacher or peer (Staton, Shuy, Peyton, & Reed, 1988) are all potentially rich, purposeful avenues for literacy learning. Within any one classroom, a diversity of language-producing experiences will offer the various children in any class many ways to use and to explore print (Florio & Clark, 1982).

I am, after a year of hindsight and reflection in the quiet of my living room, using Ruben and Jesse as focal points for considering the nature of the social and symbolic support system in a classroom and how that system might be manipulated or expanded to support individual child writers. Whatever the merits or flaws in my wonderings, it is this reflection on individuals and their social and symbolic worlds that resulted, for me, from coming to know Margaret and her children. And it is this sort of reflection that I hope this book about them will stimulate for other educators, allowing them to see children and classrooms in new ways.

CONCLUSION: ON FRIENDS AND WRITERS

This final chapter has been a reconsideration of the inevitable contradictions confronted not only by children, but by those who study children. Inspired by Manuel's view of the end of Maggie's thinking cap as a possible beginning, I have tried to turn around some basic developmental concepts to see how they might look from another angle. Perhaps children's written stories become embedded, not disembedded; perhaps function and form push each other along in a developmental dialectic, rather than form always trailing behind; perhaps writing develops dialectically, too, as children's internal processes transform external experiences. And, while children do indeed learn to express themselves through writing, in another sense they are expressing who they are among other people. As researcher, I have tried to move between the child and the group, studying children as individual artists in the company of friends.

Recently there has been much debate about literacy and its consequences for human behavior and thought (e.g., Cole & Nicolopoulou, in press; Gee, 1988). Does learning the alphabetic, written system lead inevitably to more logical, more "abstract" thought (Olson, 1977)? If not, what sorts of literacy practices lead to what sorts of ends (Scribner & Cole, 1981)? In the classroom, such theoretical debates may seem deceptively irrelevant. Parents and children alike expect students to learn to read and write in school, presumably to the eventual betterment of children's social and economic futures. And, for children whose background is considered out of the "mainstream," for whatever reason (most often because the children are not middle class and/or not Anglo), becoming literate is considered a process of moving, through individual achievement, beyond present ground, beyond their families and neighborhoods.

This way of thinking about school literacy needs some rethinking. Within the context of this project, children's growth as literate people was linked to the social practices that surrounded them, that is, to their discovery of literacy's rich relevance to their present interactions with friends and to their reflections on their experiences. Literacy that helps children to articulate their todays and to make ongoing connections with others may be more likely to grow with them into their tomorrows.

In a book about reading and literature, Margaret Meek (1988) suggests that the difficulties of inexperienced readers "lie not in the words but in understanding something that lies behind the words, embedded in the sense" (p. 20). Children who know childhood lore about such figures as Humpty Dumpty or all the king's men will know "how to recognize bits and pieces of other texts in what they read [and] find it is like the discovery of old friend in new places. . . . They become insiders in the [literacy] network" (p. 22).

In a broader sense, Meek's comments capture the experiences of the children whose stories have filled this book. But, not only were they recognizing familiar characters—Jake's bubble cars, Manuel's snowman—they were coming to understand that people themselves are in stories, that stories are not something set apart from their experienced worlds. The meaning embedded in stories exists because those stories are embedded in people's lives. As writers, they can enter into story worlds; moreover, they can invite their friends in as well. As readers, they can enter into the stories of others, thereby entering their play. But that play is no longer on a stage, like the one Vivian Paley creates with masking tape on the rug. Children can create the stage internally. And from inside that world of possibilities, they can explore the outside world of actions, characters, and feelings, and in the process, they can solidify their own ongoing relationships, their shared world.

In Maxine Greene's (1988) words,

> Authorship does not imply invention *ex nihilo*. Nor does it imply the composition of texts or scripts in some space apart from the common world. The term carries with it the feeling of temporality, the sense of being in communication, the awareness of perspective in a constructed world. . . . To be aware of authorship is to be aware of situationality and of the relation between the ways in which one interprets one's situation and the possibilities of action and of choice. This means that one's "reality" [or, I would add, one's invented reality] is a perpetual emergent, becoming increasingly multiplex, as more perspectives are taken, more texts are opened, more friendships are made. [p. 23]

As I think of the futures of Regina, Jake, Manuel, Mitzi, and all of Margaret's children, I can wish for no more than that literacy will continue to be, as it was for them in primary school, a place for new perspectives, new possible worlds, new friends.

Epilogue

During the year I spent writing this book, I stayed away from the primary school where I made my observations. New children entered Margaret's classroom. The "original eight," as I came to call my focal children, were down to three. "First graders" Jake, Manuel, Mitzi, and Sonia had graduated to fourth grade in another school. "Kindergarteners" Regina, Ruben, and Maggie were still in the school—third graders all—but Jesse had moved away from the city.

In my living room, though, the original eight went again through their early years of schooling, as I pored over products and listened again to tapes. In the midst of children writing, talking, and drawing in my mind, I reread two books by very different authors, both of whom pay tribute to the living memory. In *One Writer's Beginning*, Eudora Welty (1983) writes of time and space and memory: "It is our inward journey that leads us through time. . . . As we discover, we remember; remembering, we discover" (p. 102). In this discovery, we escape from clock time and step into the stories of our memories, to use an image from Toni Morrison's *Beloved* (1987). In that book, her character Sethe explains that "thought pictures" are always there waiting to be lived through again (p. 38).

When my "thought pictures"—the chapters of this book—were nearly done, I returned to Margaret's classroom. This year's kindergarteners were in her room, working in their journals. They were drawing, talking, and writing in familiar ways. There were the good guys and bad guys doing battle on the pages; there were drawings of little girls with happy smiles under colorful rainbows. On this May day, there were even children arguing about who told them that they could put them in their story.

Nothing was "new," but nothing was old. The children did not know me. And I did not know them—no names, no best friends, no past stories to make sense of current ones. A discomforting feeling, to know classroom procedures and routines and, even, composing processes and products so very well—and to not know the children at all.

Hilde, a little girl with a long braid, brought into focus my own awkwardness—my own tensions—as I stood with one foot in my own remembered classroom and one foot in the ongoing one. Hilde was having difficulty spelling out a sentence in her journal. I tried to help, but I had trouble understanding her soft voice ("Could you say that one more time?"), and she seemed to have trouble understanding mine ("That's not what I want."). Finally, she went off to find Carol Heller, who had been helping Margaret in the kindergarten that year.

Feeling quite disoriented, I stood by the side of the room. Hilde walked over to me. She held up her journal.

HILDE: Do you know what this is? (sincerely)
DYSON: I think so. (tentatively)
HILDE: What? (demanding)
DYSON: A journal?
HILDE: Right. (nodding)

To Hilde, I was a rather ignorant stranger, one whose knowledge about journals and journal time was questionable. And yet just the day before, alone in my living room, I had been such an intimate member of the classroom.

Hilde was only partially right. I was not ignorant, but I was outside the picture. And being on the outside made me appreciative of having been inside the picture with Jake, Manuel, Mitzi, Regina, their peers, and, of course, Margaret. We who share memories with children as teachers or researchers are privileged—if at times perplexed—observer/actors in a fascinating world, a world of people beginning the lifelong process of learning how to be scholars, artists, and friends.

Data Work Sheets

WORK SHEET FOR INTEGRATING DATA
COLLECTED DURING CHILDREN'S DRAWING

Child's name _____ Date _____

Observation session* No. _____ Composing event** No. _____

Child's drawing:

Numbers indicate the order in which the particular elements of the product were produced. Circled numbers indicate that talk occurred at this point; talk is indicated in notes in the bottom half of this form.

Notes on behavior, including transcribed talk (coded functions in parentheses)

---

* Each day I visited Margaret's classroom was an "observation session"; the observation session number, then, referred to the number of days spent in Margaret's classroom.
**While observation sessions were specific to *days* spent in Margaret's classroom, composing events were specific to *focal children*. For example, on the twenty-third observation session, Mitzi served as a focal child; she was in the midst of her third, completely observed composing event.

281

WORK SHEET FOR INTEGRATING DATA
COLLECTED DURING CHILDREN'S WRITING

Child's name _____ Date _____

Observation session* No. _____ Composing event** No. _____

Child's text	Composing behavior code	Notes, transcribed talk (coded functions)

KEY: *Dialogue*: IS-P—interruption solicited from peer; IS-T—interruption solicited from teacher; IU-P—interruption unsolicited from peer; IU-T—interruption unsolicited from teacher (or other adult—indicate who). *Monologue*: OV—overt language; RR—reread; PR—proofread (make a change in text). *Other*: S—silence; P—pause; R—resource use; DR—drawing; / / /—erasing.

SOURCE: Form adapted from Graves, D. (1973). *Children's writing: Research directions and hypotheses based upon an examination of the writing process of seven-year-old children.* Unpublished doctoral dissertation, State University of New York at Buffalo.

Coding Categories

Since this project focused on young children's talk, drawing, and writing, I used inductive analysis procedures to develop coding categories for describing the children's symbolic behavior. These coding categories became the vocabulary I then used to construct each focal child's case history.

Inductive analysis procedures involve, first of all, segmenting children's behavior into units; second, comparing like units; and, third, composing descriptors to specify how those units vary.

The basic organizational unit used in this project was the *composing event*. As described in Chapter 1, a composing event refers to all behaviors involved in the production of one journal entry, that is, to a focal child's talking, drawing, and composing. Within each event, then, I needed categories—a vocabulary—for describing the children's talk, drawing, and writing. These basic categories included descriptors for *language functions*, *meaning elements*, and *topics*.

LANGUAGE FUNCTIONS

To analyze talk, I began by comparing the children's utterances (an utterance being the unit of behavior studied) in order to identify the range of functions for which children used talk. I based the analysis on the data gathered from all focal children during the first two months of data collection, although the resulting categories were continually modified and refined during the construction of the case studies. This system was adapted from one developed in a previous study of young children's talk during writing (Dyson, 1983); that system was modified to suit the collected data. The resulting classification system is two-tiered, with five major *functions* and the accompanying *strategies* used to effect each function. These functions and strategies, which should not be viewed as mutually exclusive categories, are as follows:

1. *Representational* language serves to give information about events and situations (real or imagined, past or present). The strategies used to carry out this function are
    a. *Labeling* or naming; for example, a child is drawing a sun and says, "This is the sun."
    b. *Elaborating* or detailing; for example, a child is adding a mouth to a drawn sun and says, "He [the sun] has his mouth full of raspberries—I mean jelly beans."
    c. *Associating* or comparing with earlier experiences; for example, a child has just drawn a little girl with long hair; she comments on the girl's long hair [elaborating] and then remarks, "Crystal Gayle—the only one who wears wigs was Crystal Gayle and Diana Ross. Those are the only ones who wear long wigs."
    d. *Reporting* an action or event; for example, a child is drawing an egg in a nest and says, "And the egg popped up, 'cause the egg is popping up."
    e. *Narrating* a series of actions or events; for example, while drawing, a child says, "She [a mother bird] um takes the egg—I mean the baby, and she puts it to sleep."
    f. *Dramatizing* or acting out a series of actions, for example, a child is drawing the path of an airplane and makes an airplane sound: "Eeeeeeeeeeeeeeewwwwwwwwwwwwww."
    g. *Reasoning*; for example, a child says, "How about [if I write] 'won the race'? Maybe they [the characters] could have been famous because they won lots of races."
2. *Directive* language serves to direct the actions of self and/or others. The strategies used to carry out this function are
    a. *Monitoring* (strategy through which ongoing actions appear to be controlled and directed); for example, a child is copying someone's name and says, "An R, and then, and then, and then—a *e*."
    b. *Planning* (strategy through which future actions appear to be controlled and directed); for example, a child is drawing and says, "I'm gonna make a bird in this nest."
    c. *Encoding* (strategy through which words or phrases are transferred from the oral to the written language channel; the child pronounces sounds, letters, syllables, or the word/phrase itself); for example,

Child's Speech   *Child's Text*

/pl/   p

/p/ /p/

a plump   lump

d. *Decoding* (strategy through which sounds, syllables, words, phrases, or propositions are transferred from the written to the oral language channel; the child matches oral letter names, syllables, words, phrases, or propositions to either some segment of the written text or to the entire text); for example,

Child's Text: Once   pepperoni

                ↑   ↑

Child's Speech: Once   a

                 Once   a pon a time

                 Once   a pon a

                 Once   a pon a

e. *Accessing* (strategy used to seek or to retrieve letters or words from memory; in written language situations, this strategy involves rereading); for example, a child rereads the text in order to remember what word needs to be written next, as follows, "'Once upon a' time—I need *time*."

f. *Instructing* (strategy used to convey information perceived as required or needed by someone else; language used to "teach"); for example, a child reads a peer's text and instructs him to erase the ungrammatical *a*, as follows, "'There is [a] three designs in the sky.' Erase the *a*."

g. *Requesting*; for example, a child says, "I need a red [marker]."

h. *Offering*; for example, a child says, "You can use mine. Use mine."

3. *Heuristic* language is used to explore or to seek information or learn about reality. In reference to written language in particular, heuristic language may be used to seek information regarding encoding, decoding, mechanically producing print (i.e., handwriting), or content; the print being focused on could be letters, words, phrases, or propositions (although the child may not know what linguistic unit is being focused on). Strategies include

a. *Seeking confirmation*; for example, a child has spelled *ruff* as *rofe* and seeks confirmation of her decision, saying "Is this how you spell *ruff*: R-O-F-E?"

b. *Seeking fact*; for example, a child seeks the identity of unknown characters in a peer's story, asking "Who's the 'them'?"

c.   *Seeking demonstration*; for example, a child asks, "Mitzi, do you know how to make a back like a bunny['s] right here?"

d.   *Seeking to test*; for example, a child has just written *Home Sweet Home* on her picture and is now testing a peer's ability to spell that phrase: "Do you know how to spell *sweet*?"

4.   *Personal language* is used to express one's feelings and attitudes. Examples are, "Oh great. I love this. God. I don't know how I made up those words." and "You're making me mad." Three strategies specifically identified that serve this broad function are

a.   *Evaluating others*; for example, "That's very pretty, Maggie."

b.   *Evaluating self*; for example, "I got a good idea."

c.   *Playing with language*; for example, "For some reason, I just made a bubble car. Sounds fun. Bubble car."

5.   *Interactional language* serves to initiate, maintain, and terminate social relationships. No division into strategies was done. Examples of this function are, "Know what I'm doing?" and "Do you like my [drawn] girl?"

MEANING ELEMENTS

The *meaning elements* described the meanings the children expressed not only in their talk, but also in their drawings and in their written products. The unit of behavior being studied here, then, was an expressed basic concept for structuring world knowledge (e.g., objects, actors, actions). To develop categories for describing the kinds of basic concepts contained in the children's work, I focused first on the children's representational talk, which they used to give information about the worlds they were deliberately forming during journal time. I next focused on the completed pictures, although it was at times necessary to use the child's talk to identify a depicted figure. (Since the interest was in what the child represented, the quality of the representation was not relevant.) Two of the case children, Ruben and Jesse, used gesture (i.e., exaggerated arm movements) as they dramatized actions during drawing. While it is difficult to separate gesture from the drawing act itself, gesture could convey meaning and thus was examined as an aspect of the drawing process. Finally, I focused on the content of the completed texts.

In formulating the meaning elements categories, I was influenced by work on children's behavior in a variety of symbolic media (for a discussion of this work, see Dyson, 1986a). Based on the literature in symbol development and my own inductive analysis of the children's work, I identified the following categories: objects, actors, actions, placement in

time (past, present, future) and space (location), and sensorimotor qualities (direction, force, speed, volume).

For each observed composing event, I compared the meaning elements contained in the child's drawing, talking, and composing. Table
B.1 presents my analysis of the meaning elements contained in Jesse's
"time-bomb" event (see discussion in Chapter 4); that analysis clarified
the information-rich nature of Jesse's talk during drawing.

TOPICS

Finally, I examined the *topics* of the focal children's talk; that is, I
asked, What sorts of things did the children speak about as they drew and
wrote? I compared these topics, noting their distinguishing characteristics and then writing descriptors for them. Major differences were noted
in the degree of relevancy of the children's talk to their ongoing journal
activity. The following topic categories describe these differences.

1. *Task-involved* talk is perceived as directly relevant to the child's own
   ongoing journal entry. Variations were noted in the following areas:
   a. *Degree of symbolic involvement* in the task
      i. A child might focus on her or his *own feelings and actions*,
         commenting on procedures or process; for example, saying
         while drawing, "I'm gonna make a bird in that nest."
      ii. A child might enter the boundaries of the symbolic world,
         focusing on the *actions or state of the depicted figures and
         events*; for example, saying while drawing, "And she's [a
         drawn bird] looking at her egg."
      iii. A child might differentiate between the depicted figures and
         events and the imagined *figures or events being or to be
         rendered* (i.e., the referent); for example, saying while plan-
         ning her written text, "She's [the little girl] just in the
         Brownies, but I'm not gonna say [I'm not gonna write] that
         she's in the Brownies."
      iv. A child might focus on *the symbolic vehicle itself*, separate
         from the imagined or depicted experience; for example,
         saying, in order to focus a peer's attention on the grammati-
         cality of his written sentence, "'There is [a] three designs in
         the sky.' Erase that *a*."
   b. *Nature of the time frame created*
      i. A child might create a *static* time frame in which the de-
         picted figures did not move through time; for example,

TABLE B.1. Meaning Elements Contained in Jesse's "Time-Bomb" Event

Medium	Meaning Elements				
	Sensorimotor Qualities	Time/Space	Objects	Actors	Actions
Talk during drawing	Speed of countdown	Placement of bomb on moon	Bomb		Countdown
	Volume/force of explosion		Many little moons		Explosion
	Volume/speed of airplane	Passage of time in present tense	Airplane		Movement of plane
Gestures during drawing	Direction/speed of plane				
Actual drawing (see Figure 4.1)*		Placement in sky	Bomb		Countdown numbers
			Many little moons		Path of plane
Dictation (composing)		Present (bomb)	Bomb		Explosion
		Present (on a light)			
		Past (explosion)			

288

* Children use lines, dots, shapes, and the sensorimotor qualities of these elements to represent their meaning. The presence of sensorimotor information is therefore simply assumed for drawing. Further, it is both difficult and conceptually problematic to separate children's gestures (arm movements that symbolize meaning) from the results of those gestures. Therefore, Jesse's clear use of observable gestures is acknowledged but not separated from the actual drawing.

saying while drawing, "Mine's got—all of my girls—two girls have red high heel shoes on."

    ii.   A child might create a *dynamic* time frame in which the depicted figure or figures do move through time; for example, by making the sound of a motorcycle being driven by a motorcycle racer: "Errrrrrrrrrrrrrrrrrrrrrrrrrrrr—And he falls off, and he hurts himself, and he gets back up."

2. *Other's-task-involved* talk is perceived as directly relevant to a peer's composing event; that is, a child has entered into the task of a peer. The child's talk can thus be coded for degree of symbolic involvement and for the nature of the time frame governing that talk (e.g., a child's talk could move a peer's world forward in time or it could elaborate upon a moment in time). For example, a child says, "I hope it [a peer's drawn bomb] explodes in the next century." This talk is other's-task-involved, focused on the depicted figure, and within the other child's static picture frame, anticipating but not actually moving through time. To have created a *dynamic* time frame, the child would have had to say something like, "Oh no, it's exploding!"

3. *Talk involving other in one's own task* is perceived as focused both on the child's own ongoing task (task-involved) *and* on another in the child's ongoing social world. An example is when Jake says, "Look out, Manuel!" thus warning him that he [Manuel] is about to be blown up inside Jake's own written story.

4. *Task-related* talk is any utterance that is not focused on the particular imaginary world the child is forming but is clearly related to that world. Variations were noted in the *degree of personal involvement in the related topic* and fell into two areas:

    a.   The use of *thematically related experiences*; for example, a child who has been observing a peer write a story about her mother, "a witch," says, "I have a real witch mother. My mother's a friend of a witch."

    b.   The use of *the referent category* of the objects or events being depicted; for example, a child has observed a peer drawing a pink-shirted Brownie Scout and says, "Brownies do not wear pink."

5. *Nontask-involved* talk is perceived as not falling into any of the preceding categories. The relevance of talk initially perceived as nontask-involved, however, could eventually become apparent, such as when a child has been talking with peers about an upcoming birthday party, a subject that has no clear relevance to her ongoing composing event. After completing that journal entry, though, she

immediately begins another about her party. In relation to the composing event she was engaged in *as she spoke,* the talk about her party was nontask-involved; however, in relation to her new composing event, that same talk was task-involved and focused on the event to be rendered.

Informal Assessment Tasks

During the first month of formal data collection in Year 1 of this study, I examined the kindergarten case study children's knowledge of literacy conventions through a series of tasks: (1) an alphabet identification task; (2) an initial-consonant identification task (i.e., "Write the letter that begins this word."); and (3) a set of reading and writing tasks based on Ferreiro (1978) and Ferreiro and Teberosky (1982), which required the child to write a small number of words and a sentence and to identify (through pointing) the individual words in a sentence I had just read aloud. These latter tasks were designed to allow insight into children's understanding of the relationship between print and the formal aspects of speech. I repeated these tasks in the initial and final months of observation during Year 2.

Jesse, Regina, and Christopher were similar in their responses to these tasks. During the very first assessment, all conveyed some understanding of the alphabetic principle. Regina's performance across the first two assessments is summarized in the following section. In addition, I summarize Ruben's performance across all assessments, as his was notably different from that of the other children and also changed dramatically over the months of the project.

REGINA

Year 1, Assessment 1 (February 1985)

Regina knew the names of all letters. She could identify some sound/symbol connections: F, J, V, Z, R, B, P, T, K. She spelled the words I dictated to her by putting down an orthographically sensible initial letter and following it with a string of what were apparently randomly selected letters. These are some examples:

Dictated words	*Regina's spelling*
candy	**KRUCLOX**
ball	**BAMOP**

Dictated sentence	*Regina's spelling*
The girl kicked the ball.	**DBAYPEMN**

Regina reread her sentence [DBAYPEMN] as follows:

REGINA: The [De] girl (runs her hand over over all letters) kicked (runs her hand over all letters) the ball (runs her hand again over all)

Then Regina must have realized that the same letters could not be read over three times. She then read the letters as simply, "The girl." She added a *K* and a *D*, erased the earlier *B* in the first group of letters, and then added another *B*. Then she read:

REGINA'S TEXT: D AYPEMN K D B [spacing added]

REGINA'S READING: The girl kicked the ball.

In reading the sentence I had read for her, Regina attempted to match voice and print, but she had trouble separating articles from their surrounding utterances:

TEXT: The baby dropped the bottle.

REGINA'S READING: The baby dropped / dropped the the bottle.

TEXT: The boy ate the cake.

REGINA'S READING: The boy ate the cake.

In their daily journal activity, all of the case study children, with the exception of Mitzi, at times neglected to write articles, sometimes reading them as if they were attached to a noun, just as Regina did in the example above—and just as Ferreiro and Teberosky (1982) describe. This task was certainly a very familiar one for the children, particularly the kindergarteners, as Margaret regularly had the children read their dictated stories.

Year 2, Assessment 1 (February, 1986)

Regina now was much more at ease with sound/symbol correspondence. Further, she relied on both visual recall and phonological analysis to reason her way through a word, no longer writing strings of what seemed random letters. The following compares the results from both testings.

Dictated words or sentence	Regina's kindergarten spelling	First-grade spelling
candy	KRUCLOX	Cande
ball	BAMOP	Bole
The girl kicked the ball.	DAYPEMNKDB	The Girl kit The Bole.

Finally, in reading the sentences, Regina performed perfectly. She no longer evidenced difficulty separating articles from their surrounding utterances in the assessment sentences.

RUBEN

Year 1, Assessment 1 (February, 1985)

As a kindergartener, Ruben knew the names of some alphabet letters, particularly the uppercase ones: A, E, H, M, O, P, Q, R, S, T, W, X, e, g, r. He displayed no knowledge of sound/symbol associations. He did not attempt to spell words I dictated, but he did spontaneously spell (and correctly identify) his brother's and sister's names. Ruben performed in the reading task similarly to all other kindergarteners, having difficulty only with identifying articles.

Year 2, Assessment 1 (February, 1986)

Ruben now displayed much more knowledge about the written system. He was able to name all upper- and lowercase letters. He also correctly identified initial consonant sounds, with the exceptions of C, S, H, and Y, and had no difficulty with the reading task. Ruben also willingly attempted to spell the dictated words, as follows:

Dictated words	Ruben's spelling
candy	CDE
ball	bill
jacket	GK

Ruben attempted only part of the dictated sentence (The girl kicked the ball.). While repeatedly saying the word *girl* or *the girl*, he wrote G, then *The* before the G, and finally added *RO* after G, resulting in

The GRO

He then announced, "I can't do the rest."

Year 2, Assessment 2 (May, 1986)

Ruben performed confidently in all assessment tasks and demonstrated further growth. His spellings of dictated words were closer approximations of the conventional:

Dictated word	Year 2, Assessment 1	Year 2, Assessment 2
candy	CDE	CAD
ball	bill	bill
jacket	GK	JACT

Most remarkably, he had little trouble with the dictated sentence:

The grol kac the bill.

Product Analyses

PERSONAL STANCE IN CHILDREN'S TEXTS

As described in Chapter 5, the observed children could adopt varied stances as authors. To document changes in these stances, a research assistant, Jim Slagel, and I, regularly joined by an additional assistant, Mark McCarvel, studied the collected written products. As adult readers, we identified the roles or stances children appeared to be taking vis-à-vis their written worlds, refining categories initially developed during the construction of the case studies.

In our judgment, a child author might assume the role of *commentator* on the pictured world; such products were labeled "art notes." These texts pointed to the pictures with deictic expressions (*"This* little girl") and/or progressive verbs ("is jumping").

At other times, a child might assume the role of *observer* of a world forming within the text itself. This stance was reflected in a third-person construction in a text that was not an art note. The following is an example:

the Suprise Party

Once there was a bunch of cats.
Then all of a sudden there came a
flock of birds. This was a big surprise
to the cats. At once the cats started
to kill them and eat them.
The End

A child might also assume the role of *actor* within the text world. This stance was reflected in a first-person construction in a non–art-note text; for example,

how My liFe was

I said to My sister one day that I
Was going to run away. My sister
screamed, "oh, no." My Mother
and father ran down the stairs. "What
happened?" they said. My sister was beginning
to say that I was going to run away
Whan I ran across the room
and covered her Mouth. the End

Finally, a child might appear to change stances abruptly; such texts were classified as shifting between different stances. For example, the following text was coded "observer/actor," as the author shifted from an observer of an imagined cowboy to an actor who hated that cowboy:

Once there was a cowboy. I hated the cowboy a lot. Do You LIke cowboy's? but I like YOu alot. Sometimes I LIke The cowboy. TueSdaYs I LiKe The cowboy. The End.

In our analysis of these stances, we each independently coded the 346 products and discussed all products with discrepant coding. To measure our consistency as judges, we coded and then determined interrater reliability for a random selection of 50 products, drawn from all eight cases; we agreed in our judgment of 94% of the products. The results of our analysis are presented in Table D.1.

The table illustrates that, as a group of child authors, the observed children gradually became less governed by their drawings as time went on. They moved away from the early tendency to comment on pictures, toward a tendency to observe scenes and, finally, to act within their textual worlds. Those imaginary worlds were increasingly dynamic, a change also connected with the texts' decreased domination by drawing; this change is illustrated by the product coding to be described next.

MOVEMENT IN CHILDREN'S TEXTS

As also discussed in Chapter 5, the children conveyed narrative time in varied ways within their texts. To develop a relatively precise vocabulary for describing time, I adapted Labov and Waletsky's (1967) definition of narrative movement. In my analysis, narrative movement existed if there were two temporally ordered, independent clauses presenting action or a character's reaction. A text with such movement suggested a movie,

TABLE D.1. Personal Stance in Children's Texts, by Percentage and Number of Products

Grade*	Art Notes % No.	Art Notes/ Observer % No.	Art Notes/ Actor % No.	Observer/ Actor % No.	Observer % No.	Actor % No.
K '85						
Pre-obs**	67 66	16 16	5 5	0 0	5 5	6 6
Obs	57 38	37 25	0 0	0 0	6 4	0 0
1st '86	18 12	9 6	6 4	0 0	46 31	21 14
1st '85	19 10	15 8	2 1	24 13	20 11	20 11
2nd '86	7 4	5 3	3 2	16 9	28 16	41 24
Totals	38 130	17 58	3 12	6 22	19 67	16 55

* "K '85" and "1st '86" refer to the products collected from Maggie, Regina, Jesse, and Ruben. "1st '85" and "2nd '86" refer to the products collected from Sonia, Mitzi, Jake and Manuel.

** These products were collected by the classroom teacher before the project formally began.

as in the preceding texts, "how my life was" and "the surprise party."

Texts without narrative movement suggested a slide; that is, characters and their actions were frozen in time, as in the following text:

the frog story

My pet is a little cute frog.
I love him. I care about him and
I take care of him too. He is a
baby frog. We wears clothes alot.
We bothe live in the woods.
are friends are the animals
We live by a pond. My frogy
has a girlfriend. The End.

Texts could also *imply* movement, although that movement was not actually accomplished. Such texts suggested a frame lifted from a movie, in that the frozen moment had linguistic sprockets. These sprockets were most often tense shifts that implied accomplished movement or imminent movement, as in the following example:

Once there WAs a three head bubble car an a jet that is running
out of gasoline. Then the bulbble CAr is going to Crash. But the
jet is going to blow up be cause it is out of gasoline.
    the end

In analyzing the products for evidence of movement, we followed the
procedures described for coding author stance; interrater reliability for a
random selection of 50 products was 92%. The results of our analysis are
presented in Table D.2. This analysis does not consider the intentions
of individual children and, moreover, masks individual variation. Nonetheless, it does indicate that, although the children were primarily concerned with creating imaginary worlds, which existed through their
deliberate symbolic efforts, the majority of their texts did not contain
narrative movement, as here defined. However, while approximately two-
thirds of the older children's first-grade texts contained no movement,
approximately two-thirds of their second-grade texts at least implied
movement.

TABLE D.2. Presence of Movement in Children's Texts, by
            Percentage and Number of Products

Grade*	No Movement %	No.	Implied Movement %	No.	Movement %	No.
K '85						
Pre-obs**	65	64	20	20	14	14
Obs	43	29	22	15	34	23
1st '86	45	30	28	19	27	18
1st '85	65	35	19	10	17	9
2nd '86	28	16	26	15	47	27
Totals	51	174	23	79	26	91

* "K '85" and "1st '86" refer to the products collected from
Maggie, Regina, Jesse, and Ruben. "1st '85" and "2nd '86"
refer to the products collected from Sonia, Mitzi, Jake,
and Manuel.

** These products were collected by the classroom teacher
before the project formally began. Two texts were
eliminated, as they were copied from the chalkboard due
to the direction of a substitute teacher.

References

Almy, M., & Genishi, C. (1979). *Ways of studying children.* New York: Teachers College Press.

Amarel, M. (1980). *The teacher as observer.* Occasional paper, Right to Read Office. Harrisburg, PA: U.S. Department of Education.

Ashton-Warner, S. (1963). *Teacher.* New York: Simon and Schuster.

Barthes, R. (1974). *S/Z.* New York: Hill and Wang.

Bereiter, C., & Scardamalia, M. (1982). From conversation to composition: The role of instruction in a developmental process. In R. Glaser (Ed.), *Advances in instructional psychology: Vol 2.* (pp. 1-64). Hillsdale, NJ: Lawrence Erlbaum.

Bissex, G. (1980). *Gyns at wrk: A child learns to read and write.* Cambridge, MA: Harvard University Press.

Booth, W. C. (1961). *The rhetoric of fiction.* Chicago: The University of Chicago Press.

Britton, J. (1984). Viewpoints: The distinction between participant and spectator role language in research and practice. *Research in the Teaching of English, 18,* 320-331.

Brown, A., & Ferrara, R. (1985). Diagnosing zones of proximal development. In J. Wertsch (Ed.), *Culture, communications and cognition: Vygotskian perspectives* (pp. 273-305). New York: Cambridge University Press.

Bruner, J. (1986). *Actual minds, possible worlds.* Cambridge, MA: Harvard University Press.

Bussis, A. M., Chittenden, E. A., Amarel, M., & Klausner, E. (1985). *Inquiry into meaning: An investigation of learning to read.* Hillsdale, NJ: Lawrence Erlbaum.

Calkins, L. (1983). *Lessons from a child: On the teaching and learning of writing.* Exeter, NH: Heinemann.

Calkins, L. (1987). *The art of teaching writing.* Portsmouth, NH: Heinemann.

Carini, P. (1985, November). *Valuing children's language: An observational approach.* Paper presented at the annual meeting of the National Council of Teachers of English, Philadelphia.

Cazden, C. (1971). Language programs for young children. In C. S. Lavatelli

(Ed.), *Language training in early childhood education* (pp. 119-156). Urbana, IL: University of Illinois.

Cazden, C. (1979). Peekaboo as an instructional model: Discourse development at home and at school. *Papers and Reports on Child Language Development, 17*, 1-19.

Cazden, C. (1986). Classroom discourse. In M. C. Wittrock (Ed.), *Handbook of research on teaching* (3rd ed.) (pp. 432-463). New York: Macmillan.

Cazden, C., Cordeiro, P., & Giacobbe, M. (1985). Spontaneous and scientific concepts: Young children's learning of punctuation. In G. Wells & J. Nicholls (Eds.), *Language and learning: An interactional perspective* (pp. 107-124). London: The Falmer Press.

Chafe, W. (1982). Integration and involvement in speaking, writing, and oral literature. In D. Tannen (Ed.), *Spoken and written language: Exploring orality and literacy* (pp. 35-54). Norwood, NJ: Ablex.

Clay, M. (1966). *Emergent reading behavior.* Unpublished doctoral dissertation. University of Auckland, Auckland, New Zealand.

Clay, M. (1975). *What did I write?*, Auckland: Heinemann.

Clay, M. (1979). *Reading: The patterning of complex behavior* (2nd ed.). Auckland, New Zealand: Heinemann.

Cole, M., & Nicolopoulou, A. (in press). The intellectual consequences of literacy. In *The Oxford international encyclopedia of linguistics.* London: Oxford University Press.

Cook-Gumperz, J., & Gumperz, J. (1981). From oral to written culture: The transition to literacy. In M. Farr Whiteman (Ed.), *Variation in writing: Functional and linguistic-cultural differences: Vol. I of Writing: The nature, development and teaching of written communication* (pp. 89-110). Hillsdale, NJ: Lawrence Erlbaum.

Corsaro, W. (1981). Entering the child's world: Research strategies for field entry and data collection in a preschool setting. In J. Green & C. Wallat (Eds.), *Ethnography and language in educational settings* (pp. 117-146). Norwood, NJ: Ablex.

Corsaro, W. (1985). *Friendship and peer culture in the early years.* Norwood, NJ: Ablex.

Daiute, C. (1988, July). *Play as thought. Thinking strategies of young writers.* Paper presented at the Institute of Critical Thinking, Harvard Graduate School of Education, Cambridge, MA.

Dixon, J., & Stratta, L. (1986). *Writing narrative—and beyond.* Upper Montclair, NJ: Boynton/Cook.

Donaldson, M. (1978). *Children's minds.* New York: Norton.

Dyson, A. H. (1982). The emergence of visible language: Interrelationships between drawing and early writing. *Visible Language, 6*, 360-381.

Dyson, A. H. (1983). The role of oral language in early writing processes. *Research in the Teaching of English, 17*, 1-30.

Dyson. A. H. (1984). Reading, writing, and language: Young children solving the written language puzzle. In J. M. Jensen (Ed.), *Composing and comprehending* (pp. 167–176). Urbana, IL: National Council of Teachers of English.

Dyson, A. H. (1985). Individual differences in emerging writing. In M. Farr (Ed.), *Advances in writing research: Vol. 1. Children's early writing development* (pp. 59–126). Norwood, NJ: Ablex.

Dyson, A. H. (1986a). Transitions and tensions: Interrelationships between the drawing, talking, and dictating of young children. *Research in the Teaching of English, 20,* 379–409.

Dyson, A. H. (1986b). Staying free to dance with the children: The dangers of sanctifying activities in the language arts curriculum. *English Education, 18,* 135–146.

Dyson, A. H. (1987a). Individual differences in beginning composing: An orchestral vision of learning to compose. *Written Communication, 4,* 411–442.

Dyson, A. H. (1987b.). The value of "time off task": Young children's spontaneous talk and deliberate text. *Harvard Educational Review, 57,* 396–420.

Dyson, A. H. (1988a). Negotiating among multiple worlds: The space/time dimensions of young children's composing. *Research in the Teaching of English, 22,* 355–390.

Dyson, A. H. (1988b). Unintentional helping in the primary grades: Writing in the children's world. In B. A. Rafoth & D. L. Rubin (Eds.), *The social construction of written communication* (pp. 218–248). Norwood, NJ: Ablex. Also: (1987). Technical Report No. 2. Center for the Study of Writing, University of California—Berkeley.

Edelsky, C. (1983). Segmentation and punctuation: Developmental data from young writers in a bilingual program. *Research in the Teaching of English, 21,* 121–145.

Edelsky, C. (1986). *Writing in a bilingual program: Habia una vez.* Norwood, NJ: Ablex.

Elasser, N., & Irvine, P. (1985). English and Creole: The dialectics of choice in a college writing program. *Harvard Educational Review, 55,* 399–415.

Elasser, N., & John-Steiner, V. (1977). An interactionist approach to advancing literacy. *Harvard Educational Review, 47,* 355–369.

Ferreiro, E. (1978). What is written in a written sentence? A developmental answer. *Journal of Education, 160*(4), 23–39.

Ferreiro, E. (1980, May). *The relationship between oral and written language: The children's viewpoints.* Paper presented at the preconvention of the International Reading Association, St. Louis, MO.

Ferreiro, E. (1986). The interplay between information and assimilation in beginning literacy. In W. Teale & E. Sulzby (Eds.), *Emergent literacy: Writing and reading* (pp. 15–49). Norwood, NJ: Ablex.

Ferreiro, E., & Teberosky, A. (1982). *Literacy before schooling.* Exeter, NH: Heinemann.

Florio, S., & Clark, C. (1982). The functions of writing in an elementary classroom. *Research in the Teaching of English, 16,* 115–129.

Freire, P. (1985). Reading the world and reading the word: An interview with Paulo Freire. *Language Arts, 62,* 15–21.

Gardner, H. (1980). *Artful scribbles.* New York: Basic Books.

Gardner, H., Wolf, D., & Smith, A. (1982). Max and Mollie: Individual differences in early artistic symbolization. In H. Gardner (ed.), *Art, mind, and brain: A cognitive approach to creativity* (pp. 110–127). New York: Basic Books.

Garvey, C. (1977). *Play.* Cambridge, MA: Harvard University Press.

Gee, J. (1988). The legacies of literacy: From Plato to Freire through Harvey Graff. *Harvard Educational Review, 58,* 195–212.

Geertz, C. (1983). *Local knowledge.* New York: Basic Books.

Genishi, C. (1982). Observational research methods for early childhood education. In B. Spodek (Ed.), *Handbook of research in early childhood education* (pp. 516–537). New York: Free Press.

Genishi, C., & Di Paolo, M. (1982). Learning through argument in a preschool. In L. C. Wilkinson (Ed.), *Communicating in the classroom* (pp. 49–68). New York: Academic Press.

Genishi, C., & Dyson, A. H. (1984). *Language assessment in the early years.* Norwood, NJ: Ablex.

Gilbert, S. H., & Gay, G. (1985). Improving the success in school of poor black children. *Phi Delta Kappan, 67,* 133–137.

Gillmore, P. (1983). Spelling "Mississippi": Recontextualizing a literacy-related speech event. *Anthropology and Education Quarterly, 14,* 235–256.

Glazer, J. (1981). *Literature for young children.* Columbus, OH: Merrill.

Goffman, E. (1961). *Asylums.* Garden City, NY: Anchor Books.

Golomb, C. (1974). *Young children's sculpture and drawing.* Cambridge, MA: Harvard University Press.

Goodman, K., & Goodman, Y. (1979). Learning to read is natural. In L. B. Resnick & P. B. Weaver (Eds.), *Theory and practice of early reading: Vol. 1* (pp. 137–154). Hillsdale, NJ: Lawrence Erlbaum.

Goodnow, J. (1977). *Children's drawing.* Cambridge, MA: Harvard University Press.

Gould, S. J. (1987). *An urchin in the storm: Essays about books and ideas.* New York: Norton.

Graves, D. (1973). *Children's writing: Research directions and hypotheses based upon an examination of the writing process of seven-year-old children.* Unpublished doctoral dissertation, State University of New York at Buffalo.

Graves, D. (1982). Research update: How do writers develop? *Language Arts, 59,* 173–179.

Graves, D. (1983). *Writing: Teachers and children at work.* Exeter, NH: Heinemann.

Greene, M. (1988). *The dialectic of freedom.* New York: Teachers College Press.

Gundlach, R. (1982). Children as writers: The beginnings of learning to write. In M. Nystrand (Ed.), *What writers know* (pp. 129–147). New York: Academic Press.

Gundlach, R., McLane, J. B., Stott, F. M., & McNamee, G. D. (1985). The social foundations of children's early writing development. In M. Farr (Ed.), *Advances in writing: Vol. 1. Children's early writing development* (pp. 1–58). Norwood, NJ: Ablex.

Hall, N. (1987). *The emergence of literacy.* Portsmouth, NH: Heinemann.

Halliday, M. A. K. (1973). *Explorations in the functions of language.* London: Edward Arnold.

Halliday, M. A. K. (1977). *Learning how to mean.* London: Edward Arnold.

Halliday, M. A. K. (1978). *Language as social semiotic.* Victoria, Australia: Edward Arnold.

Harris, J., & Wilkinson, J. (1986). *Reading children's writing: A linguistic view.* London: Allen & Unwin.

Harste, J. C., Woodward, V. A., & Burke, C. L. (1984). *Language stories and literacy lessons.* Portsmouth, NH: Heinemann.

Heath, S. B. (1983). *Ways with words: Language, life, and work in communities and classrooms.* New York: Cambridge University Press.

Heath, S. B. (1986). Critical factors in literacy development. In S. deCastell, A. Luke, & K. Egan (Eds.), *Literacy, society, and schooling: A reader* (pp. 209–229). Cambridge: Cambridge University Press.

Hennings, D. (1986). *Communication in action: Teaching the language arts.* Boston: Houghton Mifflin.

Holdaway, D. (1979). *The foundations of literacy.* Sydney: Ashton Scholastic.

Hough, R. A., Nurss, J. R., & Wood, D. (1987). Tell me a story: Opportunities for elaborated language in early childhood. *Young Children, 43,* 6–15.

Iser, W. (1974). *The implied reader.* Baltimore: Johns Hopkins University Press.

Jacob, S. E. (1985). The development of children's writing: Language acquisition and divided attention. *Written Communication, 2,* 414–433.

Johnston, P. (1984). Assessment in reading. In P. D. Pearson (Ed.), *Handbook of reading research* (147–184). New York: Longman.

King, M., & Rentel, V. (1981). *How children learn to write: A longitudinal study.* Columbus, OH: Ohio State University.

Labov, W. (1972). *Language in the inner city.* Philadelphia: University of Pennsylvania Press.

Labov, W. (1982). Competing value systems in inner-city schools. In P. Gilmore & A. A. Glatthorn (Eds.), *Children in and out of school* (pp. 148–171). Washington, DC: Center for Applied Linguistics.

Labov, W., & Waletsky, J. (1967). Narrative analysis: Oral versions of personal experience. In *Essays on the verbal and visual arts, Proceedings of the 1966 spring meeting of the American Ethnological Society* (pp. 12–44). Seattle: University of Washington Press.

Leondar, B. (1977). Hatching plots: Genesis of storymaking. In D. Perkins & B. Leondar (Eds.), *The arts and cognition* (pp. 172–191). Baltimore: Johns Hopkins University Press.

Lindfors, J. W. (1987). *Children's language and learning* (2nd ed.). Englewood Cliffs, NJ: Prentice-Hall.

Luria, A. (1983). The development of writing in the child. In M. Martlew (Ed.), *The psychology of written language* (pp. 237–277). New York: John Wiley.

McCaig, R. (1981). A district-wide plan for the evaluation of student writing. In S. Haley-James (Ed.), *Perspectives on writing in grades 1–8* (pp. 73–92). Urbana, IL: National Council of Teachers of English.

McCormick, C. E., & Mason, J. (1986). Intervention procedures for increasing preschool children's interest in knowledge about reading. In W. H. Teale & E. Sulzby (Eds.), *Emergent literacy: Writing and reading* (pp. 90–115). Norwood, NJ: Ablex.

McNamee, G. D., McLane, J. G., Cooper, P. M., & Kerwin, S. (1985). Cognition and affect in early literacy development. *Early child development and care, 20*, 229–244.

McNamee, G. D. (1987). The social origins of narrative skills. In M. Hickmann (Ed.), *Social and functional approaches to language and thought* (287–304). Orlando: Academic Press.

Mason, J. M. (1980). When do children begin to read?: An exploration of four-year-old children's letter and word reading competencies. *Reading Research Quarterly, 15*, 203–227.

Meek, M. (1988). *How texts teach what readers learn.* Lockwood, Gloucestershire: The Thimble Press.

Morrison, T. (1987). *Beloved.* New York: Knopf.

Nelson, K. (1981). Individual differences in language development: Implications for development and language. *Developmental Psychology, 17*, 170–187.

Nelson, K. (1985). *Making sense: The acquisition of shared meaning.* Orlando: Academic Press.

Nelson, K. E., & Nelson, K. (1978). Cognitive pendulums and their linguistic realizations. In K. E. Nelson (Ed.), *Children's language* (Vol. 2.) New York: Gardner.

Newkirk, T. (1987). The non-narrative writing of young children. *Research in the Teaching of English, 21*, 121–145.

Newkirk, T., & Atwell, N. (Eds.). (1982). *Understanding writing.* Chelmsford, MA: Northwest Regional Exchange.

Nystrand, M. (1982). The structure of textual space. In M. Nystrand (Ed.), *What writers know: The language, process, and structure of written discourse* (pp. 75–86). New York: Academic Press.

Ogbu, J. (1985). Research currents: Cultural-ecological influences on minority school learning. *Language Arts, 62*, 860–869.

Olson, D. (1977). From utterance to text. *Harvard Educational Review, 47*, 257–279.

Paley, V. G. (1981). *Wally's stories.* Cambridge, MA: Harvard University Press.

Paley, V. G. (1986). *Mollie is three: Growing up in school.* Chicago: The University of Chicago Press.

Paley, V. G. (1988, July). *Research the real curriculum: Studying the child's imagination.* Paper presented at A New Look at Language Arts in Childhood, conference cosponsored by the Harold E. Jones Child Study Center and the Extension Program of the University of California—Berkeley, Berkeley, CA.

Pappas, C., & Brown, E. (1987). Learning to read by reading: Learning how to extend the functional potential of language. *Research in the Teaching of English, 21*, 160–184.

Philips, S. U. (1972). Participant structure and communicative competence: Warm Springs children in community and classroom. In C. Cazden, D. Hymes, & V. John (Eds.), *Functions of language in the classroom* (pp. 370–394). New York: Teachers College Press.

Piaget, J., & Inhelder, B. (1969). *The psychology of the child.* New York: Basic Books.

Polanyi, L. (1982). Literacy complexity in everyday storytelling. In D. Tannen (Ed.), *Spoken and written language: Exploring orality and literacy* (pp. 155–170). Norwood, NJ: Ablex.

Purcell-Gates, V. (1988). Lexical and syntactic knowledge of written narrative held by well-read-to kindergarteners and second graders. *Research in the Teaching of English, 22*, 128–160.

Rader, M. (1982). Context in written language: The case of imaginative fiction. In D. Tannen (Ed.), *Spoken and written language: Exploring orality and literacy* (pp. 185–197). Norwood, NJ: Ablex.

Read, C. (1975). *Children's categorizations of speech sounds in English* (Research report no. 17). Urbana, IL: National Council of Teachers of English.

Read, C. (1986). *Children's creative spelling.* London: Routledge & Kegan Paul.

Rosen, H. (n.d.). *Stories and meaning.* Upper Montclair, NJ: Boynton-Cook.

Rubin, Z. (1980). *Children's friendships.* Cambridge, MA: Harvard University Press.

Schieffelin, B., & Cochran-Smith, M. (1984). Learning to read culturally: Literacy before schooling. In H. Goelman, A. A. Oberg, & F. Smith (Eds.), *Awakening to literacy* (pp. 3–23). Exeter, NH: Heinemann.

Scribner, S., & Cole, M. (1981). *The psychology of literacy.* Cambridge, MA: Harvard University Press.

Slobin, D. (1979). *Psycholinguistics* (2nd ed.). Glenview, IL: Scott, Foresman.

Smith, N. R. (1983). *Experience and art.* New York: Teachers College Press.

Sowers, S. (1985). Learning to write in a classroom workshop: A study in grades one through four. In M. F. Whiteman (Ed.), *Advances in writing research: Vol. 1. Children's early writing development* (pp. 297–342). Norwood: NJ: Ablex.

Staton, J., Shuy, R., Peyton, J., & Reed, L. (1988). *Dialogue journal communication.* Norwood: NJ: Ablex.

Sulzby, E. (1982). Oral and written language mode adaptations in stories by kindergarten children. *Journal of Reading Behavior, 14*, 51–59.

Sulzby, E. (1985). Kindergarteners as writers and readers. In M. F. Whiteman (Ed.), *Advances in writing research: Vol. 1. Children's early writing development* (pp. 127–200). Norwood: NJ: Ablex.

Tannen, D. (1985). Relative focus on involvement in oral and written discourse.

In D. R. Olson, N. Torrance, & A. Hildyard (Eds.), *Literacy, language, and learning: The nature and consequences of reading and writing* (pp. 124–147). Cambridge: Cambridge University Press.

Tannen, D. (1987). The orality of literature and the literacy of conversation. In J. Langer (Ed.), *Language, literacy, and culture: Issues of society and schooling* (pp. 67–88). Norwood, NJ: Ablex.

Taylor, D. (1983). *Family literacy: Young children learning to read and write.* Exeter, NH: Heinemann.

Teale, W. H. (1982). Toward a theory of how children learn to read and write naturally. *Language Arts, 59,* 555–570.

Teale, W. H. (1986). Home background and young children's literacy development. In W. H. Teale & E. Sulzby (Eds.), *Emergent literacy: Writing and reading* (pp. 173–206). Norwood: NJ: Ablex.

Teale, W. H. (1987). Emergent literacy: Reading and writing development in early childhood. In J. Readence & R. Baldwin (Eds.), *Research literacy: Merging perspectives* (pp. 45–74). Thirty-sixth Yearbook of the National Reading Conference. Rochester, NY: National Reading Conference.

Tharp, R., Jordan, C., Speidel, G. E., Au, K., Klein, T., Calkins, R., Sloat, K., & Gallimore, R. (1984). Product and process in applied developmental research: Education and the children of a minority. In M. E. Lamb, A. L. Brown, & B. Rogoff (Eds.), *Advances in developmental psychology* (pp. 91–144). Hillsdale, NJ: Lawrence Erlbaum.

Tizard, B., & Hughes, M. (1984). *Young children learning.* Cambridge, MA: Harvard University Press.

Veatch, J. (1978). *Reading in the elementary school* (2nd ed.). New York: Richard C. Owen.

Veatch, J., Sawacki, F., Elliott, G., Barnette, E., & J. Blakey (1973). *Key words to reading: The language experience approach begins.* Columbus, OH: Merrill.

Villaume, S. K. (1988). Creating context within text: An investigation of primary-grade children's character introductions in original stories. *Research in the Teaching of English, 22,* 161–182.

Vygotsky, L. S. (1962). *Thought and language.* Cambridge, MA: Massachusetts Institute of Technology Press.

Vygotsky, L. S. (1978). *Mind in Society.* Cambridge, MA: Harvard University Press.

Vygotsky, L. S. (1987). Perception and its development in childhood. In L. S. Vygotsky, *Collected works: Vol. 1. Problems of general psychology* (pp. 289–300). New York: Plenum Press.

Wagner, B. J. (1985). Evaluating the written word through the spoken: Dorothy Heathcote and a group of 9- to 10-year-olds as monks. *Theory into Practice, 24,* 166–172.

Weaver (1982). Welcoming errors as signs of growth. *Language Arts, 59,* 438–444.

Wells, G. (1985). Preschool literacy-related activities and success in school. In D. Olson, N. Torrance, & A. Hildyard (Eds.), *Literacy, language, and learning* (pp. 229–255). Cambridge: Cambridge University Press.

Wells, G. (1986). Variation in child language. In P. Fletcher & M. Garman (Eds.), *Language acquisition* (2nd ed.) (pp. 109–140). Cambridge: Cambridge University Press.

Welty, E. (1983). *One writer's beginnings.* New York: Warner Books.

Werner, H., & Kaplan, B. (1963). *Symbol formation: An organismic developmental approach to language and the expression of thought.* New York: John Wiley.

Wolf, D., Davidson, L., Davis, M., Walters, J., Hodges, M. & Scripp, L. (1988). Beyond A, B, and C: A broader and deeper view of literacy. In A. D. Pellegrini (Ed.), *Psychological bases for early education* (pp. 123–152). New York: John Wiley.

Wolf, D., & Gardner, H. (1979). Style and sequence in early symbolic play. In N. R. Smith & M. B. Franklin (Eds.), *Symbolic functioning in childhood* (pp. 117–119). Hillsdale, NJ: Lawrence Erlbaum.

Wolf, D., & Hicks, D. (in press). The voices within narratives: The development of intertextuality in young children's stories. *Discourse Processes.*

Wolf, D., Rygh, J., & Altshuler, J. (1984). Agency and experience: Actions and states in play narrative. In I. Bretherton (Ed.), *Symbolic play: The development of social understanding* (pp. 195–217). New York: Academic Press.

Zalusky, V. (1983). Relationships: What did I write? What did I draw? In W. Frawley (Ed.), *Linguistics and literacy* (pp. 91–124). New York: Plenum Press.

Index

About the Author

Anne Haas Dyson is an Associate Professor of Education in Language and Literacy in the Graduate School of Education, University of California—Berkeley. A former classroom teacher, her research concentrates on children's oral and written language use in classroom settings. She has written about her work in many articles and book chapters. She has also coauthored *Language Assessment in the Early Years* (Norwood, NJ: Ablex, 1984) with Celia Genishi, with whom she has coedited the research column in *Language Arts*. Most recently she has served as a project director in the area of emergent literacy for the Center for the Study of Writing (CSW) in Berkeley; and, as a part of CSW's collaborative work with the Center for the Study of Reading, she has edited a book on the interrelationships between writing and reading, entitled *Collaboration through writing and reading: Exploring possibilities.* (Urbana, IL: National Council of Teachers of English, in press).